P9-DHC-358

Melrose Public Library
DISCARDED

ALSO BY MICHAEL J. ARLEN

Say Goodbye to Sam

The Camera Age

Thirty Seconds

The View from Highway 1

Passage to Ararat

Exiles

An American Verdict

Living-Room War

ALSO BY ALICE ARLEN

Cissy Patterson

THE HUNTRESS

THE HUNTRESS

THE ADVENTURES, ESCAPADES, AND TRIUMPHS OF ALICIA PATTERSON

AVIATRIX, SPORTSWOMAN, JOURNALIST, PUBLISHER

ALICE ARLEN AND MICHAEL J. ARLEN

PANTHEON BOOKS, NEW YORK

Library of Congress Cataloging-in-Publication Data
Names: Arlen, Alice, 1940–2016. Arlen, Michael J.
Title: The huntress : the adventures, escapades, and triumphs of Alicia Patterson: aviatrix, sportswoman, journalist, publisher / Alice Arlen and Michael J. Arlen.
Description: New York : Pantheon, 2016.
Identifiers: LCCN 2015048178.
ISBN 978-1-101-87113-3 (hardback). ISBN 978-1-101-87114-0 (ebook)
Subjects: LCSH: Patterson, Alicia, 1906–1963. Women publishers—United States—Biography. Women journalists—United States—Biography. Newsday (Hempstead, N.Y.)—History. Women air pilots—United States—Biography. Women adventurers—United States—Biography. Horsemen and horsewomen—United States—Biography. BISAC: BIOGRAPHY & AUTOBIOGRAPHY/General. BIOGRAPHY & AUTOBIOGRAPHY/Editors, Journalists, Publishers. BIOGRAPHY & AUTOBIOGRAPHY/Women.
Classification: LCC CT275.P417 A75 2016. DDC070.5092/273—dc23. LC record available at lccn.loc.gov/2015048178

www.pantheonbooks.com

Jacket images: Alicia Patterson, in 1943. Reproduced from Hofstra University Special Collections. All other photographs, courtesy of a family collection.
Jacket design by Janet Hansen

Printed in the United States of America
First Edition

2 4 6 8 9 7 5 3 1

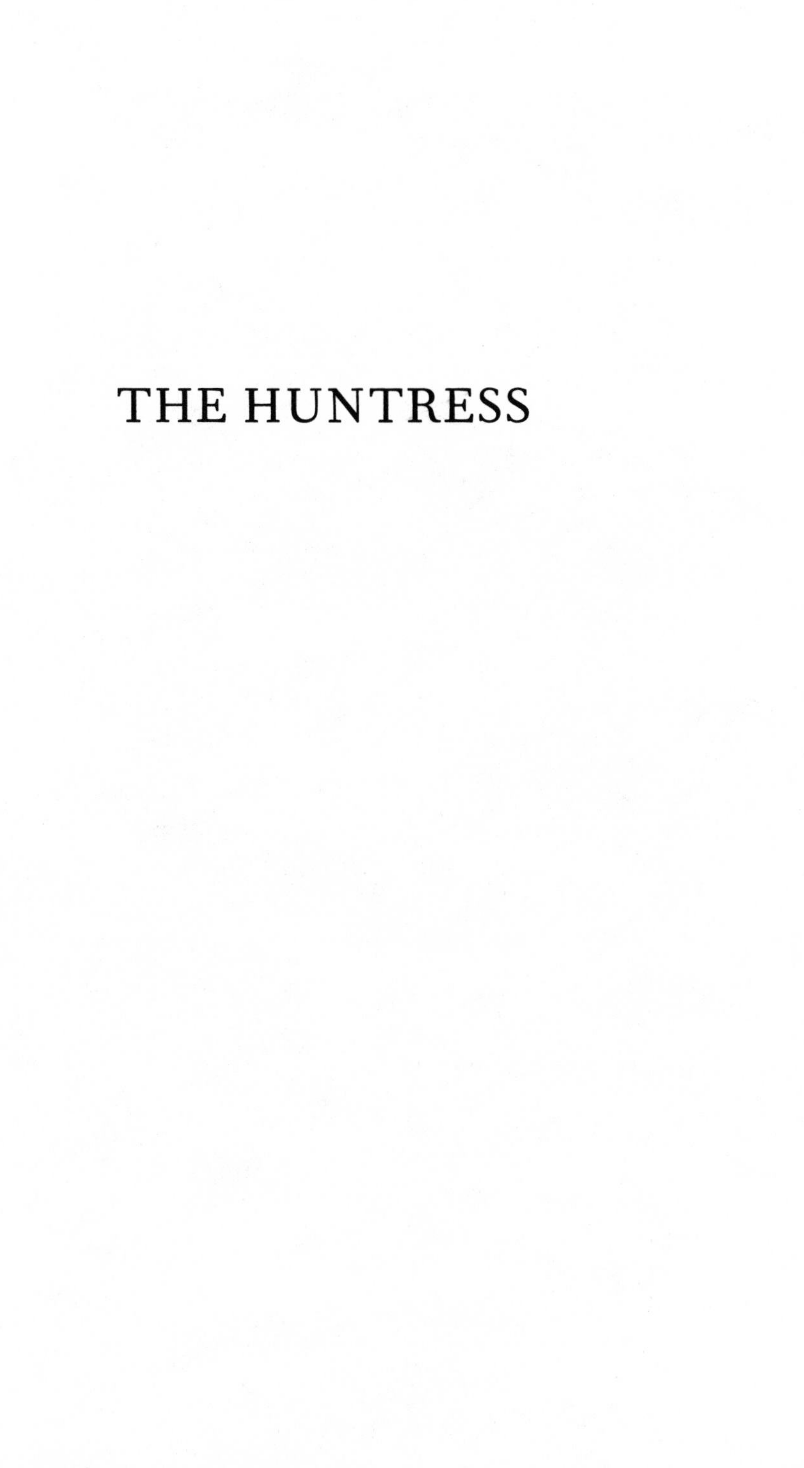

THE HUNTRESS

PROLOGUE

OLD SCRAPBOOKS HAVE AN ENTROPY of their own, especially when it comes to newspaper clippings, whose newsprint, often dry as parchment, threatens to crumble at a touch, and whose faded photos (none too well-defined to begin with) seem to be reaching out to contemporary eyes like faint light from an ancient starburst. *This* old scrapbook, the one under observation, with its worn blue leather cover, has had its contents protected after a fashion with filmy shields of what must have been a new product at the time, cellophane; though after the passage of 112 years, cellophane or no, the unravelings of time have barely been slowed, let alone arrested. Today the columns of print are hazy on the page; the figures in the ancient photographs stare out from their stiff poses (in their now "historical" costumes) as if from a long-vanished country.

The newspaper thus preserved is Hearst's *Chicago Morning American*, and the date is November 20, 1902. On this news-filled day—which apparently also provided readers with such stories as "Two Saloons Blown Up, Many Dead"; "College Students March to Protest Vaccinations"; "Remorseless Convict Hanged"; and (not without interest) "40,000 Troops Mass on Canadian Border"—the *American*'s major story begins on page 1 with a hefty four-column headline, then spreads out inside to cover most of five other pages. The headline (a bit on the wordy side, in the style of the day) reads as follows: "Higinbotham-Patterson Wedding Acme of Elegant Simplicity." Several subheadlines follow in a similar vein: "Social Event of the Year"; "Rare Taste Displayed"; "Bishop Addresses Throng." Also on the first page, an artist's sketch of "The Bride at Church" extends across several columns and down below the fold, causing the report of the Canadian invasion to be cut short. Inside, beginning on page 3, are many related features, long and short, furnishing additional wedding information: Most but not all the bridesmaids wore plumes of mauve feathers; the ceremony

WILL DISPUTE BRITISH RULE IN CANADA.

Frenchmen in This Country Organize a Canadian Republican Army to Invade and Take Possession of Northern Territory.

WILL JOIN FORCES WITH DOUKHOBORS

Plan Is to Organize a Large Force and March to Winnipeg, Where Juncture Will Be Made With 40,000 at That Point.

HIGINBOTHAM-PATTERSON WEDDING THE ACME OF ELEGANT SIMPLICITY

THE BRIDE AT THE CHURCH.

BRIDE MADE A BEAUTIFUL PICTURE.

As at Her Mother's and Grandmother's Marriages, Religious Ceremony Dominated Over All the Elaborate Arrangements.

FASHIONABLE THRONG AT CHURCH AND HOUSE

Rare Taste Displayed in Decorations, in Which White Plays Principal Part — Venerable Bishop MacLaren Officiates.

GEORGE W. CABLE must have had in mind just such a wedding as that of Miss Alice Higinbotham and Joseph Medill Patterson at Grace Episcopal Church yesterday when he wrote of a wedding in his "Bylow Hill":

"There never was as pretty a wedding so simple, nor so simple a wedding so pretty."

Only in this case he might have said instead:

"There never was as elaborate a wedding which looked so simple."

Married as Her Mother Had Been.

The *Chicago Morning American*'s front-page account of Alice Higinbotham's wedding to Joseph Medill Patterson, 1902.

was performed at an hour (4:00 p.m.) only lately made fashionable in New York City; the procession of carriages arriving at Grace Church had caused a complete shutdown of Wabash Avenue. Elsewhere there are profiles of the seven ushers ("mostly Yale men with an affiliation to Scroll and Key"); individual portrait photos of each bridesmaid; and a complete list of all six hundred guests—a list heavy with the names of Gilded Age great families of Chicago such as Armour, Swift, Pullman, McCormick, and Field—plus a special section devoted to "Members of the Smart Set of the Eastern Cities" who had traveled west to grace Grace Church with their presence.

As to the principals in this grand event, the bride and groom, they are more than amply celebrated on the broad bleached pages of the *Morning American.* Alice Higinbotham, the bride, portrayed in numerous photos in addition to the artist's sketch, invariably described as beautiful, elegant, comely, and of course radiant, with her "dark hair and laughing eyes," is seemingly already well-known to many Chicagoans as the daughter of Rachel and Harlow Higinbotham—himself the former president of the 1893 Chicago World's Fair (with its Venetian lagoons, gorillas from Africa, and thrilling Ferris wheel—the fabulous "White City" on the Midway), and before that the shrewd finance executive who led the remarkable retail expansion of Marshall Field & Company.

On an inside page, in a decorously gossipy feature attributed to "the Bystander," one of the bridesmaids, Miss Kate Lancaster, recalled the "charming story" of Alice's adventure, or misadventure, one winter's night two years before while iceboating on a moonlit Wisconsin lake with "some college fellows." An unexpected gap in the ice had caused the boat to overturn, spilling eighteen-year-old Alice into the freezing water; although she herself was tiny, weighing next to nothing, her soggy fur coat and boots made it impossible for her companions to pull her out. But little Alice had gamely shouted that she would "hold on and stick it out," and this she had done for close to twenty minutes in frozen Lake Geneva, until the college men returned with ropes and hauled her to safety, later much praising her for her "pluck and grit." According to "the Bystander," this story had almost certainly reached the ears of the future groom (a young man "much drawn to derring-do"), who had spent the better part of the next year "in romantic pursuit" of Alice Higinbotham—literally a pursuit: she being whisked off by her family to view the cherry blossoms in Japan; he contriving to intercept the returning travelers in California—before finally obtaining her and her parents' consent to an engagement.

A grainy photograph on page 4 shows Joe Patterson surrounded by his seven ushers. He is tall for his time (six feet even; taller than the others, with the exception of his cousin Robert McCormick, who is six feet four), and broad shouldered, doubtless from his years on the Yale crew. On the whole he seems a fine-looking young man, with brownish hair, a wide forehead, and a somewhat indecipherable or indeterminate expression, which might be simple optimism or youthful wariness: hard to tell since the primitive nature of the old engravings doesn't permit much nuance or show of personality. On that November afternoon in 1902, Patterson is twenty-three years old, barely two years out of college—not so youthful as he would be considered now but none too old either. At the groom's "farewell dinner," according to the *American*, one of the ushers toasted "Joe Pat's restless energy—or was it energetic restlessness?" Another spoke of his "Rough-Rider spirit," referring to his unsuccessful attempt to join Col. Teddy Roosevelt's "Rough Rider" regiment in the summer of his freshman year; alluding also to a subsequent summer spent "rough-necking on a ranch in Wyoming" (during which time he'd apparently befriended another restless young man, the outlaw Butch Cassidy); and one year later to his going even farther afield, across the wide Pacific to China, then in the throes of the Boxer Rebellion. For at the age of twenty Joe Pat had somehow made his way inland, not as far as "the palace of the Manchu Empress in Peking" as the *American* playfully averred, but nonetheless as far as the fighting at Tientsin, tagging along with a company of U.S. Marines, after which he'd sent back dispatches to Chicago newspapers, notably the *American* and the *Chicago Tribune*—the last described as "a publication where the correspondent was not entirely unknown."

What the Hearst editors saw no need to explain—what most readers of any Chicago newspaper in those days already knew—was that young Joe Patterson was the son of Robert Wilson Patterson, editor of the *Chicago Tribune*, the most prosperous newspaper in the country; moreover, perhaps of greater local consequence, on his mother's side he was the grandson of the redoubtable Joseph Medill, founder and owner of the *Tribune*; early antislavery voice in the Republican Party, one of the original "Lincoln men" in Illinois, and while two years dead still venerated as one of the early titans of Chicago. In other words Joseph Medill Patterson right then is very much a young prince of the city, whether he wishes to be or no; and possibly any ambivalence on his smooth face derives from his somehow knowing this while at the same time not quite knowing what it means.

Finally, after many column inches, the *American*'s Homeric account of the great wedding concludes with a description of Alice Higinbotham Patterson's reappearance, at the finale of her parents' "chrysanthemum-strewn reception," in her "dark-blue cloth traveling gown and sable-trimmed cloak and hat," bound with her husband for a brief honeymoon in Thomasville, Georgia, after which, it is reported, the couple will return, not to Chicago but to the state capital in Springfield, where "Mr. Patterson will attend to his new duties in the State legislature." Today's reader, peering in from modern times, looks perhaps sentimentally for a photo, portrait, artist's sketch of the bride and groom in the process of shape-shifting into husband and wife, about to step into the future. But amid this cornucopia of wedding pictures on these old pages, there seems to be none—none at all—showing the two principals actually together in the same frame, as it were.

· 1 ·

IT WOULD LIKELY BE UNFAIR and uncharitable (though maybe temptingly ironic) to suggest that Joe Patterson and Alice Higinbotham's brilliant wedding represented the high point in their marriage. For one thing, most marriages—even the discordant and implausible ones, even those that in hindsight might seem challenged from the beginning—are surely voyages with many stops and starts, surprises, sideline excursions, and not all of them unpleasing. For instance, years later a middle-aged Joe Patterson recalled for his twenty-six-year-old daughter, Alicia, that on their Georgia honeymoon his young wife had been "good in the hay," a snippet of information that, among other things, gives some notion of the oddly familiar relationship that came to evolve between father and daughter.

On the other hand, on the subject of that same honeymoon—two young people alone together for the first time, at a resort in the piney woods of Georgia—what the bride mostly remembered (not being one to chat easily with daughters, or anyone else, about "the hay") was the impatience and disapproval of her new husband. "He liked it that I rode," she once told her youngest daughter, Josephine, "but he was down on me for not shooting although I just didn't like to. And he was always scolding me for fussing with my hair and trying to get dressed properly." More tellingly she could sense that he was already becoming bored with her company. In fact, soon after their return he was writing glumly to his mother to the effect that Alice, "in spite of three years at Miss Porter's School," appeared to know little more than "how to read and speak a little in the French language"; indeed, save for "her interest in the decorative arts," he continued, his new wife knew little "in the way of History or Politics"—a deficiency, he said, he was doing his best to remedy by compiling a reading list for her.

In January of next year, as planned, the Pattersons settled into a modest apartment near the railroad tracks in Springfield, then a town of some forty thousand, embedded in the great, flat downstate prairie, far from the familiar sophistications of Chicago. Alice worked at learning to keep house with the help of a Swedish farm girl, who did most of the heavy lifting in an era of washtubs, laundry lines, and weighty hand irons, to say nothing of the chores and crafts of the kitchen. In her free time she tried to get through her mountain of wedding thank-you letters, and wrote almost daily to her mother, who remained doggedly skeptical of the Swedish girl's domestic skills. "Inger prepared a fine breakfast for Joe," Alice declared in one letter, "using fresh eggs obtained from her cousin, although J. was as usual in a great rush to get to his office." Joe Patterson's office was a half mile away in the statehouse, where he was just then the youngest member of the Illinois legislature—a Republican assemblyman from Chicago's Eighth District: a job he'd strenuously campaigned for in the months before his wedding, having come to the conclusion that he could accomplish more in politics than he could as a lowly reporter on the *Chicago Tribune* in the shadow of his august father.

In the beginning Patterson's experience of statehouse politics was much to his liking—the noisy, often raucous speechifying of downstate politicos, the slow-motion give-and-take of lengthy sessions, and then afterward the late-hours camaraderie and tavern talk, almost like a Yale fraternity without the Yale men. For much of that spring the legislature was occupied with the heated issue of Chicago street railways; at the time there existed dozens and dozens of small, mostly inefficient trolley car operators, and inevitably there were the usual forces wishing to consolidate them. Patterson instinctively regarded himself as a man of the people, and soon devoted much energy and many words trying to push forward a populist agenda. But which was the populist agenda? The one favoring small operators? Or the one backing municipal consolidators? Legislative sessions grew noisier and then violent. Fistfights often broke out on the floor. Joe himself was named in a newspaper account for throwing an inkwell at the Speaker, an accusation he accepted noncommitally if not cheerfully, which horrified his wife. "Of course I like him to be working hard," she wrote her mother, "but not so lathered up, and not letting his good name be trampled in the mud." But in the end the great street-railway debate led to one of those typical legislative compromises, which didn't do much to change Chicago transportation one way or the other, but which put Joe Patterson on what he thought to be the wrong side of the fight and sent him back to Chicago, for the time being disillusioned with politics and thankful to have a desk he could return to at the *Tribune*. By then, too, Alice was pregnant with what her husband felt certain would be their first boy: his son and heir. Not all men in those days placed sons at such a premium, but many did, and certainly Joseph Patterson was one of them.

Joe Patterson, a very young father, with baby Elinor, ornamentally seated on a table.

By the time Alice was ready to have her baby, she and Patterson were living on Stratford Place in Chicago, another rental on the not entirely acceptable North Side; which was one among several reasons she moved back into her parents' huge mansion on Prairie Avenue for her accouchement, as proper people called it, a female ritual best managed in the comforts and cleanliness of a well-appointed home (as opposed to the unsanitary conditions prevalent in most hospitals). Here the Higinbothams' family physician was in attendance, maids were everywhere, and a young German wet nurse waited in a room down the hall to breast-feed the newborn. In due course, and without notable trauma to Alice, who had the benefit of chloroform, a fine baby girl was produced—in fact, more than fine, everyone agreed: a beautiful, quite perfect little creature. Even Joe

Patterson, summoned from his office at the *Tribune*, doubtless surprised himself a little at his gruff satisfaction with the lovely little female, who was instantly named after his mother: Elinor Medill Patterson.

Indeed, she would remain remarkably beautiful for most of her long life (and in that one respect at least prove a tough act to follow); although as Joe soon wrote his mother, he was now more confident than ever that their next child would be a boy.

· 2 ·

GIVEN THAT JOE PATTERSON was now a father, a family man, there were those—with Alice Patterson surely at the head of the pack—who rather hoped, even assumed, that he might take this opportunity (under his nose, so to speak) as a signal to buckle down after that first false start in Springfield and settle in at the *Tribune*. His job was on the editorial board, surely a nice level for a young man to begin his employment, and one with the potential for providing a public platform that greatly appealed to him, given his growing interest in populist matters. The *Tribune*, of course, was not merely Chicago's leading Republican newspaper (with its editor, Robert Patterson, consequently a major force in the Republican Party) but for decades it had been speaking to and for the so-called sound business interests of the city. Nationally it was considered a topflight paper, employing talented reporters and editors; it had been a pioneer in publishing well-regarded cultural coverage on art and architecture, books, and music; it was also excellent on sports. But one thing it wasn't, and had never been, was a journal for the masses. Accordingly Joe Patterson's decision as a junior editorial writer to embrace not only the city's new Democratic mayor, but also the mayor's push for city ownership of those blessed street railways, meant that from the start he was in constant conflict, first with his immediate boss, James Keeley, who steadfastly declined to print his editorial submissions, and farther up the line, inevitably, with Keeley's boss, his own father, an increasingly aloof and taciturn figure whom he rarely saw except at a distance, and who in due course turned out to be having plenty of his own problems.

It's worth noting that Joe Patterson wasn't wrong about the city and its evolving demographics; with the middle class expanding more rapidly than the *Tribune* elders seemed aware of, with the lower classes becoming steadily better educated and more literate, and with neither group deserving of being abandoned to Hearst. He was also mainly right, as he would often turn out to be, in his intuitions about, and empathy for, ordinary people. But while capable of forward and imaginative thinking, he could also be obstinate and stubbornly righteous in that off-putting way of true believers, stirring up a frothy mix of well-meaning impulse and quick-study certitude, which sometimes played out to those around him as visionary charm, though at other times more like restless instability.

It also probably didn't help matters much that, more or less offstage, Patterson's parents' own marriage was fast sliding downhill, in a mostly buttoned-up Gilded Age version of marital dysfunction. His father, Robert, by nature grave, hardworking, and undemonstrative (himself the son of another lately deceased Chicago great man: the charismatic Presbyterian preacher Rev. Robert Patterson), had been trying hard to steer the *Tribune* into the new century without provoking the wrath of Joe Medill's ghost or the incessant, clumsy interferences of his wife, Nellie, who with her sister, Kate McCormick, was a cotrustee of the powerful Tribune Trust: interferences lately transmitted mostly by telegram, because soon after Joseph Medill's death she had by and large decamped to Washington, D.C., where on fashionable Dupont Circle she had decreed a mighty pleasure dome (in fact, a twenty-eight-room mansion) to be built by Stanford White, furnished in the grand manner, and intended to at least rival the mansion already erected down the street by her sister, where such bellwethers of Eastern society as Mr. Henry James, Jr., and Mr. and Mrs. Henry Adams had reportedly taken tea. This left Robert Patterson not so much free as duty bound to run the *Tribune*, by his own choice bleakly domiciled in a hotel room near Chicago's Loop, where he had the bellboys bring him occasional corned-beef sandwiches from a tavern across the street, also more than occasional pints of bourbon whiskey, which he unfortunately preferred to tea.

· 3 ·

BY EARLY 1904 Joe Patterson had taken the hint—surely numerous hints—from senior *Tribune* editors as to his slim chances of slipping even modestly progressive editorials into the paper. But instead of entirely backing off (as Alice begged him to do, once reminding him to "think about which side your bread is buttered on"), he only shifted tactics, now devoting his energy to producing a less overtly political and more or less consumerist supplement for the Sunday edition, which he was allowed to title the "Workingman's Magazine"—a four-page insert featuring information and advice for white-collar office workers on such topics as "travelling tips" and "business opportunities"—which was generally well received by readers though scarcely noticed by those on high.

Then in March came a frantic summons from his mother for him to come immediately to Washington—alone, *sans* Alice; this was specified—to help out with a new family crisis: the wedding of his younger sister, Cissy Medill Patterson, nineteen years old, with flaming red hair, porcelain-white skin, a piquant slightly upturned nose, and the air and manner (which would stay with her all her life, for better or worse) of the proverbial "wild child." As an older brother Joe was fond of Cissy and she of him, though neither had much in common beside the bond of siblings in a family of disordered grownups. Most emphatically she was neither populist nor progressive, nor for that matter much of anything just then beyond determined to be married to a Polish-Russian nobleman by the name of Count Josef "Gigy" Gizycki, more than twenty years her senior, handsome in the then-approved international style of brushed-back hair and waxed mustache, certifiably aristocratic with a castle in eastern Poland, many acres, peasants, horses, debts—and alas very little money—and on the whole with a persona, as one might call it, that seemed fairly to shout a warning to willful nineteen-year-old American heiresses. But Cissy was intent on becoming Countess

Joe Medill, founder of the *Chicago Tribune*, one of the original "Lincoln men," with his grandchildren: (*clockwise*) Eleanor "Cissy" Patterson; Medill McCormick; Joseph Medill Patterson; Robert R. "Bertie" McCormick.

Gizycka, and had already provoked a first crisis by making a press announcement of her own engagement. The second crisis, following rapidly from the first (and thereby causing Joe's summons to Washington), stemmed from what might be called a contractual disagreement between the principals, which is to say between the dashing, impecunious Gigy, who expected to be paid for his services—and paid rather well—and Cissy's parents, notably her father, the morose, moralistic Robert Patterson, who took the position that upstanding Americans neither wished to sell their daughters nor for that matter wanted to buy a son-in-law, even one with an impressively unpronounceable title.

By the time Joe arrived in Washington on the morning of March 4, entering the marbled splendor of 15 Dupont Circle with a valise in one hand and a copy of the "Workingman's Magazine" in the other (in the hope that his father might finally consent to read it), the Patterson-Gizycki nuptials were in ever-more-serious disarray. The bride was locked in her room upstairs, threatening suicide should the wedding not take place. Somewhere downstairs Nellie Patterson was attempting to placate a Roman Catholic bishop and a trio of priests who had been hastily enlisted, first to consecrate the vast secular edifice by sprinkling holy water about the premises, then to perform the ceremony—a liturgical compromise presumably between the Pattersons' stern Protestantism and the count's smoky Russian Orthodoxy. The father of the bride, perhaps understandably, was nowhere to be seen. The putative bridegroom himself was reported to be defiantly incommunicado a mile or so distant, behind the walls of the Russian Embassy.

Much against his will, or at least his commonsense impulses, Joe was persuaded by his mother (who seemed to have evolved a rather more flexible attitude to dowries than her husband) to take a hansom cab over to the czar's embassy and there try to arrange a compromise with the haughty Gizycki. This too turned out to be more easily said than done. Joe Patterson, a Yale man and prince of Chicago, was accustomed to a certain high level of American sophistication and behavior. But with Count Gigy and the other Russian aristocrats gathered around him at the embassy, he quickly found himself out of his league. When Patterson showed up in the embassy billiard room, Gigy just laughed at him, and not a kindly laugh either; and when Joe, repeating the family line, told the count that in America they did things differently, Gigy snidely replied to the effect that that was why America was so provincial, so uncultivated, and so on. In the end, for better or worse, an understanding was achieved, which is to say the Pattersons gave in: A "distribution" to Count Gizycki of so many dollars was agreed on, payable in such-and-such a way, according to such-and-such a schedule. Whereupon the wedding took place. The Catholic bishop, assisted by the trio of priests, united the unlikely couple in Holy Roman matrimony; flowers, champagne, and even a wedding cake were produced. However this was still not the end of the drama, for the groom was expecting not merely the promise of future dollars but an actual here-and-now check, a down payment, so to speak. This in turn was the last straw for Robert Patterson, citizen of Chicago and the Middle West, plain-spoken son of the Great Presbyterian. He wouldn't write one; not then, not there. And so, while the new countess was upstairs changing into her traveling clothes, the newly married count turned on his heels and left for Union Station by himself, declaring that he would travel back to Europe without her. As it happened, Nellie Patterson (who already enjoyed being the mother of a countess) had a checkbook handy of her own, with an ample balance. She soon wrote out a check for ten thousand dollars, and once more prevailed on Joe to take another hurry-up hansom cab, this time to the train station, bringing with him both the check and his sister. Which he did, handing both over to his infuriating new brother-in-law and even staying around long enough to wave a sentimental American good-bye to the departing couple.

IT SHOULDN'T COME as much of a surprise that Countess Cissy's marriage eventually ended no better than it began; rather worse, in fact, seeing that by then there was a child involved. But that, as they say, is another story for another time. Meanwhile, let us hold for a moment on Joe Patterson, now in his second-class carriage on a Baltimore & Ohio train, heading back to Chicago. As one of those young men (and surely he is still young, though fast growing older) who stoutly claimed how he always liked to learn from his experiences—well, a biographer might unprofessionally wonder what might he have lately learned? That his father's patriarchal posture was something of a mask, that he can't even protect himself; that his mother, another character better suited to the stage, is too tightly sewn into her own costume to be of much use to anyone else; that his sister is at once spoiled, beloved, and incorrigible; and that fancy-pants Europeans are no better than one would expect, besides being snootily unreliable witnesses to the American life he cherishes? But possibly he has known much of this already. As the train travels westward into the Pennsylvania twilight, does he stare out the grimy window? Does he read? Read what? Keep in mind, moreover, that he is not really the hero of this narrative, not the key player. In any case the key player is a *she*, has not been born yet, has not even been thought of, in the way such things are thought of. In the meantime he is here in this story, one might say, to provide context, a kind of ballast. And we also know this about him, because years later, so many years later, his wife (now a grandmother) remembered it: that in his suitcase, which his mother herself had packed, beneath some shirts and whatnot, still perfectly folded, clean, and crisp, lay the same copy of the "Workingman's Journal" he had brought down and presented to his father, who had returned it to him, obivously still unread.

· 4 ·

WHAT SEEMS TRUE of many warring couples, even those who don't know or won't admit they're at war, is how firmly convinced each of the parties remains of his or her own reasonableness; and more and more this became the case with Joe and Alice Patterson. She, all too recently Alice Higinbotham, raised in the sober calm of the Higinbotham household, wherein father, mother, children moved in Newtonian predictability across the domestic universe, on the whole assumed that everyone—at least everyone at a proper social level—observed similar laws of motion. Why wouldn't they? Why wouldn't her husband, for instance, be altogether pleased to work in a successful family business, and work hard too, responsibly, in an effort to impress his superiors and gain advancement, and then come home at a decent hour to attend to his wife and child? At the same time Patterson, who had been sent off to boarding school at eight, raised neither by wolves nor exactly by himself, as he traveled through Groton, Yale, and the corridors of his grandfather's large, empty house, could see no reason why a man—a man such as he—shouldn't chart his own course, try to do some good in the world, make his mark while making things better. What could be more sensible than that?

As has been noted, Joe Patterson's choice of a platform from which to improve the imperfect city around him—the city's leading conservative newspaper—was a choice unlikely to bring satisfactory results. His editorial ideas continued to be disregarded; next his already small "Workingman's Journal" was cut down to two pages and then discontinued. At which point Patterson's response, which might be ascribed to either youthful audacity or sheer bullheadedness, was in effect to double down on his mission of converting the family newspaper to progressive politics. He proposed to the editorial board (whose invisible chief was of course his father) that the *Tribune* promptly and strongly endorse the new "People's

Candidate," Democrat George Dunne, in the upcoming mayoralty election; and when the editorial board pointedly declined, Patterson stalked out of the building, leaving behind him a curt message of resignation (a copy of which he walked over and left at the offices of Hearst's *American*), and then offered his own services to candidate Dunne.

After Dunne was elected (by a wide majority) he appointed Joe Patterson his commissioner of public works. Unsurprisingly this new political period posed new challenges to the Pattersons' strained domestic life. Joe's loud and queenly mother and Alice's quiet and not-at-all queenly mother both weighed in with admonitions and concern. For her part Alice was trying hard, after her fashion, to be a stand-by-your-man wife. True, she didn't often understand Joe's big ideas, but as a woman of her time she harbored no big ideas herself and thought that a man who did would be bound to amount to something. "Like you, I do sometimes worry about Joe," she wrote Nellie Patterson, "but I know his heart is in the right place." What neither she nor either mother nor certainly Robert Patterson expected was that Joe's first official decision as commissioner of public works would be to enforce a hitherto minor and recondite public ordinance against both the *Tribune* and its chief advertiser, Marshall Field & Co.

The regulation in question had to do with allowable storage space below sidewalk level, and until then was something few people had known or cared about. But the areas involved also happened to constitute crucial warehousing space for both the *Tribune* and Field's department store: taxable square footage, proclaimed the new public works commissioner, on which city taxes had gone unpaid for years. As can be imagined, rival papers (notably Hearst's) provided enthusiastic and ample coverage of the crusading efforts by the new commissioner, and of course the "People's Mayor, " to recover the several hundred dollars in scandalously withheld taxes from the two establishment delinquents. The issue, such as it was, buzzed along in the public consciousness for almost two months until the other papers lost interest, and then the lawyers took over and the matter once again disappeared from view. But among those close to Joe Patterson, there was not one of them, save perhaps for pretty little

Elinor, who didn't begin to worry that Joe Medill's grandson (and likely inheritor of a substantial piece of the *Tribune* pie) might be burning bridges that he would later need to cross.

Nellie Medill Patterson's all-purpose answer to many of the problems and puzzlements of marital life—to those tiresome "situations," as people spoke of them in those preanalytic days—was one she had learned from her parents and shared with her contemporaries. It was to "go abroad," which inevitably meant Europe in a general sense, though more specifically England and France: the mother ships of empire, those lodestones of culture and shopping, with their great imposing, civilizing capitals of London and Paris. Thus, she proposed directly to Alice, and indirectly to her erratically behaving son, a mother-financed holiday across the Atlantic, with the unspoken hope that the proverbial "change of air" might bring a calming and who knows a romantic effect on the alienated young couple.

Alice was thrilled; at seventeen she had spent six months at a finishing school at Versailles and sometimes remarked wistfully that she wished she had been born French. As a boy Joe had been on several excursions to Europe with his parents and liked the place well enough, though now as a grown man, with things to do and people to see, he declined the offer. Besides, hadn't anybody noticed that he was Chicago's commissioner of public works? But almost immediately his new political career began running into gusty headwinds. Apparently the serious men of the city had been having quiet talks with Mayor Dunne, with the result that the "People's Mayor" was now having second thoughts about some of his more progressive initiatives, perhaps especially those lately trumpeted by his young public works commissioner. In other words, far from it being a poor idea to take some weeks off from reforming Chicago, it now seemed a fortuitous and timely move. Thus, on September 7, Patterson, Alice, and little Elinor embarked on the *Caronia*, one of the older White Star steamships, for the seven-day crossing to Southampton.

· 5 ·

LONDON IN EARLY AUTUMN 1905 was as impressive as its postcards suggested, which Alice Patterson, seated in the writing room of the Hyde Park Hotel, inscribed in quantity and sent back to Prairie Avenue and nearby addresses. Although Queen Victoria had finally died, her stout, jovial, tirelessly lascivious son, the perennially incumbent "Prince Eddie," now ruled as Edward VII over an empire at its apogee of power, economic prosperity, and geographical reach. As did many of his own countrymen, Patterson accepted more or less as a fact of life the size, the heft, the sheer theatrical mass of the British Empire. But no longer a Groton schoolboy cheerfully bellowing Anglican hymns, and spending more time in the classroom studying British instead of American history, lately he had come to find the well-bred arrogance of the English, with their ruling-class attitudes and general stuck-upness, almost as oppressive as the czarist aristocracy. As a husbandly tourist he dutifully traipsed around the city with Alice, but his thoughts seemed elsewhere ("Spent the afternoon with J at the National Gallery but suddenly he vanished and was back at the hotel," she wrote to Nellie, who was herself in Vienna at the time). They took little Elinor to feed the ducks on the Serpentine. One night they went to the D'Oyly Carte Theatre and watched *The Mikado*, where he embarrassed Alice (as she wrote her sister) by complaining, "not as quietly as he might have thought," about "the habit of British condescension to the Asiatic races."

Matters were not much better after they crossed the Channel and made their way to Paris. He left Alice even more on her own, drifting along the rue Saint-Honoré, looking for chemises and lacework, dropping in on the Luxembourg Gardens to check on Elinor with her *mam'selle.* Joe seemed not only restless but had become interested to the point of preoccupation with ongoing events in Russia: the six-month-old revolution of 1905, which had been back in the news as students and other revolutionaries mounted renewed protests against the czarist regime. He disappeared for hours to the American Reading Room nearby the embassy, also to the *Tribune*'s little office on the rue du Louvre. Then seemingly on the spur of the moment, as Alice plaintively described it to her mother-in-law, he packed his "old valise with shirts that should have been with the laundress" and took the night train to St. Petersburg.

Once there he found what apparently he had been looking for: conflict, danger, a battle between elemental opposites. For the better part of a week, he made his way around the unstable city, with its many youthful dead and green-uniformed, saber-wielding czarist cavalry patrolling the streets. He managed interviews with student revolutionaries, as well as with the newly emerging liberal and socialist politicians who were trying vainly to achieve even a modest level of constitutional reform. In all he produced five creditable articles, a mixture of on-the-spot reporting, interviews, and political analysis, which he arranged to have smuggled out in the U.S. Embassy's diplomatic pouch (safe from Russian censors), and which were published in the *Tribune* under the pseudonym "David Macbeth." Temporarily pleased with himself, he returned to Paris, where Nellie had shown up to take Alice and the baby under her distracted protection, and where Alice, bewildered and angry as she had been at his sudden bolting, now claimed she was glad to have him back.

· 6 ·

BY FEBRUARY 1906 Alice Patterson suspected—more or less knew—that she was carrying another child, almost certainly a baby brother for Elinor, and it's hard to tell when she passed the news on to her husband, whether right away or just as likely not so immediately. Two months earlier, when Patterson had returned from Europe to resume his duties as public works commissioner, he'd found his relations with Mayor Dunne even more strained than before. Earlier he'd somehow assumed that Dunne's retreat from reform was only a tactical maneuver, a temporary change of plan, and that he would soon resume the offensive against Chicago's establishment malefactors, and with his righteous commissioner once again at his side. But the offensive was never resumed. Worse still, Dunne summoned Patterson to his chambers and told him directly, and even heatedly, that from now on he should stop working and speaking against the "sound business interests" of the city, and by inference that he should none too slowly align himself with those same interests—the business leaders who paid most of the city's bills, which of course included the *Tribune*.

Patterson's response was twofold. For a while he stayed at his job, signing forms, inspecting sites, "doing nothing," as he told his wife—although not exactly nothing, as she well knew. For after office hours, and sometimes instead of returning to the office after lunch, he had started dropping in at the new Socialist Club on State Street, where he began reading Marx, Veblen, and various of the proliferating socialist publications, in the process hanging out with the new political class, as well as doing more than his share of drinking. As the journalist Burton Rascoe later wrote of Patterson in those days: "Young Joe Patterson was all brains, brawn and pep, and tried hard to prove that being brought up wealthy hadn't made him soft. He'd walk into a rough saloon like Hinky Dink's and pick a fight with one of the tougher mugs—and of course the

SATURDAY.—Rain or snow. CHICAGO EVENING AMERICAN, MARCH 3, 1906. Rain or snow.—SATURDAY.

"What Right Have I to More Pleasure Than My Servant?"

YOUNG PATTERSON MAKES FIERCE ATTACK ON INHERITED WEALTH

JOSEPH MEDILL PATTERSON IN AN ILLUSTRATED TALK ON SOCIALISM—STRIKING SENTENCES FROM HIS LETTER OF RESIGNATION.

"Capital says there is equal opportunity for all. It lies and knows it lies."

"You are merely pattering with skin-deep measures when you stop short of socialism."

"Our laws practically make it no offense for capital to steal from the community."

"I realize that to fight privilege under present laws would be a jest."

"The whole body of our laws at present is ridiculous and obsolete."

"I cannot see why money should not be more or less evenly distributed."

Joe Patterson, "the renegade heir."

other tough mugs would all knock him about and pitch him onto the sidewalk. But he felt he'd made his point." In April he officially quit his job and resigned from Dunne's administration, but not without first sending off a pugnacious public letter to the mayor: "You of all people know how many of our laws are obsolete and ridiculous. When Capital says it offers equal opportunity, you know that is a lie. And you also know that any efforts that stop short of Socialism are no better than skin-deep measures."

It was troublesome enough that Joe Patterson had taken a potshot at Chicago's mayor in the city newspapers, especially in competing papers such as Hearst's *American*, which took obvious delight in running with the story. But next, when approached by a Hearst reporter looking for a follow-up, young Patterson more than obliged, unleashing a tirade on an even broader front. "By what right does Mr. Rockefeller enjoy a monopoly on the oil that God put in the ground?" he declared in full voice. "By what right does Mr. Vanderbilt own all those railroads, employing so many thousands of workers, when in fact it's those workers who support and carry Vanderbilt, and all wealthy capitalists, on their shoulders?" And then, as if tiring of attacking others, he attacked himself: "Consider my own undeserved good fortune. I can go to the theater or opera any time I like, and sit in the best of seats, but only because my grandfather worked hard for sixty years and left us money." And: "I own two horses, and have a groom to take care of them, and yet he has to touch his cap to me and call me Sir, despite his being a better horseman than I am, all because he was born poor."

Twenty-six-year-old Patterson's seemingly sudden and all-too-public transformation into a class warrior finally got the attention of his father. Prodded into action by his wife, Nellie (who almost certainly had been sharply elbowed on the subject by Kate McCormick, her older sister and *Tribune* cotrustee), Robert Patterson initially played the part of the bemused-though-tolerant parent. "Don't worry about Joe," he amiably told a gathering of reporters. "He's all right. He just needs to feel his way around for a while. Young fellows like him have to sow their wild oats. Besides, if all sons thought just like their fathers we should still be in the land of Abraham." Then, on his way out, he added, "I don't mind telling you boys, I think Socialism is one of the wildest fanaticisms of the age," which provoked a burst of sympathetic laughter from the crowd. However, such was the nearly scandalous nature of the story, especially in the context of Chicago's rule-bound, moralistic establishment, that reporters even sought out Alice Patterson at home, to ask her for a statement about her rebellious husband. Pale and visibly pregnant, she met them at the door, with one reporter describing her as "the most daintily incongruous ideal of a Socialist one could imagine," while another wrote of "her delicate face and violet eyes, the lady looking like a butterfly poised for flight rather than the wife of one of the city's most talked-about Socialists." Loyally the lady declared: "I don't know much about Socialism but I am sure of one thing. Whatever my husband is, then so am I. If he is a Socialist, I suppose I am one too." After which she added: "He tried so hard as Commissioner but nobody appreciated his sincerity and effort, and then he received not one word of thanks from anyone in the city. Now he is worn out and exhausted and I hope he will rest for a long time."

Instead of resting, or for that matter spending any more time at home than he had to, Patterson only accelerated his political activities. In the process he went back to journalism, though not to the *Tribune*. In May, to the consternation of his wife and parents, he became editor of the *Daily Socialist*, a Chicago-based, blue-collar workingman's journal that at the time was one of the leading advocates for the national political ambitions of former labor agitator Eugene V. Debs. Moreover, it was widely reported that not only would Debs be giving the principal speech at a Sons of Labor July 4 picnic outside Milwaukee, but that one of the preliminary speakers would be a new convert, Joseph Medill Patterson. On the day appointed, warm and sunny, with a large crowd already milling about in the open field where a makeshift platform had been constructed by Sons of Labor carpenters, and around which Joe Patterson was happily consorting in the company of such prominent socialists as Carl Sandburg, Emma Goldman, and the notorious Debs himself, all of a sudden he received a tap on the shoulder by a special messenger from the *Chicago Tribune*. Alice Patterson, it seemed, had unexpectedly and dangerously gone into early labor, for which she was receiving urgent medical attention. Patterson rushed home immediately, distraught and guilty at having pushed things so far, only to find on his arrival a situation by all appearances far from dire. He ran into the family doctor taking his leave, who seemed as blandly affable as always, pronouncing the patient healthy, with everything normal save for the usual discomforts. Upstairs he found his wife in bed but crocheting, also to his surprise his mother, both of them with the look of coconspirators, pretending astonishment at seeing him home so early, and of course regrets at his having to miss his moment at the socialist rally, both of them equally bad dissemblers.

If Joseph Patterson was already reluctant (or, some might argue, too restless, innately distracted, or self-involved) to let himself become conventionally domesticated, then his being so clumsily tricked into leaving the July 4 socialist picnic, and before delivering the speech he had put much work into, was almost guaranteed to turn an already disaffected husband into an even looser cannon. Since he could no longer deliver his speech at its intended venue, instead he published it at greater length in the *Daily Socialist*; and such was its singularly provocative nature that the little newspaper, struggling along with a modest blue-collar circulation, soon began receiving requests for thousands of reprints. "I have not done a particle of productive work, or have added one jot of wealth to the larger community," Patterson's statement began, with its odd, arresting mingling of autobiographical mea culpa and upside-down grandiosity. "For I am a member of the Capitalist class, the slave-owning class of the Twentieth Century. The rest of you have served me all my life and unless you wake up to the situation you will continue to do so; and when I am dead you will construct a handsome marble headstone over my head to keep me down."

One immediate result of Patterson's new notoriety was an invitation from the *Saturday Evening Post*, an important, mainstream national magazine, to expand his piece for wider publication. This he did, and now titled "Confessions of a Drone" ("drone" was a contemporary synonym for a do-nothing social parasite), it appeared in subscribers' mailboxes across the country to even greater effect, earning its author the sobriquet the "Renegade Heir," and thus infuriating his parents even more, also worrying his wife, who was far along in her pregnancy and not looking for more trouble. After the *Saturday Evening Post* piece came more magazine offers. In *Collier's Weekly* for a second time he challenged Marshall Field & Company, or more precisely the Field family, on the subject of a recently probated will that showed a failure to pay income taxes. What people at the time called muckraking (and what we now call investigative reporting) was fast becoming popular, and other things being equal, Joe Patterson might have continued in this vein, in the tradition of such journalistic battlers of the era as Frank Norris and Ida Tarbell. But other things are rarely equal, or remain equal for long. On October 16 Alice Patterson finally went into labor, once again in her parents' large, safe, stable household, and once again with a minimum of duress was delivered of a daughter.

· 7 ·

AT LONG LAST the subject of our story has made her appearance, in that upstairs bedroom in the grand Higinbotham mansion on Michigan Avenue. Her name was, or soon would be, Alicia Patterson; that is to say her Patterson surname was clear from the start, although it revealed a certain lack of acclamation at her debut—one might even call it an atmosphere of downright letdown—that her birth certificate stayed incomplete for many years: "Female Child Patterson." As Alicia years afterward characterized the moment: "No bells rang at my arrival." Few would have disagreed; indeed, some recollections go so far as to describe the disappointed father thudding down the Higinbotham stairs, then slamming the front door on his way out of the house. Or was it only out of his wife's birthing room? Or possibly out of all the doors and all the rooms? Again in Alicia's later words: "Father had much wanted a boy."

Fortunately Patterson's bark was usually (which is not the same as always) worse than his bite. Granted, the new baby was not as compellingly adorable as Elinor, not a showcase, demonstration-level beautiful baby. But it was a healthy kid, however unremarkable, with the right number of fingers and toes, despite of course all too evidently not being a boy. And soon enough Patterson was on companionable terms with the new arrival, referring to her affectionately and a bit abstractly as "Baby"; who in any case, in keeping with the practices of the time, was rarely visible, being nursed offstage, though not by Alice but by a wet nurse hired for the occasion, a young German girl with a baby of her own at home.

Besides, Patterson's thoughts as usual were elsewhere. He was still committed to socialism and continued to edit and write for the *Daily Socialist*. But he had lately shifted, or rather expanded, his perspective on social justice from urban politics to agrarian reform. In this he was a disciple of sorts of Count Leo Tolstoy, the great

Baby Alicia with her mother, Alice Patterson,
and older sister, Elinor.

Russian novelist, who had startled many in his country, beginning with his own family, by leading an idealistic back-to-the-land movement, freeing his two hundred serfs, and trying to institute modern farming methods on his large estate. Patterson himself had no serfs to free, and no estate, large or small, but with Alicia barely three months old, and with Alice and Elinor in tow, plus two domestics and the prospect of hiring another wet nurse from a local farm, he moved his family eighty miles north of Chicago to Madison, Wisconsin. There he installed them in a rented cottage, not far from the campus of the Wisconsin State Agricultural School, in which he had enthusiastically enrolled, so as to learn something about progressive agriculture while he looked around for a farm to buy.

It was there in March 1907 that a reporter from *World* magazine braved the snow-covered fields outside Madison to interview "Chicago's former golden society couple." In his piece he described Patterson as "handsome, all bone and muscle, now wanting to lead an honest life by learning to plough and furrow, milk a cow." Mrs. Patterson told him that "each day she walks a mile and back along the railroad tracks to the provision store," while their cottage was portrayed as "no more or less than any dairyman might afford, shared by two pretty children, a charming wife and only two servants." The novice agriculturist was apparently "reluctant to be interviewed until the subject turned to Socialism, at which point his dark brown eyes lit up"; whereupon he told the reporter that he had "sold his automobile and in a general fashion turned his back on Society," setting himself a goal for the future of "providing high-class dairy products to the sick and ailing."

By midsummer, with the Wisconsin landscape suffocating in heat instead of buried by snow, Alice Patterson was more than ready to return to Chicago and civilization. She thought she had an ally in her mother-in-law on Dupont Circle, with whom she corresponded on a regular basis. "Joe does mean so well," she wrote in one letter, "and he is so much healthier away from certain temptations. But I worry that out here he is too far removed from things that matter to him." Nellie, however, while perfectly willing to take a few swats at her rebellious son ("I do get so angry at him, and he is so bland and rude to me at times") doesn't rise to the bait. "True, he is exasperating, turbulent, willful, stubborn," she writes to Alice, "but who is to say he has not a touch of genius? Besides, I think he never did a mean, dishonorable thing in his life. I am satisfied with him." And then, to demonstrate her satisfaction, she takes for her the rare step of loosening her purse strings and advances Joe the necessary funds for him to buy and improve a farm in Illinois he's had his eye on.

THE PROPERTY was a three-hundred-acre farm in Libertyville, Illinois, a sparsely settled rural community some twenty-five country miles west of Lake Forest or, to put it another way, a two-hour journey by horse cart down a rough dirt path to a decidedly unsuburban destination, far removed in fact and spirit from the softening influences of familiar shops and neighbors. In Alicia's recollection: "I don't think father was any expert on farming, but he knew enough to see that the topsoil was deep and black, and that the corn grew as tall as you could want it—taller, in fact. The farm was bang in the middle of that bounteously rich farmland that marched in straight section-lines right to the horizon. So, fertile it certainly might be, but also unbelievably flat and bleak, fiery hot in summer, freezing in winter. And few trees anywhere, except along the fence lines or beside a muddy stream, or in little clusters we called 'the woods.' I remember April and May were always glorious, many wildflowers—trillium, hepatica, spring beauties—sometimes growing so thick you had to walk carefully not to crush them. But I don't think mother ever really made a connection to the *farming* part of the place, which of course is what it was; it was a farm. Even when the corn started growing to the sky, you knew she just didn't give a tinker's dam about such things, about corn or grain or hogs. The truth is, she thought all that kind of thing was a bit vulgar, ought to be left to the laboring classes, the Sons of the Soil as she called them. In Libertyville, even the wildflowers didn't quite meet her standard of how flowers are supposed to look. If you had to live in the country, she thought, better do it as the English do, with deer tripping daintily on lush lawns, and graceful sheep grazing in the distance. An English country house had style and presence, not an Illinois farmhouse. So, from the start, I think she and father had a kind of unspoken pact. The farm was his, the isolation and discomfort all of ours; but the house and its garden were hers. And over the years, she tried as hard as she could, with the help of architects and landscape people, to simply block out the Illinois prairie behind a screen of imported stately elms and assorted shrubbery. I don't think it was ever a marriage of two minds."

Both Pattersons, Joe and Alice, were still in their twenties, young enough to have some good days together from time to time on their remote, experimental farm. In the beginning Alicia, barely two years old, was in no position to remember much of anything beyond a blurry sense of fields and animals. Elinor at six, later claimed to

Two-year-old Alicia ponders her future.

remember that thrilling moment in their first year, the early morning when they could see that the alfalfa crop had come in: those little green shoots poking above the soil, with her father stomping about in the fields, welcoming the event with happy shouts; then marching up and down the furrows, singing some music-hall ballad, followed by his running back to the house to lift his tiny wife Alice off her feet and carry her out in his arms to show her their triumph—well, surely his triumph. Unfortunately much more of the time seems to have been passed in an atmosphere less resembling a pact than a chilly stand-off between two people who had painfully little in common: With Patterson out all day in the fields or in the barns, usually in the company of his Swedish farmhands, trying hard to be a farmer; with Alice either indoors, suffering from allergies or "nervous exhaustion" as she struggled to match fabrics to wallpaper, writing voluminous instructions to Chicago decorators, or else outside, on what she insistently called "the grounds," trailing about with her Scots gardener, trying hard to be a country lady.

Then, too, with Joe Patterson, there was nearly always the problem of focus, or perhaps of its opposite, distractedness. No matter how sincerely he might have wished to devote himself, say, to the challenge of feeding the sick and ailing, at the same time there was so often the rival challenge of keeping his attention fixed in one place. Thus, in addition to plowing and planting, to raising pigs and milking cows, to training as well as breeding workhorses, he soon went back to journalism. On the ground floor of the red-brick farmhouse, just off the front door, was a square, plain, low-ceilinged room which he took for his own, paying one of the rawboned Swedes to saw planks and install bookshelves, dragging in an old green sofa, a desk and chair, and various writerly implements, including one of the new Underwood typewriters. He called it his library, and when he wasn't out in the fields or jogging along the fence lines (sometimes skipping rope and shadowboxing) to keep in shape, he was at his desk, writing signed editorials for the *Daily Socialist*, unsigned editorials for the *Chicago Tribune*; also a growing number of articles for magazines, national and regional; also fiction, in the form of the beginnings of a novel provisionally titled "Little Brother of the Rich." All things considered it was not a bad life on the farm; there were strains and disagreements though also a kind of balance. But then, in early June 1908, seemingly on the spur of the moment, Patterson accepted a request from the leaders of the Socialist Party to serve as manager of Eugene Debs's next run for the presidency.

· 8 ·

PATTERSON'S REENLISTMENT in the Debs campaign turned out to be one straw too many for his beleaguered wife. As Alice Patterson saw it, two years earlier she and her children had been uprooted from decent society and removed to a wilderness of pigs and cornstalks; now she was being asked to undergo public humiliation because of her husband's perverse decision to align himself (and thus her) with those Reds and assorted troublemakers who were proposing the notorious, and possibly criminal, Debs for the highest office in the land. In late June a cross and embattled Alice left the farm for Chicago, where she linked up with Mother and Father Higinbotham (both of them as tiny as she), and then all three took the train east to Manchester-by-the-Sea, an hour or so north of Boston, where her older sister, Florence, and her lately acquired husband had rented an immense house close by the water.

The former Florence Higinbotham, now Florence Crane, or rather Mrs. Richard Teller Crane, seemed continually to be grabbing the gold rings that, by simple justice or some principle of sisterly fairness, should at least now and then go to Alice but somehow never did. Younger sister Alice had married first, and married well, so it appeared, into a family with all those imposing Medills and Pattersons, to say nothing of Groton and Yale. But then look where it had got her: an alfalfa crop in Libertyville and Eugene Debs. Big sister Florence, on the other hand, with her brassy voice and bossy manner, had just married into the greatest plumbing fortune in the country: Wherever and whenever bathtubs, sinks, and especially flush toilets were being installed, a mighty river of dollars flowed into the Crane bank accounts. Moreover, Mr. Richard Teller Crane was definitely not a renegade heir, was by no means ashamed of having dollars in his bank account. Indeed, in the harbor just below their summerhouse he kept a fine white yacht at anchor; in the garage was parked one of the new Renault touring cars; and upstairs in the airy nursery, thanks to Florence who obviously managed everything better, a newborn son.

After a week or so of having her nerves restored by the sea air and soothed by the comforting nearness of her diminutive parents, Alice Patterson for the first time in her marriage found the voice, at least on paper, to send back a coolish reply to Nellie Patterson, who had been pursuing her across the country with letters of concern since her decampment to the East. "Dear Mrs. Patterson," she wrote her mother-in-law: "Your last letter was forwarded to me here although I have been leading such a strenuous life I haven't had a minute to answer it. Last week we motored by way of Newport to New London and the Yale-Harvard boat races in Mr. Crane's splendid new automobile—a Renault it is. And here in town, Florence gave a big Tea in my honor, which was well-attended and most delightful. I can also report that Mr. Vanderbilt has been visiting from Newport for a few days, his wife being still abroad, and that later this week we have been promised a yachting excursion."

THERE IS POSSIBLY some arithmetic of revolt, whether of wives or Russian students, that suggests that, should the rebellion not be violent or alarming enough to actually frighten the authorities, these same authorities will either pretend not to notice it or notice it only with disdain, as a gesture of the powerless and neurotic. Granted, Alice's deft dropping of Mr. Vanderbilt's name into her letter to Dupont Circle might have scored a temporary point or two with Nellie Patterson. But it was a sign of how far apart the Pattersons had grown, with their paths not merely diverging but opposing, that in roughly the same time frame that Alice was proudly picturing herself with her Crane in-laws and all the other plutocrats, in the parade of straw boaters and white flannels at the Yale-Harvard regatta, Joe Patterson, her Son of the Soil husband, just then was putting the finishing touches on his novel, still titled *Little Brother of the Rich*, and lately accepted by a Chicago publishing house, Reilly & Britton, which energetically attacked and satirized those same kinds of people.

When Alice finally returned to Libertyville, she said she was glad to be back, which was almost the same as saying she was glad to be home, and was happily greeted by her husband and two children. All three were glad to see her, to have the household recompleted, although each one of them had evidently done quite well in her absence. In fact both girls, in the way of children who have watched their mother disappear for no reason, and now reappear for no better reason, reacted for the most part as if they couldn't tell the difference. Elinor remained engrossed in her dolls, while Alicia was engrossed in Elinor, at least when permitted access, otherwise suffering more or less cheerfully her lackadaisical supervision by Inger, the maid, and Mrs. Swenson, the cook, and being ever alert to the overexciting possibility that her father might make another of his sudden, boisterous incursions into whichever room or corridor she was stumbling about in. Alice noted, on the whole mildly, that in her absence Joe had resumed the habit of wearing his dusty farm boots inside the house, as well as of tossing the baby a little higher in the air than was probably safe. But otherwise everything seemed in order—perhaps not quite the order she had had in mind six years ago, walking down the aisle of Grace Church, but what had she known then about anything?

· 9 ·

IN THOSE FIRST YEARS out at the farm, Libertyville was barely a speck on the map of Illinois: by one measure only some thirty miles north of Chicago, a dozen miles inland from the western shore of Lake Michigan, but the terrain was for the most part sparsely populated farmland—what people still called the prairie, at least the outskirts of the prairie. The nearest town of any size or substance was Lake Forest—actually a "village," not a town—and essentially a weekend retreat for a few rich Chicagoans, one whose origins, as it happens, had much to do with Joe Patterson's own family. Back in the spring of 1855, Patterson's other grandfather, his father's father, the Reverend Robert Patterson, leader of the city's important Second Presbyterian Church, had taken an expedition of church elders north on the Chicago & Milwaukee Railway, a line so new that the track beyond the Wisconsin border was still in the process of being laid. Ten miles before the line ended at Waukegan, Rev. Patterson and his colleagues had asked the conductor to stop the train and let them off in the middle of a scraggly section of brush and scrub oak, where they stomped around for an afternoon in their frock coats and stovepipe hats until they were satisfied they had found what they were looking for—the site for a model Presbyterian community, which by its arcadian remoteness should be free from both the taints of urbanity and the heresies of rival Presbyterian factions, and which they agreed to name Lake Forest, given that the steely waters of Lake Michigan could be more or less glimpsed through the surrounding trees.

Despite his family's role in its founding (also in the establishment of Lake Forest College, built with bricks from Rev. Patterson's church, destroyed in the Great Chicago Fire), Joe Patterson himself had no special fondness for the place, especially as it evolved into a suburb of faux-Tudor mansions for Chicago industrialists.

His wife, on the other hand, looked on Lake Forest as an oasis in the bleak landscape of farm country, if not a kind of Camelot at least an aspirational enclave of English gardens and properly countrified ladies and gentlemen: alas so near and yet so far, since to travel the dozen or so miles to get there required two slow challenging hours in a horse cart over corrugated dirt roads, difficult enough in good weather and impossible in bad. Eventually, in fact in the matter of a few years, new asphalt roads would be built across the vanishing prairie, and the railroad that already linked Lake Forest to Chicago would extend a spur inland so as to include Libertyville. But for the time being the four Pattersons, young and old, Tolstoyan and not so Tolstoyan, were very much up there, on their own, on a farm in farm country.

What a grown-up Alicia remembered of her mother from those early days was a slight, cool, determined figure, often a kind of theatrically costumed presence, with her face hidden beneath the wide brim and ribbons of an English gardening hat, her small hands and arms encased in elbow-length gardening gloves. Outdoors, pacing about her "grounds" like a military commander, usually with her gardener, the stoic Mr. McGregor, at her side, she staked out the dimensions of a French orchard and supervised the planting of two long rows of young saplings, which she hoped would one day become an allée of stately elms at a European level of impressiveness, suitable for welcoming the Lake Forest Garden Club. Indoors lay a similar challenge, as she struggled with Higinbotham persistence to effect the transformation of a nondescript red-brick Illinois farmhouse into a proper "country-house," a place that would have a cedar-lined closet for the good linen, English chests for the good silver, a display case for the good china, and so on, all the while waging a never-ending and mostly useless campaign to persuade, bully, or shame the servants and the rest of her own family into showing some little respect for the niceties of civilized life.

The two children, Elinor and Alicia, seem mostly to have kept out of the way, in their own geographies and routines, maintaining separate orbits from their variously preoccupied parents, and often from each other, since there was a nearly three-year difference in their ages. Day in and day out the Patterson sisters were buttoned

Alicia ready to ride, age seven, at the house in Libertyville, Illinois.

into clothes, fed, nudged about, and more or less watched over by a sequence of Swedish farm girls masquerading as maids, also on occasion by suddenly arriving and mysteriously departing French governesses, those ubiquitous *mam'selles* of the era, whose task it was to teach "deportment" to both girls (that is, table manners, sitting up straight, and other emblems of the well-brought-up child) when not engaged in the ceremonial ritual of brushing Elinor's hair; for as Elinor had grown in size and loveliness (accompanied by a mostly amiable placidity), so too had the general importance of her hair, her long blond tresses, almost perfect, virtually perfect, but which governesses, Swedish farm girls, as well as Alice Patterson herself were always eager to improve by a fond lashing of fifty strokes with an English hairbrush.

While youthful Elinor, blond and blue eyed, seemed to be growing into the kind of cool, composed, almost languid beauty that caused young and old, males and females, to gush their approval, her younger sister, Alicia, was, from infancy, cast as a supporting player: so sweet, as people said (at least for a while), with her round, wide-open face, her dark eyes and dark hair, so demonstrably untresslike, always flopping this way and that in defiance of English hairbrushes, which in any case were only seldom applied. As did everyone else, Joe Patterson duly noted Elinor's perfections, her loveliness, what might later be called her star quality, but more often than not it was little Alicia, all knees and elbows and tousled hair, her imperfections cheerfully on display, whom he went out of his way to run after, seize, and toss into the air; "she seems to *want* to be thrown into the air," he more than once remarked to his wife, somewhat puzzled.

As for Patterson himself at this point, he might fairly be described as active on many fronts, a jack of several trades though proverbially still master of none. The farm of course took up much of his daytime energy, and while some of it was going well—sometimes quite well, other times not too badly—he was discovering (as had much of humanity before him) that farmwork was never done, that last season's good luck could just as easily turn bad for no discernible reason, and that just waiting for the alfalfa to grow could somehow cost you money. As for politics, his second (or was it his first?) vocation, despite his heartfelt dreams of social justice he could scarcely pretend much surprise at Socialist candidate Eugene Debs's disastrous showing in the presidential elections, or for that matter the general rejection of the Socialist ticket across the country. "My impression of the Socialist faction in Illinois," he wrote in a rueful farewell to the *Daily Socialist*, "is one of endless bickering, argument, and in-fighting between persons who would rather out-talk one another than advance their cause." This left a third vocation remaining, one in fact where he was finally beginning to see a little success. For his novel, *Little Brother of the Rich*, had been published in March 1909, and while its publisher, Reilly & Britton, was a Chicago firm and thus its readership was mainly in the Chicago area, all the same the book had brought appreciative reviews ("A timely and sardonic satire of spoiled Eastern collegiates . . . ," said one) and sold eleven hundred copies, enough to compel a third edition. There was even talk of a stage adaptation for a trial run in Chicago, before moving east to New York's Broadway. Out in Libertyville,

Joe Patterson now took to disappearing into his study soon after dinner, remaining behind the closed door until late at night, with the only sounds in the dark house, as Alicia remembered, being the "machine-like metallic clatter of the typewriter keys and the almost cheerful ping of the carriage bell."

· 10 ·

SOONER OR LATER Patterson would have had to return his exiled family to the city, if only to put his children, beginning with Elinor, into a proper school, at least one that offered a broader field of study than governess-taught rules of posture and memorization of the kings of France in chronological order. Stubborn as he was, however, and determined to try things on his own and not be pulled back into his family's spheres of influence, he might have stayed longer at the farm, tending to his tractor and his typewriter. But then on April 1, 1910, the sudden, unexpected death of his father changed many things for many people: one of those seemingly out-of-nowhere grand disruptions that turn out to shift the riverbeds of family narrative.

In truth, for some time Robert Patterson had been viewed, at least by those paying attention, as not the strongest iron in the fire: For years he had suffered from increasing "attacks of melancholia" as people then called depression, which lately had only been getting worse and, combined with a long habit of solitary drinking, regularly sent him off on covert visits to spas and sanatoriums as far away as Europe. Then, too, in recent months he had felt the mounting pressure from the *Tribune*'s two principal owners, his wife and her sister, Kate, to find a buyer for the paper: in other words, to sell the hallowed though financially struggling daily for cold profit, and not only out from under his own editorship, but also, as he saw it, in direct violation of the trust once placed in him by his father-in-law, Joseph Medill. Even so, as wintry March held the Midwest deep in snow, Patterson showed no outward signs of unusual problems. Late in the month he had traveled first to Atlantic City, New Jersey, to be near his ailing eighty-nine-year-old mother, then on to Philadelphia, where she was brought with pneumonia, and where in fact she died on the morning of April 1: a doubtless sad though neither surprising nor untimely event that, as a minor Chicago-related news item, began slowly to make its way back to the Midwest via the

Morse code signals of the telegraph system. But barely five hours after old Mrs. Patterson's death, a new report was being received at *Tribune* headquarters in Chicago by means of the newer, speedier, codeless circuitry of the telephone: Robert Patterson himself had just been found dead, alone, in his Philadelphia hotel room.

In those pious judgmental times, the good people of Chicago (and most everywhere else) had little tolerance for suicide, least of all the suicide of such a pillar of the community. Promptly both family and *Tribune* put out an official explanation that Robert Patterson had died from "a stroke of apoplexy" brought on by the same "winter fevers" that had just felled his mother. Although there were surely many who suspected otherwise, and some in the inner circle who seemed to know more than a thing or two about what else might have been found in that hotel room. In his biography of Robert McCormick, *The Colonel*, Richard Norton Smith quotes an April 2 message to McCormick from his mother, Kate: "I've just heard RP is dead—alone of course. He died of an overdose of Veronal. I say this in case I do not go to Chicago for the funeral for I do not want to."

Even so, when the time came, imperious Kate McCormick was on the train from Washington, unable to pass up the opportunity to deck herself in mourning and take her place in the front pew of what, even by the overblown standards of the day, had become a mammoth and bizarre ceremony: a double funeral no less, with twin coffins—aged mother and melancholic son—lying side by side in the wreath-decked transept of the Second Presbyterian Church, *tout* Chicago in attendance, and with surely much discreet murmuring among the rows of distinguished mourners. According to Alice Patterson (who had it from her husband, who heard it from his mother), at the close of the proceedings, with Kate McCormick installed beside Nellie Patterson in the receiving line, Kate had turned to her sister—one billowy, bosomy galleon to another—and gruffly whispered, "Well, Nellie, you got ahead of me this time": a heavy-handed drollery referring to the fact that her own failed, bullied, alcoholic husband remained so incoherently and inconveniently alive in a sanatorium in Virginia.

• • •

STILL A SMALL CHILD, Alicia had little to do with such grown-up goings-on. Older sister Elinor, tall for her age, and of course beauteous in bereavement, was taken to the church in a new dress, with velvet bows in her hair. Alicia stayed home in Libertyville, with a lifelong, muddled set of memories, many of them around the word "death," which as a child who had grown up among farm animals she was not hearing for the first time, though never before had she heard it accompanied by such adult explications and silences. However, one clear memory she retained pretty much forever was of her father in tears—a unique and startling sight, and doubtless a true memory since, in that era of painfully undemonstrative relationships, Robert Patterson's abrupt decampment must have left his once-rebellious son with a hodgepodge of discordant feelings. This was a situation not helped by a reading of his father's will, which conveyed a final dour message from the deceased: a request that "my son Joseph Medill Patterson return to the estate my gold cufflinks which were a valued gift from my own father."

All the same, discordant feelings or no, momentous changes were soon in the making, set in motion by an impromptu visit from cousin Robert McCormick to Patterson's farm in Libertyville. McCormick showed up early one afternoon, only a few days after the funeral, in a giant Hudson touring car, driver and vehicle equally mud splattered from the spring thaw. McCormick was slightly younger at thirty years old, unusually tall at six feet four, though broad of beam and somewhat soft and awkward. Trained as a lawyer, he was officially treasurer of the *Tribune*, a largely honorific title without real authority, serious responsibilities, or even salary. Patterson, as we know, was a sometime gentleman farmer, part-time dabbler in left-wing politics, currently an aspiring novelist and playwright who, however, had lately been given the news that his stage adaptation of *Little Brother*, which had played for six weeks at a theater in Chicago's Loop, had been turned down for Broadway. Therefore, when Cousin Bert proposed to Cousin Joe, both men stomping around in the steamy horse barn to keep warm, that the two of them should now do the unthinkable and step into the void and disarray at the *Tribune*, partly to preserve the family business, partly to gain a little financial traction for themselves, Patterson was of a mood to give it a try. The crucial question was, Would their mothers—who controlled everything, and who had wanted to sell the paper—agree to such a plan? The answer came over the next week. Yes, provisionally: That is to say the two "boys," as Kate and Nellie insistently called them, would each be given "significant responsibilities" at the *Tribune*, positions to be reviewed and renewable after one year.

· 11 ·

PATTERSON AND McCORMICK were cousins, both graduates of Groton and Yale, though they were by no means kindred spirits. Bert McCormick was a conservative Republican, also something of an Anglophile, given not only to wearing English suits but also to going about in full English hunting gear, complete with riding crop; Joe Patterson, as we know, was a barely reformed socialist, who sometimes forgot to wear socks with his shoes and often looked as if he had slept in his clothes. Luckily, however, their teaming up on the floundering *Tribune* was already proving to be a successful experiment, with Bert bringing order to the business side and Joe increasing advertising with his new, expanded Sunday edition; as a result, even before the first year's trial period was over, the two normally querulous Medill sisters seemed well satisfied with the results.

But while profits were on the rise at the *Tribune*, and Nellie Patterson certainly cared about profits, what she cared fully as much about were what people called "appearances," short for family appearances, or how things looked and what other people were saying about you. Herself a daughter of hardworking, rule-abiding, and mostly God-fearing parents, Nellie and her sister had inherited the fruits of such hard work and piety, namely the ability to do pretty much as they pleased. But she was chronically distressed by her son and daughter-in-law's "situation," by what she kept hearing outright, or "picking up," about the parlous state of their marriage; and never more so than in that period after their return from Libertyville to town, when stories about Joe's late hours and drinking, even rumors of possible scandal, increasingly began to reach her at Dupont Circle. By early 1911 she had made another of her decisions, with an authority, mostly unspoken, derived from the monthly allowance she meted out to her son from the Tribune Trust she partly controlled: Joe and Alice must once again go to Europe, to renew and restore their marriage; but this time as a family, and perhaps not so much to England and France, given those nations' well-known propensities for sensuality and decadence, as to Germany, just then becoming a popular destination for Americans.

Which is why, sometime around the middle of March 1911, Alicia Patterson, not yet five years old (and still called "Baby" by her father) found herself aboard a huge, bewildering steamship—the North German line's *Kaiser Friedrich*—plowing through the chop of the Atlantic, bound for an abstract destination called Bremen, in the company of Mother, Father, Elinor, and now a new kind of *mam'selle*, an unfamiliar, squarish, bespectacled person, in fact not called *Mam'selle* at all but *Fräulein*. As someone has surely observed, history is a river of forgetfulness, and one of its many forgettings is that, in the years leading up to the First World War, German *Kultur*, as people were fond of calling it, with its nonpareil depth in music, philosophy, science, archaeology, and so on, was widely regarded as the apogee of Western civilization. According to the peripatetic author Mark Twain, returning from a monthlong visit in 1910, the German public education system, all by itself, might be considered "an Eighth Wonder of the world," and with its "resolute humanism" presaged a future "free from the ignorant barbarism of war." What was good enough for Samuel Clemens (whose *Huckleberry Finn* had been warmly praised in Germany while being largely scoffed at by the English and unpublished in France) was certainly good enough for the traveling Pattersons, who left Chicago barely speaking to each other, and now hoped to thaw out the tundra of their marriage through the traditional American therapy of self-improvement and keeping busy.

Their plan, such as it was, called for a maximum of movement, mostly by train: east to Hamburg, south to Munich, back up to Nuremberg, then a boat trip down the Rhine to Würzburg and Frankfurt, and finally an overnight sleeper to Berlin. When not being actively transported, the married Pattersons plodded glumly through museums and cathedrals, gazed at much medieval brickwork, attended musical evenings. Meantime the two children were energetically pulled and pushed about by *Fräulein*, taken out in the morning for fresh air, sometimes to parks with carousels, and almost inevitably band concerts; and in the afternoons or whenever stationary, given lessons in German, both spoken and written, an enterprise much recommended by Nellie, whose view it was that while American young ladies, by which she mostly meant Elinor, might do well enough in the world with a knowledge of French (which Elinor already "had"), they would do even better with an addition of German, by all reports the language of the future.

ONLY A FEW SCRAPS of written record remain from that mainly well-intentioned expedition. For instance, from Munich a rather plaintive note from Joe to Nellie: "Dear Mother, I write you as a dutiful son but I have nothing to say. We do much traveling and looking about. The days are long and wet, this being Germany. I am frankly eager to be home." There is also a postcard, or perhaps a souvenir photo, left behind by Alice and not sent to anyone, just a photo of a nameless church on a city street, with a single word on the back in her handwriting, "church." From Berlin there is part of another letter from Joe to his mother, indicating that his spirits had at least temporarily picked up: "An impressive city, with energy and ambition. Our hotel accommodations v. agreeable, with a view, and not at all noisy. I believe we could learn something from their public transportation arrangements." But then a sort of postscript: "Had tickets for the Bruckner concert however Alice too sick to attend."

In that sketchy phrase, referring to what by then would have been the latest in a continuum of Alice Patterson's both real and perhaps less real physical complaints, lay the origins of a sequence of improbable happenings that would stick with daughter Alicia for the rest of her life. Improbable to us at any rate, who tend to approach parenthood differently than our forebears. For while many parents today would travel six thousand miles from home with two young children, indeed would do it easily, in a matter of hours, not weeks, doubtless few of these couples, with the mother sick from some undetermined though probably respiratory ailment, would leave the children behind in an unfamiliar pension, in a strange foreign city, in the charge of a not-long-employed governess, with instructions to stay put for possibly several months and improve their German. In defense of Joe and Alice Patterson, it's worth noting that their decision to leave Alicia and Elinor in Berlin with *Fräulein*, while they headed westward to Paris (and presumably better health for Alice) was not so unusual for the time. It didn't surprise *Fräulein*. It didn't surprise Nellie, who was soon informed by letter. It didn't even surprise the two children, who were accustomed (like many of their contemporaries) to spending long stretches of time by themselves, watched over by various domestic "minders." Besides, what could go wrong? In those days many parents from the privileged classes, with a certain degree of logic, regarded governesses in general, and *Fräuleins* in particular, as vastly superior to themselves in both the skills and patience required for child raising. What's more, the children weren't being left just anywhere; they were being left in one of the world's great centers of civilization, in Berlin, possibly the most advanced metropolis on earth in terms of science, medicine, culture, street railways, and much else besides.

What could go wrong indeed? Let us count the ways, beginning with the fact that twelve days after her parents' departure, four-year-old Alicia awoke in the middle of the night, in her bed next to Elinor's, on the fourth floor of the Gasthaus Lotti, screaming with pain from what would eventually be diagnosed as an ear infection. Then add another fact: that *Fräulein*, impeccably credentialed as she was in so many aspects of child supervision, was also, as it turned out, a Christian Scientist, one of the more devout believers, one who in a medical emergency, say, would no more seek human (as opposed to divine) medical attention than fly to the moon. And then perhaps a final complication, in that the Pattersons, far from waiting in Paris for Alice to recover from her bronchial problems, had taken a ship back to America and were already in Chicago when a cable reached Joe Patterson from a Mr. Edward Chambliss in Berlin.

Ned Chambliss is one of the happier accidents in this odd tale. At the time he was the *Chicago Tribune*'s correspondent in Berlin, and one afternoon found himself on the receiving end of a telephone call from a now nameless (though much alarmed) resident of the Gasthaus Lotti, passing along the plight of the little Patterson girl, whose infection by then had reached a dangerous stage but was being left untreated because of *Fräulein*'s superstitions. Moving rapidly, as a good reporter should, Chambliss first summoned a doctor to see Alicia, then arranged for her to be taken to a nearby clinic, and meantime fired off a cable to Patterson, lately and inconveniently arrived at *Tribune* headquarters in Chicago. Patterson himself was no slouch at movement, and soon was rushing worriedly, and doubtless guiltily, across the ocean, back to his sick child: a time-consuming reverse travel process requiring a sleeper to New York, then a downtown hotel, a morning's ferry ride to New Jersey, and then a six-day transatlantic crossing, landing once again at Bremen, from where another overnight train would carry him to the German capital.

ONE OUTCOME of this sorry business was that Joe Patterson and his younger daughter actually grew closer in Berlin. On his arrival at the clinic he was shocked at how pale and frail she looked, and concerned too by her seeming speechlessness, though much of that would turn out to be temporary, a result of her surprise at seeing Poppy materializing out of nowhere, so large and loud and unexpected, and at her bedside. But soon the unlikely duo, little girl and oversize father, each one kinetic, connective, voluble—each one too, as it would turn out, susceptible to private loneliness, never entirely comfortable in his or her own skin—began for the first time to discover each other, to begin in some ways what would become a kind of lifelong love affair. In his first letter back to his wife, also convalescing, Patterson sounded a note of simple happiness, and even lightness of soul, long missing from his communications, perhaps since his father's death. Thus: "Today Baby clambered out of bed, insisted on sitting on my lap, then slathered me with moist kisses. She is determined we will speak to each other only in German, which of course I don't understand, and shrieks with laughter when I get everything wrong. I think we are both much pleased that I am here." And a bit later: "Elinor has gravely explained to me the difference between 'mischievous,' which she says *she* is sometimes and which means merely naughty, and 'wild,' which she says is not *merely* anything but something a good deal worse, such as 'wild like Baby.' By the way, Baby has informed me that she has a poor opinion of the Kaiser, from the way he glares out at everyone from posters all over the city, also that her own real name is Alicia and she wishes not to be called Baby ever again."

Patterson and his two children spent ten days in Berlin, waiting for the doctors to clear Alicia for transatlantic travel, which on the whole seems to have been a pleasurable time for all of them. Then, on the night before taking the train back to Bremen, Patterson seems to have stayed up late in his hotel room, unburdening himself to his wife in a rarely personal, alternatively self-flagellating and accusatory letter, which perhaps served as a coda to the whole problematic European journey, as well as to the state of their marriage. "Of course I should prefer to be virtuous, simple, and maybe above all *level*," he wrote Alice, "a successful businessman say, an exemplary father. But I can't. We both know that. For I don't come of good blood, from the kind of stock that will let me feel contentment, or be free from worthlessness. . . ." And: "We must do our best, Alice. I know you can be brave, but you also need to be big, and big all the way through. Not peevish or small. Not like every lady you know, inert or malicious or quick to escape into those expressions of silent disapproval. Remember: if you haven't much of a husband, and I fully concede that point, you still have two pretty fine kids, whose lives will be made or marred by your influence." And finally: "If we could only get on together, I think everything else would solve itself. But it's knowing that we can't, that I grate on you across the board—my way of doing things, running the farm, arranging my books, looking out of the window of my study, just my way of talking, eating, driving the car, my whole point of view. Well, my guess is these would be your ways too, if I were your sort of fellow. But I am not, and I can't say as I blame you. All I can promise is, I will do my best on my return." And on that rueful note the family trio headed for home.

· 12 ·

UNFORTUNATELY AND PERHAPS PREDICTABLY, no sooner were the Pattersons reassembled back in Chicago than their marriage resumed its muddled course, though with one seeming improvement, and not a small one either, noted by Alice in a letter to her mother-in-law. "I seldom see J until past the dinner hour," she wrote, "but at least he is in good spirits and clear of eye." Since many of their recent problems had been attributed to Joe's fondness for stopping off at a bar or hotel or one of his clubs for the proverbial drink with friends, which then sometimes led who knew where, the part about being "clear of eye" at least seemed partial good news. It also might have struck Alice as a positive development that her husband, who not that long ago was writing editorials for a socialist paper and associating with Reds, had apparently found a place for his interests and energy at the family *Tribune*; where he had a small office, down a corridor from the newsroom, in which he put together the Sunday edition, with the help of his secretary, a young Irish Catholic woman called Mary King, whom he had inherited from a departing executive and once described to Alice as "extremely efficient, with plenty of good ideas of her own."

But this is Alicia's story, and at the time she knew little of any of these matters beyond the facts—facts as they seemed to her—that on the one hand her father, who had seemed so jolly and close at hand in Germany, was now again so distant as to be nearly invisible, and that her mother, who was usually all too visible though never exactly close, had lately spoiled everything by putting her in school with Elinor. Could anything be worse? It turned out that yes, it could. Mother was pregnant; of course not a word anyone would use in front of the children. The stork, it was explained, would soon be flying in with a baby brother to be named Joseph, though probably he could be called Joe.

One month before the stork's arrival, the girls were sent down on the train to their grandmother's house on Dupont Circle, accompanied by yet another governess and instructions to be good and mind their manners. Since goodness and manners minding were skills at which Elinor excelled, this was not likely to be a problem, even at Dupont Circle, where there were many precious objects to be careful about and rules to be observed. Indeed, Nellie Patterson was quick to write Alice of her gratitude for the presence of her granddaughters, although mentioning only one of them, Elinor, whose sweetness and amiable deportment were apparently equaled only by her beauty. Seven-year-old Alicia was not unnoticed, however, swiftly becoming the bad child, refusing to heed *Mam'selle* or any of the domestics or even Grams, not only with hair permanently unbrushed, dirty hands at table, in fact no discernible table manners at all, as her grandmother reported, but also with somewhat criminal or at least delinquent tendencies: using a pillow to toboggan down the broad marble banisters, hiding in the dumbwaiter, assaulting the chandeliers in imaginative ways. Things were no better on returning to Chicago, to the house on Bank Street, which the stork had obviously visited, though perhaps carelessly, depositing baby Josephine in the crib intended for baby Joseph. Predictably Elinor smoothly glided into the charming role of "Little Mother," earning coos of approval from the real mother, whereas Alicia, not so long ago the reigning "Baby," descended into tears and tantrums at any, or even at no, provocation. Worse still, she took her new persona to school, the relatively accommodating and progressive Francis Parker School, causing the headmistress to write Mr. and Mrs. Patterson one of those grimly polite and dreadful letters, suggesting that "Miss Alicia" might be better served at "an institution with greater structure" than her own.

Thus, with the usual inconveniences associated with such rearrangements, and in the middle of the school year, too, late in January 1914, Miss Alicia was transferred from Francis Parker to the more regimented University School on Lakeshore Drive. Roughly one month later, on February 20, with probably less outward signs of disturbance, Patterson himself left, the first in a sequence of departures, bound this time for Houston, Texas, and then on to Veracruz, Mexico. Houston was the assembly point for a U.S. Navy battle squadron as it prepared to attack—on the orders of President Woodrow Wilson—a force of some eighteen hundred Mexican "insurrectionists" who were in fact troops belonging to the sitting Mexican government (of which we disapproved), who currently held the post office and several waterfront warehouses on the Gulf of Mexico at Veracruz. In due course, after the arrival of navy cruisers off the Mexican port, the Mexican soldiers were impressively dislodged from post office as well as warehouses by eight or maybe ten shells, and then by the much-photographed wading ashore of two companies of U.S. Marines; which more or less constituted the Battle of Veracruz, after which a patriotic U.S. Congress handed out a total of fifty-two Congressional Medals of Honor—about half as many as were awarded in all of World War II.

As to why the presence of the Sunday editor of the *Chicago Tribune* was personally needed at such a faraway adventure, Patterson's first dispatches to the paper were prefaced with a note from "The Editors," explaining that their Veracruz correspondent was "a veteran reporter who in his present position as editor of the Sunday department is also leading *The Tribune's* pioneering newsreel camera crew in pursuit of motion-picture news opportunities." It was certainly true enough that Joe Patterson was an early appreciator of film, movies, motion pictures in general, and that the *Tribune*'s newsreel teams were among the first and best in the business. But there was truth of another kind in baby Josephine's observations, years later as a grown woman, that "Poppa pretty much walked out the door after learning I wasn't a boy. It was a time when the roof started to fall in on all of us."

· 13 ·

AS EVENTS WOULD PROVE, the devolution of the Pattersons' marriage had much more to do with the nature of the marriage itself, of the conflicting strengths and unhelpful limitations of the people involved, and most certainly, as we shall see, with the offstage presence of a third party. All the same the refusal of fate as well as Alice Patterson to provide a son to a man so driven and confused by tribalism was little help in an unraveling situation. Joe Patterson returned to his family and the Bank Street house after Veracruz, though taking his time about it, but by midsummer he was off again. Long afterward Alice Patterson told Alicia that she had never felt so lonely as when her husband was first away in Mexico, then added that it was almost as lonely when he came back.

In mid-August 1914, with the European great powers at war, Patterson headed back across the Atlantic, officially in charge of another *Tribune* newsreel crew, though soon leaving his supposed charges behind, with their cumbersome tripods and heavy cameras, in order to scout the German frontier on his own. As a result he was among the first correspondents to witness and report on the swift advance of German troops into Belgium, following a German battalion on its way into Liège by traveling in a rented touring car with three British reporters. Five months later, in March 1915, the war having settled into the trenches, he returned to the western front, this time in the French sector, making numerous flights above the lines with French aviators and reporting on some of the first air engagements. Next, in April 1916, finding obstacles in the way of a third reporting assignment to Europe, he impetuously signed on with the Illinois National Guard as an ordinary private, and went south into Texas, close by the Mexican border, where he played a small though energetic part (as a "mule-skinner," packing mules for the supply trains) in Gen. John Pershing's little war against Pancho Villa, eventually being promoted to sergeant.

Meanwhile on the home front, the Patterson family began what would become an extended, in fact never-ending, process of trying to redefine itself as a solar system revolving erratically around a largely absent sun. Mother and Elinor on the whole seemed to find a natural alignment with each other, perhaps around a shared bond of stoicism mixed in with not a small amount of denial, plus an understandable impulse to present the best face on things to the outside world. Baby Josephine of course was little more than a tiny moon in Elinor and Alice's shadow. But middle daughter Alicia seemed determined to put herself in an altogether different orbit of her own, whether from conscious intent or from some intuitive response to the growing strangeness of life around her.

Not unexpectedly the tighter discipline at the University School served mainly as a challenge to break more of the rules, and soon the new pupil was notorious for the impudence as well as the creativity of her pranks. In an early example, perpetrated at a time of frequent labor agitation in Chicago, she persuaded several classmates to rise together in the classroom brandishing "Strike" placards, only to quickly sit down again herself, exposing the placard holders to scolding and demerits: an act of defiance toward both school and classmates that was at once pugnacious and self-defeating. After a few more such disturbances, Alice Patterson's imperious sister, Aunt Florence, took it on herself to step in and have Alicia removed from school, to be admonished and set on the path of righteousness by no less an admonisher than the rector of St. Chrysostom's Episcopal Church. But needless to say Alicia's career of waywardness continued, though for a while she shifted her rebellious activities from school to after school: stealing fruit from the grocer, sneaking into movie theaters through a side alley, hitching rides on the back of ice wagons like a regular townie, and of course terrorizing baby Josephine whenever possible, thus keeping her in a seemingly constant and necessary conflict with her mother.

AS TO HER FATHER, the much-missed and glamorous Poppa, inevitably more desirable in direct proportion to the length and mystery of his absences, he returned home in February 1917, after months of unsuccessfully pursuing the mustachioed Pancho Villa across the Chihuahuan desert. He was back for little more than two months, doubtless enough time to reconfuse everyone in the family including himself, when the bugle call to arms sounded once again, only much louder this time. Spurred on by the German sinking of the *Lusitania*, America was finally in the Great War, and Sergeant Patterson of the Illinois National Guard was swift to volunteer his service once more to General Pershing, who was already beginning to assemble an American Expeditionary Force (AEF) to cross the ocean and give battle to the Hun.

Were this not his daughter's story, there would be opportunity here, and more than ample material, for describing at length Joe Patterson's service in the Great War (also known at the time as "the War to End All Wars"). Enough to say that it was in the main exemplary, honorable, and harrowing, although memories of the dead and dying, the human costs he saw all about him, continued to resonate inside his head for the rest of his life. He was thirty-nine when he enlisted, definitely on the old side, but he was determined to play his part, do his bit; also, as an inveterate man of the people he was intent on enlisting in the ranks as a private or sergeant. But higher-ups (prodded by his cousin Bert McCormick, who glided in as a major) second-guessed the recent mule skinner from the Tex-Mex border and took him in instead as a lieutenant. In brief, he shipped overseas in late summer 1917, executive officer of a four-gun artillery battery, and after some few months of training exercises at an abandoned French army base in Brittany he went into action as part of the new U.S. 42nd (or Rainbow) Division, first attached to a French corps in the Champagne district, then as part of a larger American force assembling in the shadow of the Vosges Mountains. Patterson seems to have been both liked and respected by his men, who called him "Auntie" in good-natured reference to his age, also to the commonsense attention he paid to practical matters of health and sanitation. In April 1918, after his unit was shifted west, toward the center of the Allied line near Charlevoix, he was among those stricken by a German gas attack and spent several weeks recovering in a field hospital. Returned to his brigade and promoted to captain, he fought with his unit as part of the first American offensive at the notorious Saint-Mihiel salient. According to a published brigade history, "Captain J. M. Patterson first led his battery out of danger from air attack, during which his own horse, tethered nearby, was destroyed by a German bomb . . . then, when orders to advance were received, Capt. Patterson moved his cannoneers at a gallop, down a steep hill, right through the village of Ste. Etienne, four horses pulling each gun carriage, the men hanging onto the Seventy-fives . . . arriving in time for his battery to materially assist our advance on the Boche position."

By war's end he and his brigade were still in action, living in the field, taking casualties, part of the final Allied advance through the ruined woods of the Argonne. According to those who knew him, Patterson was much affected by his experience in the war, deeply troubled by the wasteful carnage as well as by, as he saw it, an almost inbred penchant for incompetence and double-dealing on the part of French and British leadership, amounting to a virtual betrayal of the troops in the trenches. But he also took away something much more positive from his many hard months in the field: both a sense of pride at having acquitted himself well with the ordinary guys in his command, and a new, or perhaps reaffirmed, confidence in knowing that he could "speak the lingo" of the common soldier, indeed that he shared many of his tastes and interests.

After the so-called Armistice that ended hostilities on November 11, 1918, a time when those who could were heading home as fast as possible, Joe Patterson, just released from active duty, made a purposive detour before crossing back across the Atlantic. In a letter from AEF Headquarters in Rouen to his mother, after saying that he is in good health though tired and dirty, he writes that he will make "one more stop to drop in on Edward Harmsworth in London, who has offered to see me." Lately knighted by King George V as Lord Northcliffe, Harmsworth was at the time publisher of the wildly successful London *Daily Mail*, one of the great swashbucklers and innovators of the newspaper era, more or less the inventor of tabloid journalism.

· 14 ·

WHEN ALICIA'S FATHER—eleven months at the front, with gas-scarred lungs and a Distinguished Service Medal—returned to Chicago on December 20, 1918, it was a moment she remembered all her life. A cold, bright morning, with the four Patterson females, mother and three daughters, in their winter coats and hats, waiting in cavernous Union Station for the overnight from New York. The train was hours late, which only added to the strain and excitement of the moment, but then there he was, walking down the platform in his army greatcoat. "Big as ever," as Alicia recalled it, "but older, weathered, and with a limp in one leg where he said he had been kicked by a supply mule. Mother lately seemed to have acquired this wry little smile, one side of her mouth turned down, and she had on that little smile just then. As I remember it, at one point he said 'I got really scared over there,' as if, I thought later, trying to share something with us, or at least with her, from the dark places he'd been to, and mother coolly saying 'Joe, I thought *nothing* scared you,' just throwing it right back. But we had a glorious Christmas that year, I think maybe the best ever, with a big tree and colored glass balls. . . . Poppa brought a new Caruso record for mother, also a new Victrola to play it on, and perhaps to balance-out Caruso he came home one afternoon with a large, green, squawking and cursing parrot." But then three weeks later, in January, right after New Year's, he was off again.

Back to New York was where he said he was going, and "on *Tribune* business" was pretty much all he told them about it. "It was just dreadful when he went right off again," Alicia remembered. "I begged and pleaded, and it felt like we were all crying, all over the house, but I think it was mostly me. Mother was just quiet and cold, and I don't know what was going on with Elinor." In due course it would turn out that Patterson's extended sojourns in New York were for the purposes of launching a new newspaper, his own tabloid, which first appeared in May 1919 as the *Illustrated Daily News*.

It was printed on rented presses in Lower Manhattan and, though financed by the *Chicago Tribune*, was viewed by *Tribune* trustees as a small, speculative venture almost certain to lose money; indeed Patterson's mother and aunt Kate had only reluctantly agreed to put up the money because they'd been assured by their advisers that it would generate useful tax losses. Of course, the way matters evolved, more or less from that time on, with the nearly instantaneous success of the *Daily News*, Joe Patterson vanished as a regular parent; perhaps not exactly vanished, because he would reappear constantly, back and forth between New York and Chicago, though from his family's perspective mostly forth. But after early 1919, he was gone, no longer really there, in the kind of fundamental way that if you were a child, you knew something was truly different, that one kind of life had stopped and another had started, even if none of the grown-ups would tell you what kind of life that might be.

As for Alicia in those days, there remains an April 1919 letter from Patterson to his mother, trying his best to make things sound as if her grandchildren's lives were normal, even prospering. "All are doing very well," he blithely wrote. "Elinor is sometimes a bit moody as befits her age, but you will be pleased to know that Alicia has turned a corner, passing her exams or most of them, and seems to be coming into her own as an equestrienne. Mr. Rasmussen, the riding teacher, says she is the best young rider he has seen, not scared of anything. One tough kid, if you ask me." At the time, at least among families who could afford it, almost everyone could ride, could sit or handle a horse correctly, as Alice Patterson and certainly Elinor could do. But few females then rode athletically or embraced riding as a sport, with its immediate and unladylike risks—the jumps, the falls, the bruises and breaks. Patterson was an athletic horseman himself, in his own fashion; an enthusiastic polo player who could also ride to hounds, not graceful but fearless and fond of taking chances. Would it after all be such a surprise if his second daughter, the one who was not an American Beauty rose, who was not naturally cool and self-contained like her mother and older sister, might conceivably, for no reason at all, begin developing an identity in which fearlessness and risk taking were paramount, where being a tough kid was a goal to play for?

There is a saying about time healing all wounds, which like most such sayings is probably true enough except when it isn't. Time at any rate was surely moving faster and to better purpose just then for Joseph Patterson, whose *Daily News* with its splashy photos of actresses and gangsters, its "ordinary guy" approach to sports and sports heroes, its "new woman's" regard for homemaking practicalities was selling more copies almost day by day, than for the quartet of Patterson females left by the hearth in Chicago. In point of fact Alicia was not doing well at school or even well enough; she had turned no corners academically. But she could and did throw herself into horseback activities, both at Mr. Rasmussen's riding academy in town (located where the John Hancock Tower now stands) and out in Libertyville. And she lived for the periodic, all-too-brief, inevitably disruptive reappearances of her father in their seemingly abandoned Bank Street house, materializing out of the distant jazzy grandeur of New York, with his gruff and sometimes goofy manner, his pretending not to notice Mother's disapproval, and most of all for the sense he gave her of someone who—despite his overt and courtly attentions to Elinor and little Josephine—basically "got" her the way no one else did, where nothing more needed to be said about it.

BUT THEN AS ONE YEAR rolled into the next, as the strange new rhythms of the diminished household settled almost into routine, everything shifted once again. Father didn't show up for a long time, and then he was in and out of the house, and without his usual leather valise, as if he were staying somewhere else. Mother too seemed in a new phase, often out of the house herself, and when she was in she was even less fun than usual, not infrequently in the company of Aunt Florence, she of the dramatic hats and loud reedy voice echoing through the downstairs rooms, proffering advice (as was her habit) on anything and everything. The truth of the matter was that, if there now seemed to be an inchoate and unspoken feeling in the air at Bank Street of another shoe having somehow dropped, it was probably because one had; perhaps nothing so satisfyingly tangible as a shoe, perhaps something more in the nature of rumor, gossip, smoke, though the kind of smoke that all too often indicates a fire.

The rumor, gossip, smoke in question, not to be too metaphoric about it, were reports of varying substance and detail blowing in from the East, such as had lately reached even the wife-is-the-last-to-know ears of Alice Patterson, to the effect that her husband, in moving to New York, had acquired not only another paper but another woman. Ironically, as well as perhaps puzzlingly to those who didn't know him, the alleged usurper was in most ways the opposite of what Alice might have expected: some dazzling sophisticate from the fleshpots of Gotham. In fact she had a name, and besides we have already met her: Mary S. King, his now thirty-one-year-old former secretary at the *Tribune*'s Sunday department, lately moved to New York as assistant editor at the *Daily News* and now Patterson's second in command and apparently much else besides.

Of course none of this marital mess was revealed to the children, either talked about with them or even mentioned in their presence. Alice Patterson was at heart too disbelieving of the situation, also much too pained to take action. Her big sister, Florence, however, was not one to take such matters lying down, or in this instance to let her younger sister lie about passively, feeling sorry for herself. Accordingly, in October 1921, more than a month into the school year, Elinor and Alicia were suddenly yanked out of the University School, and with trunks and suitcases packed by Mother in a flurry of tissue paper and tears, with Josephine and her nanny in the rear, with Mother pulling them along from the front, they made still another transatlantic escape to the supposedly soothing environment of Europe: first a week of shopping and museum trudging in Paris; then off to Switzerland and the sedate correctness of Lausanne, where the two older girls were boarded at Mme. Gautier's École Internationale, to resume their schooling. Alicia hated everything about the new arrangements from the start: certainly prim Mme. Gautier herself, most of her equally prissy fellow students, then the tragic lack of riding (for herself, that is, since she or somebody had forgotten to pack her riding stuff), and perhaps most of all the farawayness of her father. She wrote him incessantly, detailing her loneliness, making jokes about Mme. Gautier, begging him to come and rescue her, and of course reminding him to be sure to bring her riding gear when he came to join them at Christmas. But come Christmas break, he never showed, eventually replying to her distraught letters with a confusingly self-pitying letter of his own: "Dear Alicia, you bet I miss you too . . . besides, for your information, you are practically the only person anywhere who is writing to me now. I think Josephine quit writing when she changed nannies, and Elinor stopped writing for some other reason, ditto mother." When school resumed at the École Internationale, Alicia was once again in constant trouble. She wrote her father that "Mother now is threatening to stay in Europe for another year," and vowed that she herself would "stow away on a ship" to get back to him. When nothing else appeared to work, she climbed out of her dormitory window after curfew and escaped briefly into town, causing the headmistress finally to expel her. But Mother was still in no mood to return to the all-too-American Midwest, and instead moved everyone to England, to a country inn at Stratford-on-Avon, there to obtain the benefits of a six-week Shakespeare festival.

THE LITTLE GROUP CAME BACK to America in mid-September 1922, with Patterson there to meet them on the New Jersey docks: perhaps not a great reunion, since his jaw was almost swollen shut from an abcessed tooth, and from that or other causes he seemed especially distracted, though probably better than none. He stayed long enough to escort them across the Hudson and see them into a hotel, but then he was gone; and then suddenly, as it were, Mother, Elinor and Josephine were also gone, or about to get on a train back to Chicago; and Alicia was now on another train, heading south to Baltimore, from which city arrangements had been made by Nellie Patterson for her to be met at the station and then driven out to St. Timothy's School for Girls, where (the school year having already started) she had been enrolled in the fourth form, or tenth grade. In days to come she received a letter from her mother, back in Chicago, combining advice as well as uplift: "Make up your mind that you are going to like everything and that people are going to like you, and you will see that they will. But if they see you whimpering and wearing that bleak and angry expression you get when things do not go your way, I am afraid your schoolmates will decide that you are not a good sport. So try to be sweet and polite always. It is not so hard as all that, and believe me it pays. And remember, it is not how someone else behaves to you that matters, it is how you behave towards them. Love, Mother."

Her father went down to visit in October and reported back to Alice: "Alicia seems to be doing all right, but I can't help but notice that she has already collected a whole bunch of new bruises and scars. . . . The fact is, I never saw such a child for damaging herself. Her latest achievement was to slide down a rope fire-escape from an upper story, in some way losing her grip so the rope burned through her fingers almost to the bone." Alicia hung on at snooty, snobby "St. Tim's" almost to the end of the year. But her grades were poor and not improving, and her disposition for rule breaking was not showing any signs of true repentance. The final straw, it appears, was the discovery in her footlocker of a copy of *Anna Karenina*, at the time prominent on the school's list of forbidden books because of its scandalous subject matter, and perhaps characteristically (though unknowingly) sent to her from fellow troublemaker, and Tolstoy enthusiast, Poppa Joe Patterson. And once again she was out.

· 15 ·

THERE'S NO NEED for us to spend more time on boarding school miscreances, though it may be worth noting that Alicia's next educational port of call was the redoubtable Foxcroft School in Middleburg, Virginia, with its imperious Miss Charlotte at the helm, or perhaps one should say on the parade ground, given the headmistress's idiosyncratic approach to feminism, which required the girls to "form-up" once a week in platoons and march about with wooden rifles on their shoulders. On the whole Alicia managed quite well at Foxcroft, for all its old-fashioned ways, possibly a result of the school's lesser emphasis on bluestocking bookishness than, say, St. Tim's, combined with the greater availability of sports in general and riding in particular. It also doubtless made things easier that her father, who always seemed to know sometimes unlikely people "from somewhere," had apparently met up with Miss Charlotte along the way, and that the two of them were friends of a sort. At any rate, by the end of her first term Alicia had levitated herself to being second in her class academically, with several riding prizes to her credit, and returned in early December to Chicago, to the family's new home on Walton Place, expecting not unreasonably to have her turn-around performance praised, or at least noticed.

Once there, however, scarcely anyone seemed aware of her existence, let alone interested in history grades or horse-jumping awards. Walton Place, that is to say the new Patterson apartment, which left to itself was a spacious, even handsome residence, with oak paneling downstairs, and an imposing ebony piano in the drawing-room, had not been left to itself. Instead it was now a scene of startling upheaval and disarray: yards of dressmaking cloth lay strewn about the furniture; the dining-room table was mostly buried beneath a litter of lists and envelopes; Alicia's own small room upstairs was made considerably smaller by the presence of two dressmaker dummies and still more fabric; and her mother, who not long ago had been in the habit of delicately wafting in and out of the house in a kind of stoic melancholy, now marched in from winter streets (and often just as quickly out again) with the brisk stride of a military commander planning great things. And true enough, great things were afoot. For Alice Patterson was engaged in orchestrating the debut, the presentation to Chicago society, of her eldest daughter, the lovely Elinor, to take place on December 21. Thus caterers must be interviewed and then reinterviewed; pastry chefs need be consulted; bandleaders had been visited in their gloomy offices in the Loop, who later sent over pale young men with lists of music for Madam to approve or disapprove. Meanwhile Madame Chloe, the milliner, followed by her assistants, bustled in and out of the house as if it were her own; hats and hatboxes were now everywhere; also sewing girls with German accents, dropping pins about the floor; and last but not least the right coiffeur yet had to be decided on, from a waiting list of temperamental men with little mustaches and charming names, all from the best hotels, alternately pleading with and trying to bully the debutante, her mother, indeed any of the womenfolk they could get their hands on into trying *this* or not doing *that.*

In the end, of course, Elinor's coming-out party was a brilliant success. The grand ballroom of the Blackstone Hotel was decked in flowers, and two bands played, one for waltzes in the first part of the evening, another later on for the new "young people's" dances, the Castle walk, the turkey trot, the Charleston, currently all the rage in New York. Some said there were four hundred guests, others thought six hundred if you counted the party crashers. The next morning all the Chicago papers splashed the glamorous event across their society pages, with large photos of the deb's mother, looking almost serene in a plum velvet gown, wearing pearls borrowed from her sister, Florence; also of the deb's father, clearly present, much in family mode, and resplendent, as the saying goes, in white tie and tails; and most naturally of Elinor, now widely acclaimed as "the Deb of the Year" (though not, it should be said, in the *Tribune*), standing beneath one of the ballroom arches in her pale green gown, with her beautiful blond hair so perfectly coiffed (enhanced for the evening with a little Egyptian tiara), and with her agreeable features arranged in an expression, neither stuck-up nor overmodest, that seemed to be saying, Well, why *not* me? As for Second Daughter, with her report card and riding ribbons still sitting in her suitcase, Alicia found herself ignominiously grouped with little Josephine in the underage category, and so was briefly bundled into the Blackstone for a glimpse of swank and glamour, and then bundled out again before the party began.

WHILE ALICIA AND ELINOR were buddies of a sort in their youth, thrown together in the inevitably shared situations of childhood, by the time of Elinor's debut they had less and less in common: different sensibilities, metabolisms, secrets, and so on; and over the years to come their lives would virtually cease to intersect, for practical purposes diverging into quite separate narratives. All things being equal, then, this latest Elinor moment, with her grand debut, swell party, and all the attentions that immediately followed, might be as good a time as any to bid farewell to First Daughter, who would turn out to live a long life, though one largely out of sight and out of mind from her younger siblings, especially Alicia. Farewell, lovely Elinor! But all things are seldom equal, and what more or less immediately followed Elinor's big moment in Chicago turned out to be an even bigger moment, on a wider stage, and is surely worth at least a mention here.

Where to begin? One place might be in Salzburg, Austria, where in 1920 the theatrical impresario Max Reinhardt, an Austrian Jew, had designed and staged an elaborate spectacle based distantly on the ultra-Christian passion plays of southern Germany, in which Gregorian chants, quasi-Wagnerian themes, and Roman Catholic pieties were mingled together in a smoky, soulful spectacle, set in the facsimile of a vast Gothic cathedral, centered on two female figures, one described as "the Virgin Mary," the other as "the Tragic Nun," and accompanied by an enormous cast, literally more than one hundred pilgrims, beggars, cripples, and so on, the whole thing enacted without dialogue, in pantomime. The massive production was called *The Miracle* and was a huge success, first in religiously devout Bavaria, soon after in Berlin, Paris, and then London, where the absence of dialogue proved to be an especially brilliant touch:

Alicia's sister Elinor as the Tragic Nun in an American production of *The Miracle*, 1924, with Lady Diana Manners as the Virgin Mary.

Miming added a kind of portentous dignity to the goings-on, while the not-having-to-speak made it possible to cast celebrities and society beauties in the two key roles; for example, the aristocratic, glamorous (and privately naughty) Lady Diana Manners famously played "the Virgin Mary" in the wildly acclaimed London run.

At this point a diminutive, hyperactive New York theatrical producer by the name of Morris Gest enters the story. Gest had managed to secure the financial backing of the New York financier Otto Kahn for an American tour, and was looking for an innocent American beauty to play "the Tragic Nun." On his search Gest somehow bumped into a personage already known to these pages, the lately divorced Countess Gizycka, now once again calling herself Cissy Patterson; in other words Joe Patterson's sister, the children's aunt Cissy, who mindful of her niece Elinor's recent social-page stardom, suggested that the producer and the debutante get together. In his memoir, *On My Own*, Mr. Gest described the meeting, which took place in Cleveland where he had come to scout cathedral-sized venues for his touring drama. "The little lady," he wrote, "stepped into my office, so lovely, and classy too, but modest. She said she would do anything, the smallest part. She had this look about her, so simple, almost spiritual without being actually religious. Needless to say, I at once asked her if she would agree to play 'The Nun.' The rest, as they say, is history, if sadly of the totally forgotten kind.

The Miracle had its American opening in Boston on December 16, 1924, to sell-out crowds and awestruck reviews, with Lady Diana Manners reprising her role as the Virgin Mary, and Miss Elinor Patterson, in a magnificently costumed nun's habit, with eyes wonderingly cast upward or somberly cast downward, as the Tragic Nun. The production then moved to New York's giant Hippodrome Arena (one of the few venues with enough space for setting up a satisfactory Gothic cathedral), where it stayed for many hugely profitable months before traveling off across the country to equally welcoming destinations, very much including Chicago. There its arrival coincided nicely (depending on one's point of view) with Alicia's own little debutante party, also at the Blackstone but with only one all-purpose band, and (so she claimed) champagne from Canada, and where much of the chatter in the receiving line was naturally about Elinor: Would she be there? Would Lady Diana? The answers being yes to the first, no to the second. And then, some months later, when *The Miracle* reached San Francisco, Elinor suddenly disappeared, leaving the show, a life on the stage (or at least a life in a plywood cathedral), and ran off to be married to Proper Bostonian Russell Codman. And so at last: farewell, lovely Elinor!

· 16 ·

LEDYARD SMITH was not Alicia's only suitor, or even the most impressive, but he seemed to be cut from different and more interesting cloth than her other beaux, as people used to call them, or "young men" or "swains" and so forth. Not that he wasn't from the same proper, prosperous Midwestern background as most of his rivals: For instance, young Daggett Harvey (of the railroad dining-car Harveys) or Sage Cowles (of the Minneapolis newspaper publishing Cowleses) or Princeton junior Adlai Stevenson (also from a newspaper publishing family, in downstate Illinois), or for that matter Smith's fellow Yale classmate, Jim Simpson, son of the president of Marshall Field & Co., and perhaps his chief competitor. As it happened, Smith and Simpson were each fair haired, tall, athletic, both formed in the same Anglophile, Eastern prep-school mold at St. Paul's, and friends of a sort. But where the Marshall Field heir was cool, assured, and self-contained sometimes to the point of arrogance, an unusually gifted college athlete who already played polo at an international level, Ledyard Smith was more of a warmhearted, enthusiastic outdoorsman with an adventurous spirit; an undergraduate archaeology student, he was sufficiently proficient to be heading south soon to Guatemala, on a dig among newly discovered Mayan ruins for the Carnegie expedition.

The time we are talking about is the summer of 1926, six months or so after Alicia's coming-out party at the Blackstone. There's a photo portrait from that period: a youthful, pretty face, though one perhaps not yet fully formed or well defined, and wearing a somewhat anomalous expression that might be described as demure or even maidenly. Given the all-too-real reputational hazards for a girl her age (nineteen and some), and in her position, of not being an actual maiden, it's more than likely she was still *intacta*, as the horrible Church Latin adjective put it; but while not being a seriously "bad" girl, she was definitely not a "good" girl either. By the conservative standards of the midwest, she was probably somewhere on the near or far edge of being "fast," as well as footloose; which is to say that, having failed her entrance exams to Bryn Mawr college, she hadn't bothered or quite got around to applying anywhere else; and what with her father busy in New York with his ever-more-successful tabloid (and ever-more-complicated personal life), and with her mother preoccupied with Elinor, and if not Elinor then with something else, Alicia was mostly content to spin her wheels as a horse-riding society girl, going to parties, shuttling between Chicago and Libertyville, and now nearby Lake Forest, with its sporty Onwentsia Club.

In July, when young Ledyard Smith disappeared into the Guatemalan jungle, "four mule-riding days from the nearest trading-post," as he put it in an early letter, for a while he seems to have had

Alicia, demure debutante, at her coming-out at the Blackstone Hotel, Chicago, 1925.

Polo-playing Jim Simpson, department store heir and Alicia's mother's favorite.

Alicia's mostly devoted and certainly romantic attention. More letters followed (most of which she kept all her life). For example: "Our little boat upriver was so crowded with Indians I couldn't stand up and for once in my life I was almost glad you weren't with me . . . but at last we are on our way to the Oaxtun mahogany camp, which I think will appeal to you if or when you come down." And: "How was our child, the little dog, and what can I bring him and you from the wilds . . . ?" And: "I love you terribly, dearest. Let me know if you love me and exactly how much you love me." Alicia replied to these endearments with her own warm protestations of love, as well as her eagerness for life in a Central American rain forest. But the truth was, she had not grown up with many examples of constancy in her life (aside from those noble sentiments expressed in the nineteenth-century poems her father loved to recite out loud). Besides, her other suitor, the impressive Jim Simpson, was not in Guatemala but right next door, so to speak, scoring goals on the polo field of the Onwentsia Club. In early December, when Ledyard emerged from his dig, he returned to Yale, sought out Simpson at Scroll and Key (the "secret society" both men belonged to) and in a spirit of Ivy League chivalry, politely asked his rival to step aside; when neither man would give up the quest, they ended up exchanging one of those sweet, weird handshakes of bygone days, accompanied by the obligatory wish that the best man win.

As for the object of all these knightly attentions, Alicia was neither especially desirous nor obviously ready to sign her life away to either boy, or man, or in fact to anyone at all. But then, in the way of large, conveniently faraway planets that suddenly change course and inconveniently start looming closer, both her parents, each in his or her own way, apparently decided to take an interest. First, her father, after returning unexpectedly to Libertyville one too many times and finding his daughter still out in the middle of the night, "driving around," decided to bring her to New York, install her in a room in his apartment, and give her a low-level reporting job on the *Daily News*. This interesting experiment lasted three months, more or less, with Alicia by no means unwilling to run errands or trot around, notebook in hand, taking notes for the society page; in the end it largely foundered on young Miss Patterson's chronic though cheerful confusion as to where exactly she was supposed to be, and when, and such details as, for example, who was it she had just interviewed? Meanwhile, back in Illinois her mother had been pursuing a different and altogether more ambitious strategy. This being a time when parents were fond, in thought and practice, of "settling down" their children by marrying them off, Alice Patterson had several businesslike conferences, or chats, with Mr. and Mrs. Simpson, and together they came to the sound conclusion that the best thing for young Jim and Alicia would be to make their evidently close friendship legal.

When Alicia first got wind of the maternal push for a Simpson marriage, she was still in New York, still corresponding with the distant, beguiling Ledyard, and was distinctly cool to the idea. "I really don't think I want to marry Jim, now or ever," she wrote her sister Josephine. "Please don't tell mother because I know they'll [*sic*] be a complete explosion when she finds out." But by June 1927 she was back on the Libertyville farm, unceremoniously bounced from her job on the *Daily News*, personally fired by none other than her pompous uncle Bert McCormick (since the war now preferring to be known as Colonel McCormick, or just "the Colonel"), feeling isolated and sorry for herself, and in a mood to agree to an August wedding to Simpson. At which point Ledyard Smith reappeared, on a two-week leave from his Guatemala excavations, first looking for his beloved in New York, next pursuing her to Libertyville, where, catching her in a different mood, he apparently persuaded Alicia instead to fly the coop with him, back to his tent in the jungle.

Alicia in white satin and lace before her Lake Forest wedding to Jim Simpson, 1927.

Some of what ensued sounds today like a scene, or several scenes, from one of the romantic comedies of that era. For instance, in the *Boston Herald*, August 19, 1927: "Society Girl Betrothed to One Man, as Another Gets License to Wed Her." From the *New York Times* of the same day: "Mr. Ledyard Smith, a young archaeologist with the Carnegie Expedition, explained that he had been in a hopeful and romantic mood" when apparently all by himself he had obtained a marriage license in Waukegan, Illinois (a town notorious for overnight marriage licenses), somehow "unaware that his intended was already engaged to another." Perhaps a better exegesis of this odd tale was that Alice Patterson, on being tipped off about her daughter's escape with Ledyard to the marriage-mills of Waukegan, had quickly sprung into action: first calling in her chips among Chicago's society reporters so as to announce her errant daughter's retroactive engagement to Simpson, and then browbeating her not-quite-ex-husband to send out a similar story to newspapers across the country.

THE HAPPY COUPLE

WEDDED AND "BEST"

The bride and groom with the maid of honor and best man. Left to right: Josephine Patterson, Alicia Patterson (the bride), James Simpson Jr. (the bridegroom) and Robert S. Pirie.

The bride and groom, with (*left*) sister Josephine, as noted in the *Chicago Evening American.*

Faced with this force-majeure countermove, Alicia folded and returned to Libertyville, while poor Ledyard fled the scene, still trying to explain to sardonic reporters how, or why, a man might take out a wedding license on his own, returning to the safety of the Guatemalan mahogany forest. (NOTE: *It's worth mentioning that Ledyard Smith stayed the course in archaeology, in due course becoming Professor Ledyard Smith, and eventually chairman of Yale University's preeminent Department of Archaeology, where by the end of a long and distinguished career he had been recognized as one of the pioneers in the excavation and interpreting of the great archipelago of Mayan ruins that runs south from Mexico into Central America.)* Two days later the recent runaway bride, her face now swollen by tears and a bad case of hives, accompanied her mother to dinner with her future Simpson in-laws at their Tudor villa in suburban Glencoe. And five

Once a farmhouse, the Patterson house in Libertyville, Illinois, early winter.

weeks later Alicia Patterson and James Simpson, Jr., were duly married, at a small, mostly private ceremony in the former Patterson farmhouse in Libertyville (by now convincingly transformed into a Georgian mansion), with the ruddy-cheeked, very Episcopal rector of St. Paul's School officiating, and the scion of a rival Chicago department store as best man. The lovely Elinor, now Mrs. Russell Codman, had been designated matron of honor but called in sick at the last moment. Uncle Bertie McCormick, recent terminator of Alicia's journalism career and copublisher of the *Tribune*, arrived in a maroon Rolls-Royce, with three bodyguards to protect him from what he called "new business competition" by the Chicago mob. For doubtless many reasons, the bride, who had seemed surprisingly self-possessed throughout the service, burst into loud sobs at its conclusion, and couldn't or wouldn't stop crying for long minutes, though apparently quieting down enough to whisper loudly to her father to the effect that, while she may have agreed to a wedding, her intention was to stay married to Simpson for only one year, no less but no more.

· 17 ·

WITH ALL THESE HAPPENINGS taking place at more or less the high-water mark of the so-called Jazz Age, also known as the Era of Easy Money (at least for those who had some), it must have seemed almost natural, or at least not too unusual, that the young, and let's admit it by no means unspoiled newlyweds, had been gifted by the groom's rich father with a yearlong honeymoon: to be spent in England mainly riding horses, refining equestrian skills on the tough venues of the top English foxhunts, trying to learn what they could from the people who thought they had invented the sport. From a date three days after the wedding, there remains a newspaper photo showing the bride and groom at the deck rail of the great, four-funnel steamship *Aquitania,* Alicia in a trim new traveling suit and fashionable cloche hat, her head not quite at a level with her much taller husband's shoulders, both of them chic, abstracted, and a bit blurry, though that might be a result of the obligatory sailing photo. Five days later they were in Liverpool, then London, and soon after back up into the English Midlands, in Leicestershire: then the heartland of English foxhunting country, where they began installing themselves in the town of Melton Mowbray.

Should anyone be interested: In the phrase "painting the town red," there actually *was* such a town; and the town was Melton Mowbray, where in 1832, or maybe 1833, the contents of three wooden buckets of red paint were splashed and flung about by the dashing, fun-loving, and mostly sodden young Earl of Somerset and his fellow huntsmen of the then-famous Quorn Hunt. Not quite one hundred years later, "the Quorn" (as it was known) was perhaps even more celebrated and esteemed, as possibly the best of the 120 or so foxhunting "packs" in England, with its meets bringing together many of the most skilled and audacious riders in the nation, a clubby gathering of mainly aristocratic riders of both sexes, in which the Simpsons had arranged to be included. Nor was this a casual, picturesque, weekend type of activity; indeed, "riding with the Quorn" was in some ways—in its physical demands and possible dangers—at least an equivalent to a long winter's skiing in the high Alps: day after day going out on difficult runs, often in bad weather, in the company of the strongest and most competitive athletes. A season with the Quorn commonly ran from autumn well into winter, with as many as five or six meets in a week, each one a hard day's outing, with sometimes sixty or seventy riders running their thoroughbreds at speed over uneven, gorse-covered fields (good protection for the fox, though with hidden hazards for horse and rider), across streams and brooks, taking high fences and stone walls at a jump, or not. Thanks to Papa Simpson's largesse, the young Simpsons' well-smoothed introduction to the British hunting scene extended to their living quarters, a suite of rooms at Bishop's Inn, where the Prince of Wales, also a member of the Quorn, kept his own of course much grander suite. Out on the field Jim Simpson was easily the better rider of the couple, a world-class equestrian who in December wrote his father "how gratifying it is to be referred to here as Mr. Simpson, American sportsman and rider, and not always merely as the son of the president of Marshall Field." For her part

The Quorn field assembles, early morning;
AP is the lone woman in the middle.

Alicia was good enough at least to hold her own in a tough crowd of women riders; what she lacked in precision and training she made up for in gumption and daring, galloping headlong when she could, and accepting the bangs and bruises that came with sometimes being thrown. For much of the season she went out three or four times a week, in the saddle for most of the day, with time-outs for a change of mounts. Even with the falls, however, the days were often easier than the nights, when she chafed under the British custom, all too easily adopted by her husband, whereby the women were left behind while the men went out to dine and drink together.

And then she had one mishap too many; as it happens not from being thrown by a horse but from a sudden, unexplained bleeding, an internal hemorrhage, while cantering across a farmer's field. Back at the inn, after a doctor's visit, the problem was revealed as a miscarriage from a pregnancy she hadn't known existed. Worse still, it was from a rare, ectopic (or tubular) pregnancy, which in the short term brought with it considerable pain, and in the long term made it impossible for her to have children (a consequence only disclosed much later). It's doubtful she told her husband about the miscarriage or that he'd have known how to respond had she done so; as things were, with his new wife pale, "under the weather," and confined to bed, Simpson apparently saw no reason to alter his own schedule of hunting and dining out. But then, as Alicia recuperated at the inn, still hurting and feeling woebegone, she received a happily distracting letter from her father in New York. Whether vaguely guilty toward his daughter or just momentarily bored himself, for the time being he seemed to have abandoned the role of stern and disapproving father (of both feckless cub reporter and runaway bride) and now reappeared as good-natured, boyish Poppa. "I just read your letter about the English hunts," he wrote, "and much like what you said and how you said it. I kid you not, you have a faculty for vivid, straightforward writing, and my guess is if you want to cultivate this you can get somewhere . . . What I'm proposing is, you write me an article of 3 or 4 thousand words for *Liberty* about the English hunts and Melton Mowbray in particular. Tell about all the different kinds of people you're around, both the nobs & ladies & the grooms etc. who do the work. . . . Not too much horsy stuff but *good* horsy stuff. Customs of the hunt. The Prince of Wales on horseback. Anything of interest to the American mass reader—actually much like what you wrote in your letter. We'd pay a fair price for it, though not sight unseen, and if you do a good job it could help you make a start in the magazine business."

This was what Alicia needed to hear, and she quickly began to regain both strength and spirits, finding a typewriter to rent at a local law firm and soon setting to work in her room. She approached the piece as if she were writing another letter to her father: At once personal and informal, she spun out a narrative from the perspective of a clueless though spunky American girl rider in the heart of the British hunting establishment, struggling to get things right; with gossipy anecdotes, such as the time when the Prince of Wales got thrown at Dugald's Gate just like everyone else; how she herself seemed to hit the dirt at least once a day, though Lady Somebody, in her sixties, had just managed five hours in the rain without a tumble. Unlike many of Alicia's previous efforts, both at school and at the *Daily News*, this time she worked hard and methodically, taking pains, checking facts, doggedly rewriting, and making sure to have her copy "clean" before mailing it off. Two weeks later she heard from her father by cable: STORY ACCEPTABLE NEEDS ANOTHER THOUSAND WORDS. She quickly wrote another thousand words, put them in the mail, and cabled her father back: WORDS ENROUTE USE MAIDEN NAME ON BYLINE.

· 18 ·

IN APRIL 1928, in the same week as her husband was off in the north of England, training to compete in the famous Aintree (or Grand National) Steeplechase, Mrs. Simpson also traveled north, to Liverpool again, where she boarded a ship and sailed for home; or rather, where she hoped her next home might be: New York, her father's new base and surely welcoming domain. Joe Patterson, however, despite his success with the *Daily News*, had more than enough domestic problems of his own, not only his highly visible though formally unacknowledged mistress, Mary King, living in an apartment down the street from his own, but also now an illegitimate son, James or Jimmy, and accordingly was less than eager for added complications. Thus, instead of being greeted by Poppa's open arms, the new *Liberty* contributor was instead rather brusquely reminded that, despite a byline carrying her maiden name, she was still Mrs. James Simpson, Jr., still married to Mr. Simpson, and properly belonged back in Chicago at her husband's side when he returned to resume the pleasures of domestic life.

Cross but more or less obedient to her father's wishes and, besides, having few alternatives, Alicia made her way back to Chicago, then out to Lake Forest, where she started looking for a house to rent for herself and Simpson; nothing substantial or with too long a lease, since her plan was still that she would soon be single again, after her year of marriage was up in late August. This time uncomfortable reality intruded in the person of her mother, another marital expert in the family, who not only disapproved of her daughter's breezy notion of dissolving a union that she, Alice Patterson, had done much to create but then, more usefully, took Alicia in to visit with an experienced lawyer: a Michigan Avenue veteran who briskly spelled out the relevant details of Illinois law, essentially that the quickest she could expect to be divorced, in any sort of binding fashion, would be after at least two years of marriage.

Stymied yet again, and now stuck in a Lake Forest rental with a husband who, on his return from England, appeared to show no greater interest in her than she in him (who in fact was currently in New England, looking into Eastern law schools), Alicia's first thought was to use her newfound magazine-writing skills to gain some needed independence and in the process get back into her father's protective orbit. Confidently she fired off a daughterly letter to New York, asking for another assignment from *Liberty* (which, by the way, was a new general-interest magazine, owned by the Tribune Company though financed from surging *Daily News* profits), but Patterson was still in no mood to be helpful. Instead of the easygoing, friendly banter of "I kid you not" encouragement, he sent back a note of blunt dismissal: "What makes you think you can write about anything *except* horses? Besides," he scrawled, "the magazine needs no more articles on that subject. . . . Next time you write for an assignment you should check the spelling in your letter."

All the same she persisted, and soon came up with an idea for a series of articles on the different challenges faced by young working women in the notoriously male-dominated Chicago job market.

Alicia clears a five-foot-seven-inch jump at the Onwentsia Club, Lake Forest, Illinois.

As she explained in her spell-checked proposal, the pieces would be "nothing too serious or sociological" but rather something informal and more personal. Patterson didn't answer for several weeks and then wrote back with a perfunctory, almost grudging sign of approval, adding that she would likely find the new assignment "harder to do than you expect, the work more difficult than you are accustomed to."

Each day she took the train into the city from Lake Forest, and with a borrowed identity (volunteered by a neighbor in Libertyville) she trudged around the Loop, responding to a variety of job-offer ads, in the process putting up with continual rejection, demeaning jokes, and outright hostility. A junior editor, doubtless instructed not to be too easy on the boss's daughter, sent her first article back for four rewrites. Patterson himself then provided the final edit, scolding her that "Coca-Cola is among our big advertisers so don't call it 'poisonous stuff,' at least not on a whim," and giving further lectures on correct style. "It's just lazy and unschooled," he wrote with his red pencil, "for a writer to shirk punctuation. And never, *never* use dashes instead of commas, parentheses and so on." The second article was even harder to complete: a supposedly humorous sequence of vignettes showing the writer making a mess of the simplest and least-demanding jobs, such as movie usher, department store greeter, and so on, but in the end she finished it and saw it published. Then in late summer, struggling to come up with something else, while at the same time trying to maintain the facade of her virtually nonexistent marriage in the dead zone of marriage-proud Lake Forest, a solution suddenly revealed itself to her, perhaps to several of her problems all at once.

· 19 ·

THE SEQUENCE OF EVENTS went something like this: Given that Joe Patterson throughout his life (doubtless to some degree in response to his own conservative origins) had been an enthusiast for the new—new ideas, new things—it followed, more or less, that first he would have been an early proponent of aviation, and next that as a fiftieth-birthday present to himself, or so he said, in the course of that same summer of 1928 he signed up for flying lessons. The problem was that Patterson, in flying as in many other activities, inclined to impatience, clumsiness especially around machinery, and a marked degree of carelessness about his own person. Thus on a mid-August morning, at the far end of a grassy airfield on Long Island, instead of waiting as he should have for his instructor to check the wind and so on, clearing him for takeoff on his first solo flight, Patterson blithely took off on his own say-so, made one wobbly circle of the field and then crash-landed, mostly destroying his plane and in the process receiving many cuts and bruises.

As *Editor & Publisher* wryly reported the incident: "On takeoff, the soloing editor's wing was observed to dip in a manner already dangerous for both machine and pilot. Then on the landing he came down early, very hard, the biplane's nose right in the ground, narrowly escaping with his life." Not surprisingly many voices were raised, among them those of his wife, his mistress, daughter Elinor, and a Greek chorus of newspaper executives, to persuade the battered though not entirely chastened pilot to act his age and remain on the ground. Only Alicia went against the consensus, dashing off a note to remind him, "You've always been right, telling us never to quit or give way to fear . . . and so you shouldn't do so now." Alicia's tough-minded, chiding words, so much like his own to her on many occasions, apparently struck a responsive nerve in Patterson, and he wrote her back right away, much more warmly than before, thanking her for "my only vote of confidence," seemingly

On a dare, AP steers a glider in for a landing,
Roosevelt Field, Long Island, 1929.

once again in Poppa mode. When she followed up with a second letter, declaring her own interest in flying lessons, perhaps as potential material for a *Liberty* series, he replied cheerfully, "I think you have a good idea, it's a grand experience," and suggested she get herself out to an airfield and persuade someone to take her up.

Almost certainly what Patterson had in mind was that his daughter should try her wings at some airfield near Lake Forest or in the Chicago area, at any rate in the Midwest, her part of the world. But Alicia, whose impulsiveness had badly misled her all too recently, now gambled once again, packed her bags, boarded the train for New York, and once more placed herself, quite literally, on her father's doorstep at Forty-First Street and Madison Avenue. By doing so she thereby left behind the Old World of mother, husband, Chicago, Lake Forest with its Scott Fitzgeraldian ambience of country club, lawn tennis, polo—the whole pure, high-WASP culture of the Midwest—seemingly determined to reinvent herself overnight, under her father's benevolent umbrella, in the New World of miscellaneously populated, urban New York, and as something she hadn't thought about till just a moment before: one of the first women, as she would turn out to be, in a small, self-selected cohort of female pilots: aviatrixes, as they were called.

As luck would have it, Poppa's goodwill was still on tap when she arrived. He was as usual preoccupied with many matters, great and small, but with a mixture of bluster and bemusement he let her "bunk in" with him, in what was in fact a large, haphazardly furnished apartment, clearly not much lived in, and waited to see what she would do. At first it was much as he had expected. After advancing her a small amount of spending money, he watched as she spent most of it on a cab ride out to Curtiss Field near Malverne, Long Island, where in her own later recollection she "walked or rather strutted like a fledgling little Amelia Earhart into the flight shack in which a handful of wind-burned pilots were lounging about." She asked if any of them would take her up for a flying lesson, but none would, or showed the least interest in the new arrival. At last one of them laconically pointed with his thumb to a sign on the wall, which spelled out the stuff you had to sign off on before getting off the ground: medical clearance, fleece-lined flying suit, helmets, goggles, and so on, plus three hundred dollars (no small sum at the time) for a minimum of four months of lessons. Over time she acquired the medical certificates and necessary gear; her skeptical father coughed up the three hundred dollars on condition she used public transportation. And with the patient tutoring of a Bulgarian flight instructor

Flying solo: As an early aviatrix, Alicia went on to set several women's speed and distance records.

(who got her attention right away by telling her that only one out of the twenty-five women who had started the course had been able to finish it), after forty hours in the air, with many close calls and nervous moments, she became the second: a licensed pilot.

Her father congratulated her, though not as much as she would have liked; and when she confided to him that sometimes she too had thought of quitting, he didn't seem to know what she was talking about. "You're my dirty dog, why would you quit?" she remembered him saying to her once, maybe more than once; she knew he was crazy about dogs, so took it as a compliment. Most days she found herself getting up later and later, lounging about the somewhat strange apartment in her dressing gown, smoking of course, planning something to write. Her mother sent her a postcard from San Francisco, where she'd gone to be with Aunt Florence while she waited for her husband, Mr. Richard Teller Crane, who was taking his yacht through the Panama Canal. "When are you coming home?" her mother asked, though not as if she expected a reply.

And then one morning a businesslike envelope arrived for her, by messenger from J. M. Patterson at the *Daily News*. Inside was a clipping from the magazine *Aviation News*, a brief item, or perhaps commentary, related to women and flying, noting that while it had become almost usual for women to earn a basic pilot's license (there now being 105 of them in the country, according to the magazine), only nine women so far had received the far more challenging and demanding transport pilot's license, which required two hundred hours of flying time as well as substantial expertise with navigation and engine mechanics. To this her father had added a handwritten note to the effect that, while he thought she might survive two hundred hours in the air, he strongly doubted she could ever hope to master the map reading and machinery part of the test, the "technical stuff that even men have trouble with."

Was Patterson being intentionally provocative? Unintentionally? Just making trouble? In any event Alicia took up the challenge, as she saw it, and returned to Curtiss Field, where—with another infusion of her father's money—she signed up for the extensive flight and ground training required for the more advanced license. A transport license in those days meant one could carry mail as well

AP and Poppa in matching gear, flying together, 1930.

as passengers (providing the foundation of the nascent commercial aviation industry), and was no easy matter to achieve, especially for someone such as Alicia whose formal schooling had been so erratic, whose math skills were all too basic, and whose engineering knowledge was practically nonexistent. At first, instead of flying she had to sit for two months, day after day, in a little bare-bones room at Curtiss Flying School, trying to learn about maps, grids, coordinates, and flight paths, also about the mysteries of the internal-combustion engine, from a sequence of often skeptical and condescending instructors. As for the matter of logging the necessary two hundred hours in the air—solo time, all by herself—this was its own special kind of challenge; instead of taking off from Curtiss Field and making scenic runs up and down the Long Island seashore as she'd done before, she now had to plot a course for Cleveland or Detroit, hoping the weather would hold and her fuel remain sufficient, and get herself back by sundown. On one such flight on a gray day she'd reached Detroit on schedule and made a turn for home, but then the weather closed in around her, and realizing she was lost, she brought her plane down low, flew above some railroad tracks for guidance until she found a farmer's field she could land in.

When the weather lifted she got herself in the air again and made it back in time to Curtiss, where her instructor suggested she work a little harder on her navigation skills. This she did, in the process discovering that she was turning out to be quite good after all at "the technical stuff"; good enough at any rate to get her transport pilot's license six months after she'd begun, becoming possibly the tenth woman in the country to have done so.

· 20 ·

FROM AN EARLY ISSUE of *Time*, December 9, 1929: "A score of private plane pilots in various parts of the country are watching today the progress of Editor Joseph M. Patterson's ten-thousand mile 'air-cruise' to the Caribbean in his all-metal, five-ton, amphibian aeroplane, although for obvious reasons Mr. Patterson prefers the description 'flying boat' over 'air yacht,' which the manufacturer, Sikorsky Aviation, employs in its advertising. The air cruiser, christened 'Liberty' for the occasion, has two large Vought engines, enabling it to fly at 120 miles per hour, at an expected altitude of 3,000 feet. . . . In addition to Mr. Patterson and a crew of three, comprising pilot, Lt. Fred Becker, assisted by a mechanic and a radio operator, all three borrowed from the U.S. Navy, there are two guests on board: Mr. Floyd Gibbons, veteran war reporter, and Miss Alicia Patterson, the air-cruise commander's daughter." Alicia was just twenty-three that winter, not really young but not exactly old, not really married though not exactly unmarried; a last-minute addition to the Caribbean expedition, filling in for some nameless guest who had just dropped out. When she got the call from her father, already down in Florida, she packed her suitcase, took the train to Miami, where the seaplane or flying boat or air yacht was boarding, a surely strange contraption tied up to a dock in the harbor, and dutifully fit her small self in beside the luggage in the back of the cabin.

First they flew out low across the waters of Biscayne Bay, then a one-hour straight shot over to Cuba, splashing down into Havana Harbor, peering out the little porthole-type windows at the still-visible wreckage of the USS *Maine*, with Morro Castle across the bay, and a flotilla of government launches approaching to take them ashore. Everywhere they went, people were nice to them, important people, unimportant people. After some days in Havana they flew off to Santo Domingo, rode horses around a coffee plantation; then up in the air again, zigzagging back and forth across the

Caribbean: Belize in British Honduras, a small harbor not really equipped for air cruisers, where a squall came in while they were landing, Lieutenant Becker skillfully lifting off again, just in time, before two fishing boats were nearly blown right into them. Then Haiti, flying across the mountains into Port-au-Prince, where the president of Haiti gave them a big dinner, and the next day a quartet of young U.S. Marine Corps aviators took Alicia and Floyd Gibbons for a joyride in their pursuit planes, skimming over the mountaintops, diving down into the green valleys with the little tile roofs. However, in Haiti they started to have trouble: not with the plane or flying but with the pilot, Lieutenant Becker, who got so sick he had to be taken to a U.S. Navy hospital on the other side of the island. Becker said they should fly in a substitute, continue on their trip, but Patterson said he'd stick with Becker. While they were waiting around for Lt. Fred to get better, Floyd Gibbons said there was a ship in the harbor bound for Panama, only two days' steaming, Panama with its superb fishing. And so off they went, a little detour to Panama. Floyd Gibbons, Poppa's old buddy, with a patch over one eye, who'd made his name by tracking Pancho Villa through the Sierra Madre mountains for his famous scoop; and of course Poppa, who liked to fish, although he liked to move about on the spur of the moment even more than he liked to fish; and Alicia, who when she was around Poppa made it a point to be game for anything. The Swedish ship to Panama

Father and daughter, with Patterson's amphibious flying boat *Liberty*, before their 1929 "air-cruise" to the Caribbean.

was okay; Gibbons played poker through the night, also the day. In Panama, which was known as the Canal Zone, they made a quick tour of the big locks and then went off to the Chagres River to fish at the Chagres dam, one of the world's great places for landing tarpon, where you could actually see the huge steel-blue fish darting about in the water near the lip of the dam. What happened then and there probably wasn't intentional, although who's to say in the end what's intentional or not? Years later Alicia said she was certain her father had been told about her problems, abdominal problems, female problems; after all, she used his doctor back in New York, Dr. Harold Meeker, and she knew they spoke together. About six weeks earlier, Dr. Meeker had examined her at Doctors Hospital, indeed opened her up because she was in pain, found nothing (though noting significantly on her chart, "patient unlikely to bear children"), stitched her up again, told her she could do the trip but avoid strains.

Now at the Chagres dam her father kept pushing her to get up on the spillway, to pull herself up onto the ledge of concrete, teasing, prodding, and finally she did it. That's my girl, he might have said. Or maybe nothing; he wasn't really a cheerleader. Which was when she felt something tear inside her, or pull, or something. She kept quiet about it; complaints were not rewarded. The next day they left Panama, and then Haiti too, and came back home. Where she hurt for a while until she didn't, and put it out of mind. It was there the letter from the lawyer reached her; she was finally divorced from Simpson, legally single instead of make-believe single. Also a letter from Jim Simpson: "Dearest Monkee, I'm awfully glad we can part with friendly feelings. . . . If I'd been more mature I wouldn't have given you such cause for complaints. . . . For this I'm sorry, for everything else I'm glad, I wouldn't have missed that year with you as my wife for anything." She thought it a sweet letter, and kept it in a folder next to her Ledyard Smith correspondence.

· 21 ·

IN THE COURSE of her two-year, collapsed and mostly broken marriage, it would have been unlikely if Alicia hadn't found an occasional friend, acquaintance, beguiling stranger with whom to pass some afternoon or night. But there's no record of who that might have been; and had there been any real romance, she kept its identity deep in the vault, which was not the way she usually did things. She went out from time to time with Lt. Fred Becker, but these were mostly functions, formal evenings, such as the Aviators Ball, where Becker introduced her to flying aces Jimmy Doolittle and Billy Mitchell. She also left behind a scattering of letters from Philip Boyden, the handsome, savvy young Chicago lawyer who handled her divorce, suggesting a close personal relationship running along beside the legal one, though nothing necessarily more than that. But why wouldn't they be friends, even friends with a dash of electricity in the friendship? She had that effect, that ability to get up close with people, male as well as female, all her life. And then there was Joe Brooks, Big Joe Brooks, who enters her life around

From All-American footballer to infantryman on the Western Front, "Big Joe" Brooks, holding barbed-wire cutters.

this time, and who surely deserves a proper introduction to this narrative.

Big Joe Brooks because he was unusually large when men were on the whole much smaller than today, altitudinous in height, ample, as they say, in girth, and oversize too in what was even then an unusual degree of optimistic good nature. At six feet four and commensurate poundage, he had been a collegiate football star, a two-time All-American lineman, first at Colgate, then at Williams, this in the years before World War I, when professional sports didn't exist and college athletes, especially football stars, were perhaps even more celebrated than today. He'd been an infantry captain on the Western Front, emerging like many others with medals on his chest and sad memories in his head. In the lightheaded atmosphere of the Roaring Twenties, when the new people were everywhere, speaking the new language of big bucks and fast money. Everybody still loved Joe Brooks and they always would. But he had trouble gaining traction in the world.

He started a little business selling life insurance. He had a fishing camp up in the Adirondacks and rented it out in the summers to those of his Racquet Club friends who liked to fish, usually with himself as guide thrown in as part of the deal. That was another thing about Joe Brooks: He was probably better at fishing than anyone, fly casting, tying flies, knowing the river; he was unbelievable at anything to do with fishing. Which was perhaps the main reason Joe Patterson liked to be around him, liked to have Joe Brooks as his friend, although the truth was, Brooks was Patterson's kind of man: a World War I brother in arms, a stand-up guy, who fished like an artist and could fly a plane. It was almost certainly as her father's friend that Alicia first met him, probably in summertime, at his fishing camp in the woods of upstate New York, canvas tents beside the Ausable River. As her father's daughter Alicia could fish a little, but Joe Brooks taught her to be really good, he had that unbelievable touch, also an equally extraordinary patience. At first, too, it doubtless made a kind of sense, seemed appropriate, that he was nearly twenty years older. He was her father's friend, after all, the two men with so much shared background, context, the names of people and places she'd never heard of, that code of older men. The first sum-

Miss Patterson, temporarily single again.

mer she was with them at the camp, the summer before her divorce came through, he was just a friend; such a friend too, kind and careful. She could tell that her father, who had few men he looked up to, looked up to Joe Brooks when they were out together in the woods. Just when the friendship shifted into romance is hard to say, though most likely it was sometime after she was legally free. It's also hard to say how much of a romance it was; they certainly shared a tent, at least on occasion; they found pet names for each other, actually they called each other by the same pet name, "Boojums." Perhaps the main thing was that her father approved. Later on, when she tried to remember how things were at the time, what she remembered mainly was the fun, the warmth, she didn't say tenderness maybe because she hadn't known much tenderness and couldn't rightly give a name to it. After they were back in New York her normally tightfisted father told her he was buying her a little plane, a two-seater biplane, with enough range, as he informed her, to easily make the trip to the Ausable. Then Joe Brooks let her know that he was finally going to divorce his wife, a piece of news she seems to have heard without really listening to. Of course she was thrilled by the plane, how wouldn't she be? But then she reminded her father that what he'd promised her, as a reward for getting her transport license: that he'd stake her to an overseas assignment for his five-year-old magazine, *Liberty*. This was so; in one of his expansive or perhaps distracted moments, he'd indeed told her to "go anywhere," and "just work it out and tell my office." In September she made a pilgrimage back to Libertyville, where her mother was cooler than usual, sniffing betrayal in Alicia's long sojourn in the enemy camp; while little Josephine, no longer quite so little, and happy to see her sibling, seemed surprised that her older sister could feel the slightest ambivalence toward Joe Brooks, whom she had met and naturally adored, and had heard such great things about from Poppa. On her return to New York, Alicia decided, not for the first or last time, to throw some distance between herself and her various problems, dilemmas, large, tender suitors, and plan an overseas assignment, getaway and grand adventure all in one.

· 22 ·

ALICIA SAID LATER that when she was pacing around her father's empty apartment, trying to plan a trip, an imaginative destination for herself, she kept remembering a special evening some summers earlier at Joe Brooks's hunting camp, late August, a new visitor at the campfire: "The Colonel" people called him, Col. Quentin Roosevelt, President Teddy's nephew; wiry, tough, deceptively bespectacled, a seemingly much-esteemed outdoorsman, explorer, hunter, who had spoken so eloquently of the forests of Southeast Asia he'd just returned from, their wildness, beauty, inaccessibility, the amazing plants, the extraordinary animals, such as the Siamese tiger he'd tracked without success, also the immense, belligerent sladang, the Asian water buffalo, that he'd found but had not been able to bring down. Why not Southeast Asia? Why not get herself a Siamese tiger, thereby impressing Poppa as well as the readers of *Liberty* (which at the time was the second most widely read magazine in America, after the *Saturday Evening Post*)? She wasn't sure if she should make an elaborate sales pitch to her father, who was just then enmeshed in a new preoccupation, building a strange modernist house for himself up on the Hudson; but in the end she decided to keep it simple, trust to his distractedness, an approach that seemed to work.

With Poppa's okay and some *Liberty* travel and expense funds to draw on, she made her plans, such as plans were in those days, and also roped in an old Chicago friend as traveling companion, Libby Chase, another game girl, a superb horsewoman who sometimes moonlighted as a stunt rider for Zoltan's Circus at state fairs around the Midwest. With the result that, in late afternoon of September 12, 1930, the sun still high above the Golden Gate Bridge, they steamed slowly out of San Francisco Bay aboard the SS *Carnarvon*, an eighteen-thousand-ton, midsize, slow-motion workhorse of the Pacific & Orient line, headed southward across the vast Pacific, with eventual stops in Australia, Indonesia, Singapore, and finally

Saigon, in what was then known as French Indochina. Alicia at the time was not quite twenty-four.

It took them four long weeks to reach Sydney. The *Carnarvon* was British owned, and that should have counted for something, at least in the way of that reassuringly superior, apologetic British service, and perhaps in a certain level of shipshapeness or basic competence, whether on the part of first mates or waiters. But sadly the *Carnarvon* was no Cunarder; the cabins were small, cramped, metallic; the running water rarely ran and then ran discouragingly brown; bells that were supposed to summon people didn't work, and when they did the people summoned seemed to have been just awoken from long sleeps, or drink- or drug-induced siestas, or who could tell? In theory the deck designated Promenade Deck promised better things: brisk walks around for exercise, stretching out on a deck chair with one of the many books that had been brought along for the purpose. But in fact the Promenade Deck was mostly obstructed by wooden crates, sometimes lashed together, sometimes not, and thus bumping about on their own whenever the sea got rough, which seemed to be much of the time after they crossed the equator. "There is no denying, the good ship *Carnarvon* has been claustrophobic," Alicia wrote in the first of her *Liberty* articles, "which is one of the reasons Libby and I are looking forward to some shore leave in Sydney."

According to the schedule the ship was supposed to spend three days in port, unloading and then reloading, before heading northward up the coast to its next landfall at Port Moresby. "But when Mr. Mukerji, our handsome Second Officer, told us it might be three days, or four, or five, whatever the Gods willed," Alicia wrote, "Miss Chase and I decided to bet on more rather less of a layover, seeing that Mr. Mukerji's gods were now involved, and have ourselves an adventure, at least a little holiday from the *Carnarvon*." At first they thought they'd see the sights of Sydney, but Sydney then was little more than a colonial outpost and seemed to have no sights; the advertised beaches were off-limits on account of sharks. Alicia found an airfield, and there a two-engine Fokker aircraft calling itself Australian National Airlines, which flew them up the coast to Brisbane, even less cosmopolitan than Sydney, where they transferred to a rickety biplane, operated by another new entity called

Qantas Airlines, which was about to make a once-a-week run hauling mail and supplies into sheep country. "Harry Soames, our pilot, said where we were flying to was 'on the dry side right now, not much to look at,' but added that it was full of kangaroos, and maybe we'd get to see a kangaroo hunt." In the interests of journalism and keeping moving, Alicia and Libby signed on for the flight. "I had never seen real drought before," Alicia wrote in *Liberty*, "but down below us, not far below either, the land was parched and dead as far as the eye could see, not even brown but a dead kind of grey. And everywhere as flat as an anvil, the dirt and dust barely moving even when a wind-gust came up, as if all the elements were too sunbaked to move."

Charleville, the first sheep station they stopped at, was like all the others, not so much a town or even a village but a haphazard assembly of wooden outbuildings, shacks, a general store with little in it, weatherworn men and women moving slowly. Alicia noted: "Few sheep in sight, although kangaroos were everywhere but hard to get close to. Near sundown, we put down at another station in the middle of nowhere, Longreach. Mr. Soames disappeared for a while and we thought he'd abandoned us, but back he came in a borrowed Ford truck, and with a gun, told us to climb in and 'we'd get us some roos.' He drove that truck as fast as it would go, hell-bent over stony hills and ridges, down gullies, the kangaroos running, bounding all around us. Soames stopped and asked Libby to drive while he shot, but she wouldn't. So he took some shots anyway, and missed, and then gave it up. We weren't too sorry, they have such sweet faces."

They spent three days and nights in the arid sheep-ranch country of northern Australia, dropping down onto bleak, heat-blistered settlements with little packets of letters and sacks of flour. They stayed wherever they could find a place to lie down, sometimes in the back of a general store; once at an actual, self-described "inn," with rooms and beds, though the owner had auctioned off the mattresses and bedding. And then there was Birdum. "I wish there were words in the dictionary foul enough to describe that place," wrote Alicia, who was usually no pale flower when it came to camping out. "It is a settlement of about twenty persons, nineteen of them men, and most of these drunk all the time. Mr. Soames, who by then was mostly drunk himself, found us not so much a room as a section of cement floor in back of the saloon, separated from the customers by a sheet. That night, there was a gargantuan rainstorm, which brought a tide of rainwater pouring in from outside, us lying in the middle of it, in a sea of muddy water, which in some ways was a relief from bedbugs and Singapore ants." The day they left, Alicia noted, the heat was so bad that "birds were dropping dead from the trees."

· 23 ·

THE TWO TRAVELERS reached Indochina around October 20; Saigon, with its wide, well-planted boulevards, its air of torpid, prosperous colonialism, its easy mingling of automobiles, horse-drawn carriages, bicycles, and rickshaws. Reassuringly their rooms were more or less waiting for them at the Hotel Continental; spacious chambers with heavy wood furniture, new overhead electric fans slowly stirring the sultry air, enormous bathtubs with water that looked like water, though not to be tasted. But at first there were problems, disappointments. For one, friend Libby could barely walk, her knee swollen from a fall she'd taken while climbing down a hill during their layover in Java. For another, Alicia's hopes of getting up into hill country, there to roam around exploring, adventuring, tracking game in the spirit of Colonel Roosevelt—after all, the reason for her being there in the first place—seemed to have foundered on hard facts of politics and revolution. As the young Princetonian duty officer at the U.S. consulate explained, indigenous rebels were battling French troops in the highlands, and until one side or the other won, no guides would be taking Westerners into the backcountry, or much of anywhere outside the city. That was the low point of the whole trip, followed soon after by possibly an even lower one, when the doctor at the French hospital said that Libby's knee needed medical care of a kind that he couldn't provide, and she should get herself back to America.

Late the next morning, Alicia was sitting by herself in the hotel dining room (with Libby upstairs, stumbling around, getting packed), having some bitter coffee and a smoke or two, pondering her options, when, as she described it, "Into this near empty room, with its fans and sleeping waiters, marched the most splendidly uniformed Frenchman, who called my name aloud, came over, introduced himself as Capitaine someone, and would Mlle. Chase and I please follow him to the *Bureau.*" Once there, with Libby now at her

Alicia on the trail in French Indochina, showing how to hold an umbrella and read a map at the same time.

side, seated together in a room garnished with symbols of the far-flung French empire, they waited for the arrival of the deputy high commissioner, a "portly gentleman in a white suit, also amazingly with a stiff celluloid collar and necktie, but very hospitable, who said that the uncle of Mademoiselle Chase, Mr. Howard Chase, a true friend of France, had written a letter to the *Commissaire*, and that the *Bureau* was prepared to assist in any way." Soon one young officer appeared to assist Libby in getting on the next ship heading in the right direction, while another took Alicia to another part of the Colonial Office, filled with many French uniforms. When Alicia explained to an older officer in charge that she had come to hunt tigers and had been told it was impossible, he replied that, yes, it was a dangerous time; Vietminh rebels were ambushing French soldiers, there was indeed a *petite guerre*. But if Miss Patterson was looking for a hunting guide to take her into real tiger country, that of course was Laos, and if she was willing to go there, then she could have more than one hunting guide. "If I heard him right, I believe he said I could have the whole French army to assist me," she wrote afterward, "which seemed hyperbole but it was nearly true."

After suitable preparations, though sooner than she expected, Alicia departed Saigon with a military escort of twelve soldiers, first heading up the Mekong River by motor launch for many days, "until the river narrowed, and we were met by Khmer tribesmen and transferred into dugout canoes." As she wrote: "The Khmer were savage and inscrutable but paddled the lot of us, without difficulty, up the brown river, the water often completely covered over by trees." The Khmer took the hunting party to a trailhead leading into the mountains, where most of the soldiers branched off, doubtless to more conventional duties, leaving Alicia in the care of a young lieutenant and his subordinate. From a campsite in the Annam Mountains, Alicia wrote her father, "I can't believe that many white people have been here before, certainly few white women. It is all unimaginably wild and beautiful, though when it comes to vegetation too much of everything, including insects. . . . The Khmer keep to themselves but I am lucky to have Lieutenant Thierry around to protect me, should I need it." Lieutenant Thierry, unsurprisingly smitten by such proximity to this unusual American girl, wrote her romantic letters, mostly unanswered, for many years afterward, hoping to recall "the savage charm of the great forests that were our only world, our life, for many weeks."

After they came down from the Annam Mountains, the Khmer peeled off and were replaced by a cortege of Moi tribesmen, even more primitive than the Khmer, who now led the little expedition on the most challenging part of the trip. "More dugouts, more river," wrote Alicia. "We first went up the Kongquo River, then the Kongannam, to a district known to the French as Bunnethout, where more Moi appeared and took us over the Cardamom Mountains, supposed home of many tigers. . . . We saw plenty of tiger sign, more than enough to know they were in the area, and sighted extraordinary birds, a kind of Asian lynx, small black bear, but never an actual visible or huntable tiger." On the next-to-last day, before having to turn back, Lieutenant Thierry spotted a sladang, the enormous Asian water buffalo, and by many accounts the most dangerous of all Asian forest animals. Thierry took a shot at the sladang, but only wounded it, "panicking the Moi," as Alicia wrote, "who had reason to fear the violence of a wounded sladang." The injured animal escaped into the forest, but that afternoon Alicia spotted a still-larger one and brought it down with a single bullet from her Mauser rifle, on loan from the French army. "The animal was coal-black with a white face and white feet, and its horns measured four feet from tip to tip," Alicia wrote. The admiring Moi held a feast over the carcass and staged a drum ceremony, marking a cross on Alicia's forehead with blood. As the expedition returned down the several rivers toward Saigon, the news of her exploit traveled ahead of her, so that the young female sladang hunter found herself "unexpectedly greeted by drums and cheers from villages along the way."

SOON ON HER WAY HOME, without Libby but with the horns of the sladang, suitably crated, traveling in the ship's hold, Alicia made an impromptu detour, stopping in Singapore for a week's layover. There was no acknowledged reason for the stop; perhaps the charms of colonial Singapore were enough. But there was some cause to believe as attested to by Libby Chase that roughly one month earlier, when the *Carnarvon* had made harbor at Jakarta, on the Dutch-controlled island of Java, Alicia had met and been charmed by a fellow visitor, handsome, aristocratic young Dutchman Hans Hooft (whose family owned Amstel breweries), and had hopes for a reunion in Singapore. Apparently there was no reunion, at least

After the hunt, with Moi tribespeople and sladang horns, 1931.

not this time; although if she were even thinking of one it would show a young woman whose mind was not entirely made up about her future. Instead of Hooft, however, she found two other newcomers to her life: one not romantic, at least not from her point of view; the other definitely intriguing from many angles. More friend than suitor was Maj. Eugene Tempersley, one of the numerous British army officers who had dispersed to the colonies after the Great War and was now presumably being well paid in the role of military adviser to an Indian maharaja. Tempersley had already read of Alicia's hunting adventures in the *Singapore Times*, and showed up at her hotel, offering his help in arranging a proper tiger hunt in Bengal. He also introduced her to the attractive, Oxford-educated, twenty-eight-year-old son of the sultan of Johor, Abu Bakar, known as 'Bu, apparently a direct descendant of the first Muslim caliph, currently managing his father's rubber plantations across the causeway from Singapore. There's no doubt that Alicia was much taken with the beguiling and articulate 'Bu, and he with her; she left Singapore with many valuable mementos from him, including a platinum cigarette case and a portrait photo showing the heir to the sultanate in full sultanlike regalia; also with plans to write and promises to meet. Then, back aboard another ship, the *Orient Princess*, Alicia made her slow way westward across the Pacific, thinking what thoughts we do not know,

HRH Ibrahim Abu Bakar, or 'Bu, son of the sultan of Johor, AP's new friend in Singapore, with his Airedales.

though whatever they were, it's doubtful they could have prepared her for the news that greeted her on her arrival at San Francisco. It seemed that a day or so before she landed, newspapers had first carried a report that Mr. Joseph W. Brooks had crashed in Ohio in a plane, actually belonging to Miss Alicia Patterson, though with no injuries to himself; this was followed soon after by a more substantial story, with Mr. Joseph M. Patterson, the editor of New York's *Daily News*, announcing the engagement of his daughter, Miss Alicia Patterson, to Mr. Joseph W. Brooks.

· 24 ·

"FURIOUS NOT CONSULTED" Alicia cabled her father, also Brooks; a three-word message, which all things considered surely represented a bare minimum of her thoughts and feelings on the matter. She took the next train back to New York, where she learned that her father was away in Canada, inspecting newsprint timberlands with Uncle Bert. But waiting for her in the apartment was a lengthy, at least for him, overwrought letter from Joe Brooks: "Dearest Alicia, Things have been happening so fast lately. . . . I know how proud you were of your little ship, and you trusted me with it, and then to lose it seems unbelievable. . . . I took off Tuesday morning, fair skies but bucking a terrific headwind, 50 mph. Landed in Cleveland, then again South Bend. Next morning, on takeoff the motor cut out about 75 ft, straight ahead were houses, trees, etc. On my right was a small field which I tried for but didn't make. Plane crashed through top of a tree, dove into the ground, landing on its back, caught fire on impact tho I managed to get away. . . ." Brooks then concluded: "I can't tell you how grand your father was about it all. Of course, when reporting it I had to say it was yr plane I was flying, which made him think it was right to announce our engagement. Most of my clothes were burned in the crash, but I'm arranging everything so don't worry. . . . Love, yr Boojums."

Almost immediately a second letter arrived from Brooks, written after receiving her angry cable: "Dearest Boojums, I am so shocked by your cable. You are my entire life, and my only interest in living is because of my deep love for you. . . . I am prepared to go on the block under any circumstances, but when you are mad at me I am the most unhappy person in the world. . . . I know the way the accident happened was a tough break for both of us, but don't forget the person who loves you most, next to me, is your dad who's trying to protect your reputation, announcing what most people assumed anyway. I am counting the days till I can take my beloved in my arms." And signed, inevitably, "Love, Boojums."

The screwiness of the situation was surely inconceivable. And yet how, in what ways, inconceivable? Scarcely a couple of years earlier, it was her fierce, distant little mother who had roped her into a marriage with Jim Simpson, with her father (who was supposed to be her special friend) nodding his approval from the sidelines. This time around it was her father holding the lasso, her father with his Catholic mistress, and baby Jimmy, protecting *her* reputation by cornering her into marrying his old buddy Brooks. She wrote her mother in Chicago, hopeful that her mother's growing fury, at her still-married husband's domestication with his alternate or parallel family, would trump her usual impulses for correctness at any cost. But she was wrong. Her mother figuratively gave a little sigh by mail, and allowed that, given the obvious closeness of her daughter's friendship with Mr. Brooks, as indicated by her letting him use her property, marriage was certainly the outcome to be wished for. Most disappointingly, sister Josephine, whom Alicia was lately accustomed to seeing as an ally, announced herself thrilled by the engagement, wished it was herself and Joe, and so on. And then of course Boojums himself, all six feet four of him, in his insurance salesman's suit, with his Williams College tie, varyingly endearing, confident, abashed, and so apologetic for the crash, as if that was the problem between them (though come to think of it, she had really loved that plane), was pretty much instantly on her doorstep, at her arm so to speak, her escort, her more-or-less fiancé. And besides, in the flesh he was undeniably such a stolid presence, such a good guy, loving *her* so much, and of course everybody else loving *him*.

Her father came back from buying up timberland in Quebec, returning to the *Daily News* though not to the apartment; he was apparently now living up in Ossining, commuting in and out every day. She met him at a restaurant for lunch, determined to straighten out the engagement misunderstanding, debacle, whatever it was. But when she showed up, Joe Brooks was there too, both men so happy together, talking naturally about fishing, fishing in the great rivers of Quebec. Not a word about her amazing trip, flying around the sheep country of Australia, shooting a mighty sladang. Poppa (as she remembered it later) took her hand in his, as if he was about to say something personal, special, but what came out was about Canadian timberlands, his new favorite subject. Afterward Joe told her, in his big-guy-to-little-lady manner, that they should really come to a decision about a date. She said it was too soon. As it happened her mother was due to make one of her transatlantic trips, to inspect lacework and antiques on the Rive Droite in Paris, and Alicia tagged along. She also arranged for her Dutch friend from Java, Hans Hooft, to be at a nearby hotel. "We make a perfect match, mentally and physically," Hooft wrote her on a card when he sent her flowers. They went out shopping together, and, both being dog lovers, he bought her three Irish setter puppies, which she took back with her on the boat, leaving him with the understanding, if not her promise, that she wouldn't let herself be railroaded a second time into marriage. But with the Dutchman back in Holland, and she once more in New York, an aviatrix to be sure, a sportswoman, a hunter of big game in the forests of Southeast Asia, and oh, yes, a journalist too; but all the same only twenty-five years old, not very old, on her own, with an allowance from Poppa, and the use of his strange apartment, and with big, friendly, protective, faithful Boojums hovering, pressing, waiting. . . . One afternoon she took what she knew to be the coward's way out and wrote Brooks a letter, saying in effect that she was too confused, not yet ready to take the final step. Brooks wrote her back a long, rambling, miserable, obviously heartfelt scrawl in his boyish hand, saying that he was going to kill himself.

Alicia surrendered. Soon after, she wrote Hans Hooft, telling him of her decision to marry Brooks, asking him to wait one year for her to get free again, which was a variant of the same one-year plan she had tried when she married Simpson. But Hooft would have no part of one-year plans. "I can't believe your father would interfere with your life a second time, and a second time you would allow it," he wrote her angrily. "Have you thought what will happen in a year when you tell him you want a divorce? What if he threatens suicide again? What if you expect a child? What if he refuses you a divorce? And is it fair to Mr. Brooks that you marry him without his knowing all this . . . ?" But Alicia didn't answer Hooft for many months, and when she did she hadn't much to say, not being one for looking backward or second-guessing. Besides, by then she was Mrs. Joseph W. Brooks.

· 25 ·

ON SEPTEMBER 12, 1931, Alicia Patterson and Joe Brooks were married in the Broadway Tabernacle, at Ninety-Third Street and Broadway, one of the few New York churches in which divorced persons were allowed to remarry. With a seating capacity of 2,500, it was a large edifice for a small, private ceremony. On Alicia's side of the aisle were her father and her sisters, Elinor and Josephine, Aunt Florence representing her mother, and a scattering of friends. On Joe's side there were also friends, though no family. After the wedding the couple flew off (literally, with Brooks at the controls of a two-engine Bellanca on loan from the manufacturer) for a week's honeymoon on Sea Island, Georgia, where Alicia let her new husband teach her the finer points of shooting quail; at the end of the week they flew west to Chicago for a little teatime reception in Alice Patterson's apartment, which didn't go too badly, all things considered. On the way back, however, poor Joe Brooks had another of his aerial misadventures, which once again got into the papers. "Honeymooners Escape Death In Plane Crash," the *New York American* announced on its front page. "Mr. and Mrs. Joseph W. Brooks narrowly escaped death today

A flying honeymoon to Georgia, with husband Joe Brooks and hunting dogs.

in negotiating the last leg from Chicago to New York of an extended wedding trip by air. . . . Mrs. Brooks suffered a wrenched knee. Her husband was at the controls when the motor stalled, and he was forced to land in a hayfield where the plane struck the ground." In fairness, despite appearances to the contrary, Brooks was an accomplished aviator; careful, experienced, not at all accident prone like his father-in-law. Flying in those days was inherently hazardous, with weather predictions being mostly guesswork and equipment giving out without warning. All the same, it was not a propitious way to start a marriage.

In hindsight, had any of the principals known what Dr. Meeker at Doctors Hospital seems to have known, or guessed, two years earlier—when he noted on Alicia's chart that, because of her ectopic pregnancy with Simpson she was unlikely to have children—who can tell how the story would have played out, or whether there would have been that particular story in the first place? Alicia and Joe Brooks were in so many ways such an unlikely couple, neither one of them a fully developed person, this regardless of his age and seemingly greater worldliness, her appearance of youthful savvy and confidence. Doubtless her father and mother, each in their own way, somehow assumed there would be children, family stuff, so as to give structure to the marriage, settle her down (as they were always trying to settle her down), and in the process justifying their own stage-managing of their daughter's life. It also probably didn't help that both Alicia and Brooks required such extensive financial propping up by Patterson, who paid the rent on a new apartment, between Madison and Park on Eighty-Fourth Street, and increasingly subsidized Brooks's faltering insurance business with referrals from the *Daily News*.

From the start there was an oddness to the Brooks's marriage, a surface brightness with evidence of trouble underneath that calls to mind short stories of the period, early John O'Hara, for example, with their wry and rueful scenes of 1920s people adrift in the increasingly unforgiving atmosphere of the 1930s. Each weekday morning, wearing his Brooks Brothers suit, a leather briefcase at the end of a long arm, Joe Brooks would take the bus down to Forty-Second Street, then walk to his one-room office down the street from the new *Daily News* building, where he'd shuffle papers for a few hours, try to hold out into the afternoon should any calls come in from up the street, but then usually head up to the Racquet Club at Fifty-Third Street for a game of squash (another sport at which he excelled), a late lunch at the "big table," convivial, boozy, for Joe Brooks was always a favorite, followed by a few hours of backgammon in the game room, playing for sizable stakes with the rich men who loved Joe Brooks too, and who he always hoped would throw a little business his way. For her part Alicia did her best, at least at first, to play the dutiful wife, although dutifulness was never her strong suit and her experience of wifeliness was limited. Her father thought she should get a job, and she knew he was right; he was always right except when he wasn't. But she didn't want to be writing advertising copy for department stores at the Lasker Advertising Agency, which was the job he found for her.

Sisters Josephine and Alicia, New York, 1930.

What Alicia probably wanted then as much as anything—what in her primal, unexamined way must have been the underlying goal in marrying Joe Brooks—Joe Patterson's great and good friend, a man closer to her father's age than to her own (to say nothing of what the two men shared in friends and life experiences), was not only her father's approval, but that by doing so she might finally secure a safe harbor close to her charismatic, elusive parent. Joe Patterson, however, was rarely a safe man to be around, even when he tried to be one, which wasn't often. Right then, as the early months of 1932 unfolded, Patterson was in the throes of a substantial struggle, trying to get his fellow Grotonian Franklin D. Roosevelt (an underclassman he hadn't much liked at the time) elected to the Presidency. Financially he was one of the biggest backers of Governor Roosevelt's national campaign. Editorially he had been early and enthusiastic in committing the *Daily News* in support of Roosevelt's call for "a New Deal," a stance that put him in conflict with most other newspaper publishers, and more particularly with his archconservative cousin Robert McCormick, publisher of the *Daily News*'s parent, the *Chicago Tribune*. It wasn't as if he had nothing to do with Alicia and her husband; as all three of them knew though rarely spoke about, he paid most of their bills; at least somebody in his office paid them, wrote the checks. But Patterson apparently didn't see himself in a position, or perhaps in a mood, to do much fathering just then, at least not of a twenty-six-year-old married daughter. Besides, he was also now the father of a small boy, whose unmarried Catholic mother kept his feet pretty close to the fire. One weekend in April, Brooks and Alicia had driven up for dinner with Joe Patterson, in his new modernist house above the Hudson, where Alicia had been more or less quietly furious at finding Mary King holding down the distaff end of the table, with her father interested only in talking about son Jimmy's baseball exploits.

· 26 ·

DO WE REMEMBER Maj. Eugene Tempersley, whom Alicia bumped into (though it was more likely that the eager major did the bumping) on her layover in Singapore two years before? The two of them maintained a correspondence in the interim, and now a letter arrived from the major, on the thick vellum stationery of the maharaja of Jodhpur, tendering an invitation for "some prime sport": a round of pigsticking followed by a tiger hunt. An inopportune summons? Or a timely one? It might depend on the point of view. From Alicia's perspective, perhaps sad to say, given her all too recent promise to love, honor, and obey Joe Brooks, it seems to have been a proverbially heaven-sent excuse for getting out of town, for shape-shifting back into a role that had lately been so congenial, sportswoman as they called it in the newspapers. As for the problem of travel expenses, Alicia appears to have figured out that, since her father didn't have the time of day, or focus, for paying close attention to her, he wouldn't be any different when it came to requests for money, of which he then had plenty; although just to be sure, she made a case that sister Josephine, now nineteen and beginning to make trouble, would definitely benefit from journeying abroad.

There were three of them who made the trip: Alicia, Josephine, and once again Libby Chase. A French steamship was supposed to take them from New York, with several stops en route across the Mediterranean, then through the Suez Canal to Bombay. But when they reached Marseilles, Alicia persuaded her companions to disembark the plodding *Richelieu* and trust their luck to the new KLM air service, which promised speedy transportation "to Mesopotamia and the Orient." The airplane was a three-engine Fokker, with two young Dutch pilots, an onboard mechanic, a radioman, and room for six passengers (although the three women were the only ones this time). In the notebook she kept of the trip, Alicia described "the unbelievable din of the engines, the cramped quarters . . . but

Alicia pigsticking in Baroda, India, 1932.

then we crossed just above the waves of the Med, flying low up the coast of North Africa, little villages, settlements, mostly endless brown sands. . . . " The pilots let her have the controls for a spell, then when they realized how accomplished she was they cheerfully dozed and let her, as well as Josephine (another licensed pilot), fly the plane for much of each day. Tripoli, Cairo, Baghdad. Each night they'd land around sundown, try to wangle landing permits in different languages, hunt for a place to stay. There were dust storms as they crossed the Sinai, so they put down on the sand, found a Lebanese guesthouse, waited for the skies to clear. It took them ten days to reach Karachi, not much faster than by boat, another day to Jodhpur, where Major Tempersley was waiting to meet them, in shorts and pith helmet, with one of the maharaja's Rolls-Royces for the passengers and a Bentley for their bags.

Sadly, there turned out to be a problem right away. For while the maharaja of Jodhpur, Oxford educated, pro-British, ostentatiously swanky (with his cars, jewels, hundreds of servants, acres of marble in his several palaces) was outwardly hospitable to the American travelers, he held decided views on women and their place in the scheme of things. Notably they had no place in the ancient

HRH Pratap Singh Gaekwar, son of the maharaja of Baroda, with four wild boars at his feet, deceased.

ritual-sport of pigsticking. As a great concession to his military adviser, the major, he might allow the American women to observe a pigstick from a proper distance, adhering to the proper protocols. But for a woman to take part in one was out of the question. Besides, why should a woman want to? Thus no sooner arrived at Jodhpur than, disappointed, they left for Delhi, with Tempersley as an escort. But at the Delhi Horse Show, in a sea of British faces, several familiar from her days with the Quorn Hunt, Alicia was introduced to another maharaja, this one of Baroda: in Alicia's words, "white-haired but formidable, progressive, fiercely anti-British." He also took an immediate liking to Alicia, with her American pluck and sporting ambition, and on the spot invited the trio to the kingdom of Baroda for some gender-inclusive pigsticking.

Earlier in New York, before she left, when Alicia tried to explain the challenges of pigsticking to her friends, there were few who took it seriously. For one thing the name of the thing seemed to get in the way, though of course the word, "pigsticking," was part of that deliberately offhand, play-it-down vocabulary of English sporting life. The fact is the pigs were not so much pigs as wild boars, some as massive as four hundred pounds, fast, fierce, and dangerous, with tusks that could tear apart a sizable animal; and the sticks were ten-foot wooden poles with spears at the end of them, held by a rider on horseback in the manner of a lance. Also, pigsticking could be rough and local, or it could be fancy. At the maharaja of Baroda's tourney, as he liked to call it, there was an impressive venue, almost a settlement, of large and variously colored silk tents, where guests were housed and entertained the night before with music, dancers, the inevitable ten-course dinner. Next morning, and for three days afterward, the pigstickers rode out in groups of five, spears at the ready, and took their place facing a thickly wooded barrier of brush. The pigs (or boars) were inside the brush; on the far side were beaters with tin cans, trying to drive the animals forward; behind the pigstickers was open ground and possible freedom for the pigs.

As Alicia wrote of her experience: "You're mounted on this cavalry [*sic*] level horse, one you've never seen before, nor he you. From somewhere out of sight, sounds this unearthly din, as the beaters start through the brush, yelling, beating tin cans . . . then, when this great tusker breaks cover, you're told to wait, not moving, till he is well away, but when you do start after him pray your mount is sure-footed because you go full-out over ditches, rocks, fallen timber, over everything." And: "It is by far the hardest sport I ever tried. If you're after a pig and you're almost ready to spear him at a dead run, he always jumps or swerves. You can only stick him when he's on your right side and a little in front, otherwise it's too dangerous." And: "Today I was with three good lads and Josephine. The first pig gave us a corking run and the captain of our team speared him. But when the pig ran into some undergrowth, with me after him, he came out suddenly and charged the captain's horse, crashing the horse and hurting the rider rather badly."

All things considered, the maharaja's pigstick was considered a great success; with an invisible wave of the royal hand the colorful silk tents vanished, the clanging of the tin cans ceased. Then, too, Major Tempersley reappeared, migrating between maharajas, and at the usual evening banquet the question of a tiger hunt was raised. Such things might be arranged, murmured the white-haired old maharaja, and arranged they were: not overnight of course, since hunting permissions on a vast tiger preserve in a neighboring state

Alicia and Josephine (*behind her*); much heat, little shade, many hunting-camp standabouts, looking for tigers in all the wrong places.

needed to be obtained, but soon enough; and with their gear packed, with rifles and all manner of equipment on loan from the kindly maharaja, off they went. "We were a party of about twenty," Alicia wrote. "Major T, plus a fellow to scout for tigers, plus we three, plus fifteen or so porters and beaters to lug in all the stuff and tend the camp." The neighboring state, it turned out, was not so near but a long, endless day of rail travel south on an ancient, narrow-gauge train; then off in the middle of nowhere, where they waited long hours beside the tracks, sitting on jerry cans in the amazing heat, for what would turn out to be a caravan of bullock carts, plus one broken-down old truck, to take them and their supplies the rest of the way. Again Alicia: "Our hunting camp was in a clearing surrounded by thick woods. Dust was everywhere and the heat was constant, despite heavy rains that poured daily out of the gunmetal sky. Black flies appeared in daytime, mosquitoes at night, which seemed to chew their way through the netting." At first the women slept beside the campfire, but then a rabid jackal got into camp and attacked several

Alicia with the leopard she shot.

of the bearers. "The next day was spent building *machants,* or raised platforms, and from then on, when we slept, which wasn't much or often, we slept a dozen feet above the ground."

All in all they were in tiger camp for six weeks, two of which were constant thudding rain. Once the wet skies lifted, however, they moved out into the woods, where Alicia finally spotted a large tiger, took her shot, but missed. It turned out this would be her last glimpse of a tiger, though they stayed for weeks more, going out day after day with the guide and beaters. All of them by then were sick in turn with fevers and dysentery, despite the maharaja's quinine. Finally, late one afternoon Josephine spotted a full-grown male Bengal tiger moving through the brush, brought it down with one shot. Next day, a half mile from camp, coming back from another unsuccessful foray, Alicia saw a leopard moving forward in the trees, took a shot, and got her kill. It wasn't as substantial, as royal, a prize as Josephine's tiger, which the undemonstrative major admitted was "most impressive," but by then it was time to leave; and it perhaps says something of Alicia's almost helpless competitiveness that thirty years later, near the end of her life, she acknowledged that she still hadn't fully reconciled herself to the fact of Josephine having got the tiger.

· 27 ·

BACK IN NEW YORK, in the grays and blacks of the Great Depression, the exotic and extravagant colors of India must have seemed out of place, anachronistic. Moreover, *Liberty* had been sold by the Tribune Company at a substantial loss, and with new owners and a new format it was no longer a market for Alicia's intrepid-girl-adventure journalism; her notes and notebooks of pig-sticking and tiger hunting in maharajaland were stuffed into a file folder and stayed there, out of sight if not entirely out of mind. She became friends with Neysa McMein, by all accounts an interesting "new woman," a gifted illustrator and independent spirit; also with Heywood Broun and his wife, both journalists, strongly Left-leaning; all three of them members of the Algonquin Round Table group of smart, talky men and women "in the arts," who were defining the 1930s media dynamic of Manhattan. And of course she was still married to Joe Brooks. How not to be? Joe Brooks wasn't smart and talky, at least not in the way of the Algonquin wits; he told stories, jokes, some of them pretty good, but still they were those kind of stories, jokes, what people called "smoking-room humor"; and he wasn't at all leftist, he wasn't political, he would say. But the Algonquin intellectuals on West Forty-Fourth Street were happy to make room for Joe, as were the Racquet Club Republicans on Park Avenue and Fifty-Third Street. Everybody loved Joe Brooks, the former All-American; loved him too well to tell him to skip the last few rounds of drinks, loved him too well to refuse him a place at the backgammon and poker tables, which were less and less his friends.

And what of the third, perhaps one might call him the "shadow" element in the marriage: Joseph Patterson, Poppa, "Captain Patterson," as Joe Brooks, a fellow soldier, called him, and as Patterson himself liked to be called, sometimes just "Captain." The truth was that while the 1930s were unfolding unpropitiously for many people—for Joe Brooks, for example, and millions of others—for

Joe Patterson the decade had begun with much promise. The former experimental farmer and experimental socialist, the "Renegade Heir" who'd once campaigned for Eugene Debs, had placed a couple of bets that more than proved out. First, back in the 1920s, he'd launched the *Daily News*, at the time decried and ridiculed by the journalistic establishment as well as by most upright people (many called it "the housemaid's daily" and much worse, saying they wouldn't let it into their homes), which was even now, despite the Depression, continuing to mint money for its parent, the *Chicago Tribune*, while providing an ample share for its editor. Then, in 1932 he'd placed a nervy bet on Franklin Roosevelt, bet with his own money, too, also with his paper's editorials, and as a result he was a rare newspaper proprietor welcomed into FDR's circle, maybe not into his closest circle, but close enough to get "Dear Joe" letters from the president from time to time, and enjoy a measured access to The White House.

As Mrs. Joseph Brooks, Alicia felt in a chronic state of being yanked about, whipsawed, as the saying went, in her complicated relationship with her father. Although she tried not to think about the details, she could never be entirely unaware of the extent to which he sustained her marriage, kept it and them afloat with financial help, both the kind you could see and couldn't see. Joe was always a good sport about "your father's help," she knew it pained him to admit it, but how could it be otherwise? On her side she was aware that money things were strangely muddled; it pained her too that Joe—so sure, so smart, and even wise in everything to do with all the outdoor stuff that once seemed to matter so much—couldn't seem to get any traction in the everyday world, couldn't pay for the food, the rent, the cook and maid who worked for them, his secretary, her allowance. At the same time she knew she rather liked it, not entirely of course, not always, but mostly she rather liked it that her allowance came from Poppa. She even rather liked it when her father sent her one of his memos, no longer hand-scrawled but typed by Miss Josephson, suggesting this career opportunity, that person to look up, and so on. She rarely followed up because she knew the suggestions wouldn't work, but she liked the connection; she knew he was thinking of her. She liked it too, and did follow up, when the *Daily News* book editor sent her a book to review; she handed in her reviews promptly, received praise from the editor, knew her father was somehow in the loop. What she really didn't like, couldn't stand in fact, was the whole Mary King business. It wasn't that she felt much for her mother; her mother was a hard person to attach your feelings to; besides, she knew it was her mother's obduracy that was still making a divorce impossible. But she just hated Mary King, the Catholic woman who had got her hooks into Poppa; she even hated little Jimmy, which she knew was wrong and made her feel bad, but still she hated him. And what made it all worse was that she knew she didn't have to see Mary King, she was a grown-up, a married lady, who could do what she wanted. But if she and Joe wished to rent a house for the summer out on Sands Point, Long Island, as they did, then they needed to make a pilgrimage up to Ossining, mind their manners with Mrs. King, be nice to little Jimmy, and hope to get, if not her father's blessing, at least his fiscal go-ahead in return.

Alicia Brooks, Sands Point, Long Island, where she and her husband, Joe Brooks, were living in 1934.

· 28 ·

BY THE MID-1930S some things had changed, some things not. What hadn't changed, at least not for the better, were Joe Brooks's prospects; his slice of the life insurance business, which had never been large, had become ever more marginal. As a result he was spending even less time in his office and more time in a sad sequence of hotel rooms, apartments, all the assorted venues for private card games (especially poker) some lasting several days, none of which ever made him any more than briefly richer.

But if her husband was falling behind the times, giving every appearance of a man who had outrun his moment, Alicia Brooks was finally beginning to take a few, albeit tentative, strides forward into the conscious life of the period. She spent more time with Neysa McMein, long days in her sunny downtown studio, working together on a variety of graphic projects, in the process absorbing the political life of the Village. She did interview pieces for the *Daily News*, articles for Herbert Swope's *New York World*. And not exactly out of nowhere, because he'd been there all the time, though mostly there in a distant, check-writing (or check-approving) sort of way, her father began to reappear in her life, at least from time to time, and as the Poppa she so fondly remembered; the two of them no longer dirty dogs—he was too consequential for that—but all the same her good buddy. Who knows why then? Who knows what he meant by the new camaraderie, if anything? They'd go to the movies some afternoons. She'd meet him for drinks at Jack and Charlie's on Fifty-Second Street. He never said much of anything about serious subjects, the way her downtown friends were always talking about "the world." But just being there with him made her feel good. And so, one day, when he asked her if she thought her husband could spare her for a little overseas traveling, she figured he knew the answer, didn't really have to ask.

• • •

WITH HIS TWENTY-EIGHT-YEAR-OLD DAUGHTER, Alicia, as his main sidekick and traveling companion (though with Josephine and Joe Brooks tagging along on the periphery) Joe Patterson took ship for England on July 2, 1935, on one of the big new Cunarders that now docked at Southampton, much closer to London than the familiar more northerly Liverpool. The Pattersons spent the better part of one week at the newly refurbished Savoy Hotel beside the Thames, though for most of their stay they were in the energetic, officious hands of Lord Beaverbrook, Joe Patterson's new British friend.

If Joe Patterson was an important publisher on his side of the Atlantic, Sir Max Aitken, Lord Beaverbrook, was an even bigger one on the other side of the ocean; a Canadian who had risen to political power in the war as a cabinet minister and close colleague of Winston Churchill, now from his position as publisher of London's *Daily Express* (whose two-million circulation was the largest of any newspaper in England) he had become a maker and breaker of politicians and a force to be reckoned with in the seat of empire. Short, opinionated, immensely rich, Beaverbrook had been the model for Evelyn Waugh's Lord Copper, the unpredictable, tyrannical overlord of the *Daily Beast*. He was also a prototype of the modern publisher with "big ideas," his latest being an editorial proposal, lately evolved into a personal crusade, advocating what he termed "a splendid isolation" of Great Britain and its far-flung empire from the inevitable war which he, Churchill, and the mostly disregarded British anti-fascists feared was brewing on the Continent. Meanwhile, across the Atlantic, Patterson had been developing his own somewhat similar geopolitical ideas, motivated by his still-raw memories of the devastating carnage of the Great War, with its origins, as he saw it, in the inept and often devious policies of the European powers; and hoping to prevent the possibility of his countrymen being drawn into a second transatlantic conflagration, caused by weak leadership on the part of the same European powers, he had published that spring a sequence of editorials in the *Daily News*, which Beaverbrook had enthusiastically reprinted as a pamphlet titled "From Across the Atlantic" and distributed throughout England in a press run of several million copies.

Croydon Aerodrome, July 1935: Josephine, Alicia, Joe Brooks waiting to take off in Lord Beaverbrook's plane, with Sir Max and Joe Patterson, who were hoping to interview the Axis dictators.

While in London, Sir Max, or "the Beaver," as he was also known, took Patterson and Alicia in his personal charge, showing them around the new *Daily Express* building, a striking, modernist edifice constructed entirely out of steel and black glass (consequently much derided by Londoners), afterward including both of them in a round of policy discussions about the problems posed by the fascist leaders, Mussolini and Hitler. On the night of July 14, he gave a glittering ball in honor of the visiting Americans at his extraordinary residence, Stornoway House, overlooking Green Park, with its fourteen bedrooms, six salons, and its own grand ballroom, where the much-in-demand Ray Noble orchestra played that evening. It was the height of the London season, and hundreds of old and new names attended, including wicked, glamorous Lady Diana Cooper, an old flame of Max's (who once described him as "that strange attractive gnome") and whom Alicia had met more than a few times when, as Diana Manners, she played the Madonna to sister Elinor's Nun in *The Miracle*.

Two days later the serious phase of the trip began, when the Patterson party was driven out to London's Croydon Aerodrome, with its grassy runway and blowing wind socks, where Sir Max and six of his friends and associates were waiting to board a shiny new four-engine de Havilland, chartered by Beaverbrook to fly them all to Rome and possibly on to Berlin. The backstory on this at-the-time early example of airborne personal diplomacy might be said to have begun some months before, with Adolf Hitler's dramatic and disquieting announcement of German rearmament, blatantly disregarding the terms of the 1919 Versailles peace treaty, publicly defying the former Allies. This worrisome move (at least worrisome to those in Europe not blind to the German Führer's ambitions) was then somewhat offset by the appearance of Hitler's junior partner, the Italian dictator Benito Mussolini, at the Stresa conference, in April in northern Italy, where to many people's surprise he indicated a measure of independence from Hitler by joining the English and French foreign ministers in repudiating any changes to the Versailles treaty. While in London, Patterson had paid numerous visits to the German Embassy, trying to secure an interview with Hitler, either in Berlin or at his summer retreat at Berchtesgarten. As Alicia noted later, "Father had Hitler's number from the start, even when so many other poobahs were either impressed or on the fence. But he had this old-fashioned thing of wanting to 'look the other fellow in the eye,' and take his measure." In the case of Mussolini, or "Musso," as Patterson and Beaverbrook referred to him, there was real hope, in Alicia's words, "that he and Max could sit down with him, see if his peaceful impulses were real, could be counted on to any extent, and do what they could to encourage him to go his separate path." In London the Italian ambassador, Dino Grandi, had met with both publishers and assured them of Mussolini's willingness to see them and of his interest in an interview.

When the travelers finally landed in Rome, they were met out on the airfield by a cortege of officials from the British and American Embassies, commanding an array of massive automobiles, in which they were driven in stately procession into the city, where they soon expected to be received by Mussolini. But Mussolini now appeared to be having second thoughts, occasioned not surprisingly, as history would later reveal, by Hitler's fury at his junior partner's Stresa speech. For days, for the better part of one week, two of the West's more famously impatient citizens were forced to cool their heels in the Italian capital. Patterson spent his time shuttling between the American and German Embassies, still trying to arrange an interview with the German leader, still being told that the Führer was unavailable. Sometimes he took Alicia with him, "as someone to growl at since he couldn't growl at the embassy secretaries"; but mostly she was left on her own, to be happily escorted around the Colosseum, the Borghese Gardens, and so on by one or another of Beaverbrook's bright young men, particularly Sir Michael Wardell, a dashing former cavalry officer with a patch over a missing eye. Finally, on the day before they were all due to pull out, Mussolini had second, or possibly third, thoughts and declared himself ready to meet with the publishers. Alicia went in a second car, with some of Beaverbrook's staff, to the Generalissimo's white palazzo, waited downstairs "in a gloomy, marble chamber noisy with the clicking boots of Fascist officers," expecting that the interview wouldn't last long.

In fact the meeting lasted nearly three hours, most of the afternoon. Alicia noted her father's reaction: "He described Mussolini as predictably short but surprisingly massive, hard, with an odd, orange color to his skin which might have been makeup. And his voice was high and very voluble. For a long while he told stories, jokes, reminisced about his own days as a newspaperman. Whenever Max or I tried to ask him about Stresa, he'd pause, look as if he were about to say something, then change the subject. Once he said people misquoted him, or didn't understand. 'Which is it?' I asked. And then he'd tell another story. By the end, it was disappointing. I don't think he's a gangster like his Nazi friend, frankly I don't know what he is." After Rome, with Hitler still unavailable, the two publishers flew on to Belgrade and Warsaw, where as Alicia noted, "endless dinners were given by important people," and where the talk was "more about Communist agitation than Fascism." She also remembered thinking, on the boat back to America, that her smart friends in New York were so insistently pacifist, so against war, and wondering how all that was going to work.

· 29 ·

AND THEN THERE WAS THE TIME she accompanied her father to the Soviet Union. This would have been in late August 1937.

Do we remember the last time Joe Patterson visited Russia, in December 1905, when it was still called Russia; when Leningrad was St. Petersburg, Czar Nicholas II's capital; when young Patterson's obdurate aunt Kate was the wife of U.S. ambassador Robert McCormick, still half sober and only semiloony; and when the world watched with mixed feelings as the first wave of revolution, personified by Moscow University students, took to the streets against the czar's police? Thirty-two years later, more than middle-aged, still tall but stooped, Patterson, accompanied by his traveling partner, Alicia Patterson Brooks, was trying once again to pass through Leningrad, this time the Leningrad airport, on his way to the Soviet capital at Moscow; and trying too to keep his composure as casually truculent Soviet airport officials first detained father and daughter for no apparent reason, then unceremoniously emptied their suitcases onto the counters, literally turning them upside down, rummaging through their belongings in a supposed search for contraband. Alicia later recalled that she was more concerned for her father's dignity than for her possessions, though in the end both emerged more or less intact, and they were allowed to make their way into the city of Leningrad and later board the sleeper train to Moscow.

Patterson and Alicia were traveling to the Soviet Union at a time when American-Russian relations, only lately emerging from a strained period of official nonexistence after President Roosevelt's diplomatic recognition of the Soviet Union in 1932, were beginning their back-and-forth swings between friendly and frosty, between wartime partners and mistrustful allies, that eventually ended in the Cold War. Right then the Soviets seemed to have settled into what would later devolve into a familiar alternation of superficial cooperation with stony and often bewildering intransigence. For instance, two years before, with much show of reciprocal amity, the United States had finally opened an embassy in Moscow, taking over the once-palatial Spaso House, and dispatching well-regarded William C. Bullitt as ambassador. But no sooner was he installed than Bullitt had stormily requested reassignment, detailing a list of Soviet insults, some pointlessly petty, others less so, such as the Soviets' reneging on an earlier promise not to actively support the Communist Party in the United States. Bullitt, as it happened, was an old friend of Patterson's, a member of the same secret society at Yale, an old-style, speak-your-truth, no-nonsense businessman; Patterson had originally planned to visit Moscow while Bullitt was ambassador. But Bullitt had left, was now U.S. ambassador in Paris; and the new American Ambassador to Moscow was Joseph E. Davies, a smooth, well-meaning Chicago lawyer. Davies was the husband of the immensely rich Marjorie Merriweather Post and, more important, a Roosevelt loyalist who, unlike Bullitt, was doing his best to tell the president only what he wanted to hear about his new partners in the Soviet Union: one example was his notorious message to a complaisant Roosevelt to the effect that "Premier Stalin . . . in my considered opinion, is a simple, decent man who is only trying to get his house in order, despite many provocations."

Coincidentally, during the ten days in August 1937 when Alicia and her father were in Moscow, roughly a half mile from their hotel, in the high-ceilinged, grimy Hall of Justice, the second of Stalin's infamous "show trials" was winding down; with the pathetic parade of Stalin's former comrades in arms, men such as Nikolai Bukharin and Karl Radek, hollowed out by degradation and torture, forced to admit absurdities of guilt, treasonous behavior, spying for Germany. Neither Patterson nor Alicia sought admittance to the trials, though they were aware of their existence. They were also aware of the divergence of views on what was taking place between the official Soviet line, echoed by such influential voices as the *New York Times*'s Walter Duranty and Ambassador Davies, to the effect that the guilty verdicts and death sentences were clearly on the level, rough justice of a sort, and obviously justified, as proved by the prisoners' admissions of espionage; and the opposing perspective, the grim truths privately provided by junior officials at the embassy, such as a young friend Alicia made at the time, the twenty-seven-year-old George F. Kennan, later architect of the State Department's "containment policy" in the 1950s.

The Pattersons were staying at the Metropol, once a hotel in czarist days, later a Soviet office building, now more or less a hotel again. But whenever they tried to walk out the door, even to stroll around the block, there was always a so-called "guide," sometimes two of them, in their black suits, blocking their way, telling them where they could and mostly couldn't go. Partly to escape these clumsy minders, Patterson and Alicia would often stop in at the American Embassy, which Ambassador Davies was in the process of refurbishing with new electrical fixtures, including freezers for the chocolate ice cream his wife was partial to, and a phone system designed to be free of Soviet surveillance, which it never was. But the embassy itself was its own kind of dream zone, thanks to Ambassador Davies's bland confidence as to Premier Stalin's peasantlike benevolence and good intentions. After one meeting with fellow Chicagoan Davies, as Patterson told his daughter, the ambassador, speaking of Stalin, declared that he could never "distrust a fellow with such a twinkle in his eye."

Fortunately George Kennan could get free sometimes to provide a reality check; as when one afternoon, spotting her sitting in the embassy reading room, he took her out for a drive in his car, which with embassy license plates could travel unimpeded by the Intourist "guides." So for an hour they left the antiseptic main boulevards, traveled down side streets, some just next door to the big hotels and government buildings, where she could see the ordinary citizens of socialism's "great experiment" in their tattered clothing, rags on their feet instead of shoes, lined up outside shops for food and clothing that all too evidently had little food or clothing within, and sometimes, as she noted, "bent over, like peasants in a field, picking through piles of garbage for a next meal." Another unmediated glimpse of the realities of the Soviet state occurred while she and her father were actually driving in an official Intourist car to an exhibit of workers' art. The guide appeared to make a sudden detour, though to what was obviously a predetermined destination: a small square, where on first sight could be seen a listless gathering, in fact of presentably dressed men and women, leaning against a building, holding placards at their sides. However, as soon as the Intourist car came into view, the crowd leaped into action, running into the street, yelling, chanting, brandishing their placards at the Pattersons. "These are Soviet citizens," the guide explained, "who wish to praise the death of all the guilty traitors and enemies of the state." Alicia remembered her father clamping his big hand on the shoulder of their secret policeman–guide, saying, "Just get us the hell out of here."

IT'S WORTH ASKING, at least rhetorically, what Alicia took away from these two extraordinary trips, one to a Europe teetering between peace and war, the other to Stalin's Soviet Union, with its grim stage-set version of a "workers' paradise," real-world big-game expeditions, one might call them, to the true dark continents of the 1930s. Not for a moment, then or later, did she ever consider herself as anything but a bystander, a tagalong, as important personages, her father among them, shook hands with Fascists and Communists, exchanged "positions" via interpreters, breathed one another's cigarette smoke; nor did she expect, as a more-or-less young person of her time, that any of the busy, bustling men would turn to her for her opinion of larger matters, or even suppose she had one. Alicia, however, no matter how academically unschooled, was a quick study, educating herself where and how she could. In a future yet invisible, she would become a prominent liberal Democrat, an internationalist; she would strongly, and sometimes bravely, oppose the witch-hunt defamation of a generation of leftists, "pinkos," Communist sympathizers, and so on. But at the same time, even when some of the people she most admired—as if they couldn't help themselves—kept insisting over the years that the Soviet "experiment" was essentially benign, willfully misunderstood, and so on, she never forgot what she saw, and what she learned, on the side streets of Moscow.

· 30 ·

BY THE LATE THIRTIES scarcely anyone was reading Scott Fitzgerald anymore, although the glamorous, moneyed landscape he'd so lyrically and lovingly celebrated, specifically Long Island's North Shore, with its great houses and green lawns sloping down toward the Sound, seemed (unlike their fabulist) to have been barely dented by the Depression. True, one or two of the old mansions were still shuttered, while many of the remainder made do with reduced staff, for example five indoors and about the same outside, on the grounds. There was less froth but better roads; and new houses had been going up, though smaller, more sensible, as their occupants claimed, three or four bedrooms on five-acre lots being sold off by the tax-beset mansion owners. Two such newcomers to North Shore society were Mr. and Mrs. Joseph Brooks, whose strikingly (or perhaps jarringly) modernist, three-bedroom house stood close to the edge of the water on Sands Point. The house was a glass-and-brick rectangle designed by Raymond Hood, who happened to be Joseph Patterson's favorite architect, designer of his Ossining house as well as the new *Daily News* building, and whose architectural plans had been presented to Alicia and her husband along with Patterson's gift of the house. It was not always an easy house to live in, too hot in summer, too chilly in the cold months, besides being somewhat stern in its modernist configurations; but it was surely a handsome present, and well intentioned, even if part of the intentions were to prop up Alicia and Joe's marriage, which with the passing of time seemed ever more in need of propping up.

It wasn't as if Alicia herself had struck oil, landed a starring role on stage or screen, or even in her own life. She did little pieces for the *Daily News*, which in part gave her a sense of doing something, earning pocket money, in part reminded her that doing little pieces wasn't what she had in mind. She spent more and more time in Neysa McMein's studio, collaborating with the gifted and very

The Brookses' modernist Raymond Hood house at Sands Point,
more of a loan than a gift from Poppa.

professional Neysa on what seemed an endless sequence of cartoon strips and words-and-picture projects that never quite seemed to get off the ground. Even so, she could sense that she was on an escalator going up, however slowly, and sometimes fitfully, and even if she didn't yet know what her destination would be; and by the same intuition she could tell that dear old Joe was on an escalator, not merely stalled but going in an opposite direction. And more and more often, dear old Joe wasn't so dear anymore, was no longer that big bear of a man, with maybe too many drinks but still a pal, a good sport; more and more nights Joe didn't come home till late, and then as a big bear of a man who couldn't stand up, couldn't undress himself and worse, didn't even seem to have the energy for tears.

For Alicia the Sands Point house, no matter its unforgiving rectangles, was both a refuge from the trials of weekday life and a jumping-off point into the emerging vitality of the period: of course parties and drinking, the ever-present cocktails of the 1930s, but such a far cry from Onwentsia and Lake Forest, all these new, smart, talky people, stage and screen people, magazine and newspaper people, men and now and then a woman who worked in something other than the country club professions of stocks, bonds, trusts, and estates. Tall, long legged, graceful Neysa McMein was such a new woman—an example, a possibility—which was implicitly one of the reasons Alicia sought her friendship, and one might say had even followed her out to Sands Point. Neysa and her husband, Jack, rented a large white-brick house down the road from the Brookses, a roomy, welcoming place that, come summer weekends, overflowed with attractive people, for Neysa was famous for her mixing skills, Bernard Baruch and George Gershwin, Jock Whitney and Harpo Marx.

YEARS LATER, as Alicia tried to reconstruct the evening, with details and even dates by then inevitably blurred or forgotten, one thing she remembered was that it was a memorable weekend when the great J-boats were racing on the Sound; which would mean mid-July 1938, the last prewar America's Cup, between Mike Vanderbilt's *Ranger* and the British challenger, Tommy Sopwith's *Endeavour II*: the two beautiful, slender, 120-foot-long hulls, with their towering single masts, immense triangles of white sail, sliding back and forth on the blue-black waters, midway between Connecticut and Long Island. You could see the boats from Neysa's house, but they were far away, indefinite in the summer haze, and it wasn't something anyone was really watching. Alicia was at Neysa's on her own that day, as was often the case; Joe was supposedly competing in a racquets tournament in the city, though since she knew the Racquet Club courts weren't air-conditioned she assumed he was in a game somewhere, hoping for a big score. She remembered George Abbott being around, the director, one play on Broadway, another in rehearsals, who seemed to be a permanent houseguest at Neysa's that summer. Also Heywood Broun and Howard Dietz, the songwriter, from down the road. The usual chorus of young women in linen dresses, bright smiles. And then the boats were no longer racing, the sunlight was going, gone, and you could begin to see yellow houselights blink on across the water. Somebody, Alicia recalled, probably Neysa's husband, Jack, said there was a big crowd down at the Swopes' and they should all drive over—Herbert Bayard Swope, another forgotten pharaoh buried beneath the sands of time, but then the larger-than-life editor of Joseph Pulitzer's *New York World*—friend of presidents, patron of writers, consort of tycoons; also gambler, racehorse owner, party giver, whose nonstop parties, with their hundreds of guests, and lunches merging into dinner into breakfasts, had once been the model for Jay Gatsby's hospitality. By the time they all reached Swope's mansion, scores of people were literally spilling over the sides of the enormous veranda, a band was playing somewhere, waiters busied about with trays of food, buckets of champagne. Swope himself was out on the front lawn, in white flannels, shirtsleeves, playing croquet by floodlight. And then, as Alicia watched at a distance, Joe Brooks, finished with his poker game or maybe backgammon tournament in the city, drove up in a car with three other men, all four of them rumpled, cheerful, variously soft and bashful with drink. She remembered looking at Joe standing on the lawn, tieless, in his New York suit, Herb Swope's arms around him, or maybe vice versa, for the two men liked each other, both of them gamblers, one successful, the other not so much. And then, as she remembered it, out of nowhere there was the sudden crash of a huge summer storm, a cascade of water pelting down on everyone: Joe Brooks and Swope were running for the house, while she must have run back with Neysa, Jack, George Abbott, whomever, to the safety of their Packard. And then they were driving again, not far really, along some back roads close by the Sound, and then into a driveway, with what seemed to be a vast, imposing, castle-like edifice at the end of it—in fact, the facsimile of an entire thirteenth-century Normandy château. It was called Falaise, and was the property of Harry F. Guggenheim—one of "those" Guggenheims—who had apparently once told Neysa that she should come by sometime and check out his new bowling alley, and so, being Neysa, there of course they were. The rain had almost stopped but at first they stayed in the car, in the half light of the courtyard lamps; then one by one they got out, stretched their legs, walking about in the light summer drizzle, on the soft, crunchy seashell surface of the ground. What an extraordinary place, Alicia remembered thinking, with its towers and terraces, its high brick walls, its cloistered medieval elegance right at the water's edge. And then the front lights went on, the great arched door swung open, and there, apparently, was Harry Guggenheim: tall, handsome, gentlemanly, with piercing eyes, a friendly, amused smile, older but not old. She couldn't remember whether they actually went to the new bowling alley or not, how long they spent there, what anyone talked about. But she always remembered how Harry looked that night, and how he looked at her, and surely she at him.

· 31 ·

BY ALL ACCOUNTS the happiest times in the Brookses' mostly disconnected marriage were those long days, usually in late August, which they spent together at his fishing camp, in the wilderness along the east fork of the Ausable River, about sixty miles north of Lake Placid, in the shadow of Mount Marcy; a stretch of the river where forbidding boulders, brush-covered banks, cold water, and plentiful crayfish provided three species of trout—brook, brown, and rainbow—with what many aficionados thought was the best natural habitat in the eastern United States. Joe Brooks's camp had well-sited tents, employed the best camp cook in the Adirondacks, and Brooks himself, despite his size and enormous hands, was widely held in high regard for his impressive river skills. He famously used a two-ounce bamboo rod, specially made for him by Leonard & Co., so extraordinarily light that a clumsy cast could break it, and yet sufficiently precise that a superior fisherman could drop a fly just where he intended, at the edge of the most seemingly inaccessible pool, and then delicately float the fly along the surface until a rising fish took it, at which point he'd reel him in, slowly, patiently, sure of his touch—like a great saxophone player, one of his guests once said, holding an impossible note.

While Alicia hadn't originally come to fishing with the natural hand-eye coordination commonly required for expert fly casting, and in the beginning often got her line hung up on shrubs or overhanging tree branches, or sometimes lost her footing on slippery rocks and took a ride downstream (with consequent fits and curses), all the same she characteristically refused to give up trying, with the result that year by year she improved, until she herself was now at an almost expert level, successfully wielding the special three-and-a-quarter-ounce rod Joe Brooks had doggedly taught her to use. As he more than once told her sister Josephine, his idea of perfect happiness was to watch his wife working the river on a late summer afternoon; it was, he used to say, as much as he wanted out of life, which was doubtless true.

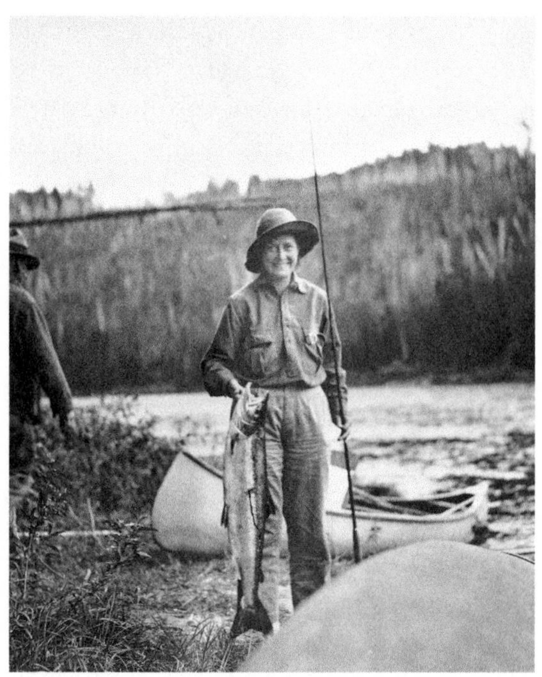
Fishing on the Ausable in the Adirondacks.

Brooks and Alicia owned a single-engine Cessna together, at least that's how they described it (a gift naturally from Joe Patterson), which they mostly used for flying in and out of fishing camp; also, toward the end of August, after a couple of weeks of living in tents, they'd sometimes stuff some proper resort clothes into a couple of valises, take off from the field outside the village of Ausable Forks where they parked the plane, and fly two hours south to the old-fashioned but thriving town of Saratoga Springs, New York, originally popular for its healing, medicinal waters, and now even more so for its August season of thoroughbred racing.

Despite its out-of-the-way, upstate location, Saratoga was an unexpectedly cosmopolitan place, where you could gamble legally on horse races, or illegally at the several casinos on the other side of the lake, where well-known big bands played, and Hollywood celebrities such as Bing Crosby and Clark Gable mingled with the Eastern racing elite. Alicia and Joe usually stayed at the United States Hotel, one of the older and better hotels, which had been around since the 1890s, when Commodore Vanderbilt's New York Central had helped make the town an attractive destination. Even in the late 1930s, Saratoga seemed to belong to a bygone era, with American flags and patriotic bunting on display, horse-drawn carriages competing with automobiles, dry-goods stores and soda fountains and a long dusty avenue called Broadway. The rich men who owned thoroughbred stables elsewhere in the country, and sent their horses by rail to Saratoga, walked about in linen suits and straw hats; their ladies sat in private boxes at the track, shaded places where "colored" butlers served mint juleps and Sazeracs, and changed their dresses throughout the day depending on hour or mood. August at Saratoga with its muted, well-bred atmosphere of carnival, drew "the best people" from all over the country, from Newport, Bar Harbor, Philadelphia, and certainly many from Long Island's North Shore: Phippses, Whitneys, Vanderbilts, and Bostwicks. Not surprisingly, in that week of late August 1938 Harry Guggenheim was there too; he almost always went up there for the season, as Alicia almost surely knew he would.

A few more words about Mr. Guggenheim. At the time he was forty-eight years old and a man of many attributes. For one thing, in an era when there were fewer than one hundred millionaires in the nation, he was immensely rich: the grandson of Meyer Guggenheim, an immigrant whose silver mine in Leadville, Colorado, began the family's mineral empire; the only son of Daniel Guggenheim, one of seven brothers who expanded the original silver business into copper mines and smelters across the American West and into South America. For another thing he was highly intelligent, both practically inquisitive as well as erudite. Privately tutored for years at home to protect him from anti-Semitism, he had enrolled at Yale, but soon after arriving at college he noted that he was refused permission even to try out for the freshman tennis squad despite his strong qualifications, and promptly left New Haven, along with his manservant, enrolling in Cambridge University across the Atlantic, where he distinguished himself in engineering studies and also won his tennis "blue." Later he worked as an engineer and project manager at the family's mines in Peru and Chile. In his late twenties he served as a distinguished United States ambassador to Cuba from 1929 to 1932. By the time he and Alicia made their initial connection, he had become a substantial power in the world of aviation, first as an early friend and patron of the still hallowed Charles Lindbergh (Lindbergh had written *We*, the famous account of his transatlantic flight, in a guest room at Falaise), and more recently as director of the important Guggenheim Fund for the Promotion of Aerodynamics. In his spare time (so to speak) he had also developed a growing interest in thoroughbred racing, deploying part of his North Shore acreage for stables and raising horses, several of which were now up in Saratoga for the races, along with their owner, who gave every appearance of being a bachelor, and a rather debonair bachelor at that, but was in fact still married to his second wife, Carol Morton, a member of the Morton Salt family, by report a kindly, nature-loving alcoholic who increasingly kept to her own world, emotionally as well as geographically.

Of course Alicia Patterson Brooks was also still married, in some ways even more married than Harry Guggenheim, since her husband was right there with her in Saratoga, although for the most part not so much with her as around the lake at the casinos. Joe Brooks had never been much of a horse fancier except for the betting part, but Alicia loved horses, always had; even though she no longer rode as an avocation, she still knew her way around stables and trainers, was known to other horse people, and during those four or five days in August it appeared that she was fast becoming known to Harry Guggenheim, who asked her to view the races with him from his private box at the track, which she did on numerous afternoons. Then, too, she began getting up early, leaving her sleeping husband in their bed at the United States Hotel for a brisk walk to the racetrack, where she stood beside Harry Guggenheim while he watched his horses work out, timed their runs, conferred with his trainer. One morning after the workouts, she remembered, he asked her to meet him later in the day, at the afternoon auction, when he said he would be bidding on some of the yearlings and would value her opinion. Tipton's Auction House was the oldest in the country, a big, dusty, barnlike structure out near the racecourse, with a small auditorium, a rectangular walking arena for the horses, and a pavilion for special guests. Alicia, who had been short of feeling special lately, seems to have felt herself a special guest of Harry Guggenheim's and later, after the bidding was over, in the course of which he'd flattered her by taking her advice on several offers, they took a walk outside, down by the New York Central tracks, past the empty boxcars for the horses, past the siding where they parked the owners' private railroad cars. She remembered, or claimed to remember, that Harry had on a dove-gray linen suit with a yellow tie; she thought she carried a straw hat in her hand because the wind was blowing; and when he took her by the arm to help her across one of the tracks, something she could easily do by herself, his hand just under the elbow, the lightest of touches but still something so definite, she knew there was going to be a lot more to it than that.

· 32 ·

IN CERTAIN OBVIOUS as well as less obvious ways, Alicia and Joe Brooks's marriage had been on shaky ground, thin ice, since its inception. Choose your metaphor. Though perhaps not teetering on a high wire, since that implies a more intense connection between the two than ever seems to have existed. As we know, the relationship had started years before they married, in fact at Brooks's fishing camp, when she was Joe Patterson's outdoorsy daughter, come to visit, and he was her father's good friend, much-esteemed wartime buddy, athlete hero, true outdoorsman, and so on, who could do no wrong as far as Poppa was concerned. When she let herself be talked or pushed (or however it was) into marrying Joe, the arrangement had seemed almost natural, logical, and if any of the three had ever paused to consider the incestuous shadows, or at least the odd dynamics, of the situation, there is no record of it. What's perhaps more surprising than her attraction to, and affair with, Harry Guggenheim is that nothing like it seems to have occurred beforehand; not that Alicia necessarily remained totally faithful to Brooks in seven years of marriage, but that there's no indication of her having entered into a serious romance with anyone, or left her husband for any length of time.

But with Guggenheim, matters were swiftly on a different footing. Two months after Saratoga, Alicia and Brooks were living apart, Alicia in their (her) New York apartment, Joe at the Williams Club. Six months later they were legally separated; a moment that evoked from Brooks another of his painfully boyish and doubtless anguished missives: "Dear One, King Booj is missing Baby Booj unbelievably. Always fly fast and safe. . . . Remember darling, I am going to do everything in my power to make your future happier than it has ever been in the past, and I am sure we will laugh and play our life long so that you will never regret me." And then, on June 15, as a mark of how fast she was flying, how decisively her life was changing, a cold legal note passed between Alicia and her father, signed by both, transferring back to "Mr. Joseph M. Patterson . . . all ownership of the aforementioned house and grounds at No. 11, Gardner Drive, Sands Point, N.Y."

Alicia seems to have anticipated that there would be problems with her leaving Brooks, who for years had been one of those larger-than-life characters beloved by many, certainly all those who didn't have to live with him, a sizable group that numbered many of her friends, her sister Josephine, and inevitably her father, who had brought them together, promoted the marriage, and then sustained it in manifold ways. When it came to Poppa, she had somehow assumed that, while he almost certainly wouldn't like the turn of events, wouldn't choose it, he would nonetheless support his daughter, take her side, at least wish her well on her new trajectory. Unfortunately, his initial response was a good deal more negative than she had expected, and his reaction didn't improve with time.

What she hadn't quite reckoned with was something she might be excused for not having taken into account; not that it hadn't been part of the world she had grown up with, and not that Poppa hadn't been part of that world; and yet Poppa had always been different, had always kept to his own course, had broken free so often from the limitations of his background. Granted, Joe Patterson had a number of sources for dismay, even anger, at this decision of his erstwhile favorite daughter's to break up with Joe Brooks, his old pal, his World War I coreligionist, everyone's friend, what was not to like about good old Joe Brooks? On some out-of-the-way, unacknowledged level of consciousness, her rejection of Brooks must have registered as a rejection of himself, which would have surely hurt. But it turned out that what really froze his soul in a manner of speaking was what she did next: her taking up with Mr. Harry F. Guggenheim of all people, scion of what was then the richest and most powerful Jewish family in the United States, indeed one of the most substantial five or six families in the country. It was as if his sometimes reckless, sometimes restless little daughter, the close one, the one who always needed him, and whom *he* could always count on, now in a chess game he didn't know he was playing, had just checkmated his king, and with her own public and powerful Jewish king. It was a sorry moment in Patterson's narrative but not the first or last; for Joe Patterson who long prided himself on his openness, his gift for getting on with anyone and everyone, a man who in a lengthy career in newspaper publishing, and lately as a New Deal supporter, surely had any number of Jewish friends. And yet there was no doubt that Harry Guggenheim's Jewishness was, as people say, a problem for him; *that*, of course and all the rest of Harry Guggenheim's situation: not just the money (though definitely the money) but the grandeur, the houses, the foundations, the family's national presence. Sister Josephine, for once unhelpful in her sympathies, reported to Alicia on a mournful, bitter lunch with her father and Joe Brooks, during which Patterson had remarked "that he wouldn't be too surprised" if Guggenheim hadn't been using "some of those European mind-control techniques like hypnosis" on his daughter.

Given the tensions surrounding her breakup with Brooks (whom she continued to care about and even love, with all sorts of mixed-up daughterly and wifely emotions), it was on the whole a lucky coincidence of timing that Joe Patterson, just then, was himself experiencing more than his usual level of distractions, both in his public and private lives, giving him little time for more heavy-handed fatherly attentions. At the *Daily News* his editorials had been growing ever more strident in advocating his own particular brand of isolationism, urging the Roosevelt administration toward two quite different international policies: In the Pacific he advocated "a well-armed America," promoting a buildup of defenses, preferably with a "ring of bases" extending from Hawaii to Asia; as to Europe, on the other hand, whose leaders had recently shown no stomach at Munich for confronting Hitler, he repeatedly advised that we should "let well enough alone"; that the British fleet was still "the most powerful military entity in the world" and could be trusted to take care of Britain and its empire; that we had "bailed out the Europeans once before and had little to show for it." Both these judgments, pugnaciously expressed, ran counter to President Roosevelt's own internationalist impulses, which had little interest in the Pacific, while at the same time sought to find ways to support European democracies in their struggle against the Fascist powers. His other distraction was much more personal: the need to legitimize his situation with Mary S. King.

For almost twenty years, despite his notorious unpredictability, his surely many inconstancies, he had remained faithful in his fashion to Mary King, the very Roman Catholic mother of his now sixteen-year-old son, Jimmy, who he hoped would be accepted as a candidate for the U.S. Military Academy at West Point. Thus he needed to have Jimmy legitimized. He needed to be able to marry Mary King, but first of all he needed, finally, to have Alice Higinbotham agree to a divorce. The solution to these several imponderables, as it turned out, lay in the hands, and lawyerly tact, of Josephine Patterson's new husband, Fred Reeve, a partner at the *Tribune* law firm in Chicago, who devised a seemingly equitable solution. All four Patterson children, Elinor, Alicia, Josephine, and Jimmy, would have equal shares in a trust, none of them would have more, none less. It goes without saying that these simple formulations were embedded in multiple pages of legal and financial stuff, with many references to something called "the Instrument," otherwise known as the McCormick-Patterson Trust, formerly known as the Joseph Medill Trust. But in due course Alice Higinbotham Patterson signed all the pages where she was supposed to sign them, and Joseph Medill Patterson signed where he was supposed to sign; then Alice went off to Mexico to be divorced, and Patterson and Mary King at long last began to plan their wedding.

AS A CODA OF SORTS to Alice and Joe Patterson's long, strange, tortuous marriage, so many more years apart than together, upon her return to Chicago from Mexico City, a newly divorced lady henceforth to be known as Mrs. A. H. Patterson, she read in her ex-husband's *Tribune* what should have been an unsurprising announcement of his impending nuptials, with a list of expected guests, and promptly fired off a fiery starburst of a letter, and not just to anyone but to her most independent daughter, always her father's favorite, his once-and-always pet, as she assumed, the still–Mrs. Joseph W. Brooks. "I am shocked and shaken," wrote Alicia's mother, "to read of your planned attendance at the June wedding festivities so brazenly announced in this morning's paper. I find it hard to believe that you would wish to humiliate yourself, as well as me, by publicly sanctioning this disgraceful affair. . . . It will certainly add nothing to your stature in your world or mine, besides placing you on record against me in a way that I am not likely to forget. . . . Looking back on these difficult years, I cannot find that my demands on your loyalty have been frequent or heavy. . . . But I am here and now putting you to the test by solemnly asking you, as I shall ask the other girls, to have nothing to do with this farce of a wedding. By your own decision I shall know where you are ranged, and what is your regard or lack of it, for me. . . . All that now matters to me in this world is that my girls are sound and true and have ideals. If not, you may come home from the party and write my epitaph: *La comédie est finie*."

The message apparently was received. On July 2 three limousines drove up to the entrance of the Bronx County Courthouse, a nine-story, fortress-like edifice recently completed as part of the New Deal public works program, and disgorged the three more than middle-aged, surviving grandchildren of Joseph Medill: Col. Robert Rutherford McCormick, Eleanor Medill "Cissy" Patterson, Joseph Medill Patterson, plus of course Mary King, and a small number of witnesses, all of whom, damp with the summer heat, trudged up the granite steps into the columned entrance, then up via elevators to the fourth floor, where in the splendiferous Art Deco courtroom of New York State Chief Justice Salvatore Cotillo, Patterson and his longtime companion were finally married. It was not the Roman Catholic wedding that Mary King might have wished for, since among Alice Patterson's conditions for divorce was a stipulation that her ex-husband not be remarried in a ceremony that required a papal annulment of his previous marriage (thus delegitimizing her own children); though all the same, at last, a legal union. None of his three daughters was present, all being unavailable for various reasons. His newly legitimate son, Jimmy, was up in the Adirondacks, on the Ausable River, being taught to fly cast by his old friend, Joe Brooks. Yet another old friend, perhaps no longer quite as friendly as before those *Daily News* editorials, though apparently still friendly enough, took time to handwrite him a warm congratulatory letter on White House stationery, signed, "As ever, Franklin," inviting him and his new wife to the cabinet dinner in the fall.

· 33 ·

SOME YEARS BEFORE, near the beginning of her marriage to Brooks, Alicia and Joe—probably in one of the little planes he used to rent or borrow—had been flying south from Hilton Head, past the Sea Islands, low above the inland waterway; just north of the Florida line she'd spotted what turned out to be the St. Mary's River, with its brown-black water, wild, cypress- and mangrove-lined riverbanks, its shorebirds taking flight as they flew over, its look of wilderness and mystery. Sometime later, visiting friends in south Georgia, she'd driven back down to the area and entered a low, Depression-era bid for a parcel of empty land on the St. Mary's, a dozen miles or so from the little town of Kingsland. In due course, after the sale closed, she put up, as she described it, a small house with a big fireplace, with a fine view of the river, and a great live oak out in front. Sometimes she and Brooks went down together to hunt quail and partridge in the woods, but mostly she was there alone; it was her retreat, her hideaway. During the many months that lapsed between her leaving Brooks and marrying Harry Guggenheim—almost a year's time, in fact—what with Harry's own uncontested divorce also having to make its way through the courts, what with Joe Brooks's unmitigated heavy sadness at being left, what with her father's fury at Guggenheim, what with the unpleasant melodrama of his remarriage, what with her mother's everlasting hurt, her sister Josephine not speaking to her, and so on, and so on, Alicia tried hard to keep out of sight; hiding out in a manner of speaking, both in her little St. Mary's place, as well as at Harry Guggenheim's altogether different, immensely grand South Carolina plantation, Cain Hoy. At the time, there were many friends of hers, not only critical of Alicia for leaving Joe Brooks but more than a little puzzled at her selection of Guggenheim. There was the Guggenheim fortune, of course, though that had been off-limits to his other wives. In so many ways they seemed such an unlikely couple: he such a cool, austere, almost mandarin figure, even older than Brooks; she an erratic, rough-and-tumble Midwesterner, hot tempered, fond of impulse. All true enough, and inevitably fault lines would appear in what was never exactly a marriage made in heaven. But right then, while they waited for legal permission to wed, such differences between them only seemed to add fuel to an already sexually heated, very definitely mutual attraction. Then, too, there was Harry's coolheaded—and to her immensely gratifying—appraisal of her ambitiousness and brains. She had "unusual intelligence," he told her, and appeared to mean it. Nobody had ever told her that before. What's more, he added, she was obviously capable of doing something on her own, something more than writing freelance journalism or comic-strip text, something substantial, something true to her background, for instance running a small newspaper on her own. As it turned out, just what she'd been thinking.

· 34 ·

IN MIDSUMMER 1939 the town of Roswell, New Mexico, was a quiet agricultural community in the southeastern part of the state, with a population of about twelve thousand, mostly farmers, sheep and cattle ranchers, and several hundred "lungers," the name for tuberculosis patients from the East who were trying to recover in the dry air. A photograph from the period shows Roswell's Main Street in the movie-set stillness of a placid, mildly prosperous, prewar American small town: dry-goods and drugstores, a cinema, two five-and-dime stores, and a line of Model A Fords and Studebakers parked diagonally against the sidewalk. Flat grassland, semidesert extended roughly seventy-five miles on all sides; hazily visible against the western horizon were the twelve-thousand-foot peaks of the Sacramento Mountains, the southernmost reach of the Rockies. The most substantial institution in the area was the New Mexico Military Institute, about twenty miles west of town. Farther west was the Mescalero Apache Indian Reservation, home so to speak for the few hundred survivors of the several Apache tribes that for much of the eighteenth and nineteenth centuries had terrorized Mexicans, Spaniards, Americans, and one another. And three miles north of Roswell, at the end of a dirt road, was an unremarkable fifteen-acre property called the Mescalero Ranch, its ranch house a many-roomed, somewhat rundown adobe structure, surrounded by several outbuildings, sheds, and a slowly pumping artesian well, which was where Harry Guggenheim brought his new wife, now Alicia Patterson Guggenheim, on their honeymoon, soon after they were married by a justice of the peace in Jacksonville, Florida; the two of them flying west in a chartered plane to the little Roswell airport, where they were met by the owner of the Mescalero Ranch, Dr. Robert H. Goddard.

Tall and thin, but with stooped shoulders that made him seem smaller, with a broad forehead, completely bald head and dark piercing eyes, Robert Hutchings Goddard had for the previous two decades been the most famous (and most elusive) scientist in America. More widely reported on than Thomas Edison, better known to the public than Albert Einstein, Goddard's specialty was rockets; in the press he was known as "The Rocket Man," sometimes "The Rocketeer." As a boy, reading Jules Verne and H. G. Wells, he dreamed of sending a projectile to the moon or Mars. As a physics student at Clark University in Massachusetts he began a mathematical study of the possibilities of using rocket power "as a means of escaping the Earth's attraction." Then in 1919, as a junior physics instructor at Clark, he published a groundbreaking paper in the obscure *Smithsonian Miscellany*, essentially proving that a rocket carrying scientific instruments might be able to escape Earth's gravity. The paper was dry, academic, mostly filled with calculations and equations, and would likely have never gained public notice save for its final paragraphs, in which, almost as an afterthought, he suggested that such a rocket, properly fired, might "reach an infinite distance," and "conceivably make impact with the dark side of the Moon." With those final conjectural paragraphs, Goddard's life changed, for the better and the worse. On the one hand his mathematics and theories caught the attention of scientists and research institutes across the nation; on the other hand, his speculations about space travel and moon landings provoked both widespread coverage and ridicule in the press, with the result that actual funding grew hard to come by. Fortunately two of the more important figures in American aviation development soon came to his rescue. First, Col. Charles A. Lindbergh, aviation hero and advocate of "air power," heard about Goddard's difficulties pursuing his research, and brought the problem to the attention of his friend Harry Guggenheim; Guggenheim in turn agreed to have the Guggenheim Aeronautical Foundation become Goddard's primary support, financing his research as well as his move to New Mexico where he could experiment with rockets, away from the public eye.

Out at the Mescalero Ranch the newlyweds were treated with a mixture of deference and distractedness by Goddard when he was around; although for two days he remained mainly out of sight in one or another of the shacklike research buildings, from where the sounds of welding and hammering could be heard starting at sunup. Then, late one afternoon the banging and hammering stopped; at dawn the next day, with the air chill and the moon still high in the clear sky, Dr. Goddard and his crew, plus Harry and Alicia, also a young man just arrived with a cardboard box of high-altitude-measuring equipment, all of them now bumping along in a variety of vehicles, drove thirty miles north into the desert, with Dr. Goddard himself in his old Ford truck, hauling an eighteen-foot rocket strapped to a John Deere gurney. In due course, in the rising heat of midmorning, the rocket was unloaded, laboriously positioned upright in an obviously homemade wooden frame, repositioned again, repositioned several times more. Two car batteries were produced, wires strung between the rocket (which had "Nell" hand-lettered in black paint on its side, this being the name of Mrs. Goddard) and the batteries. At a technician's direction, everybody stepped back about one hundred feet. Goddard began to turn dials on a gray metal box. Shortly a faint clicking sound could be heard from somewhere out front, perhaps from the box, perhaps from the rocket, a sequence of clicking sounds. And then, not right away but fairly soon, a loud roaring noise came from the direction of the rocket, then more noise, then flames and smoke, and the rocket began to rise slowly, beautifully, quite straight, but then not so straight, but then straight again, higher and higher. At about 2,250 feet (as was later calculated by the young man with the measuring equipment) the rocket began to yaw, just a little, then much more, finally veering sharply off course, smoke still pouring from its tail, flying more or less horizontally but then angling down toward the ground, which it slammed into a few miles away.

This was the ninth test of Goddard's L-series design, and as was the case with many of his tests, it was neither a success nor a total failure. There would be another test in a few days, and so Harry and Alicia decided to spend the waiting time camping in the mountains, fishing for rainbow in the Ruidosa River, which originated high in the Sacramento range, then dramatically plunged six thousand feet in about twenty miles. They returned to the Mescalero Ranch happy and grimy, in time for the next test, which fizzled completely. The problem was, Harry explained to Alicia, who liked to learn, and was thrilled to be so close to such exciting science, that Dr. Goddard, brilliant scientist though he was, kept needlessly complicating his designs, paying far too much attention to steering and balance, to gyroscopes and movable vanes, and far too little to altitude, to just getting the damned thing up there. Harry also spent a lot of time at a table in the ranch kitchen, poring over Goddard's financial ledgers, expense vouchers, budgetary outlays, in a word: spreadsheets. As Alicia remembered it, she had never before seen a man read spreadsheets with an attention bordering on pleasure. Harry in fact was at his table inside, and she was outside having a smoke, when the messenger appeared who was going to change her life for a second time in less than a week, literally a messenger: a man from the Western Union office in Roswell, driving a beat-up car, with a telegram in his hand that he took into the house. The telegram was for Harry but he brought it out and handed it to Alicia. SUITABLE NEWSPAPER PROPERTY AVAILABLE, the telegram read. NEED RESPONSE SOONEST. It was signed MAX.

NOTE: *While the prewar U.S. military and scientific establishments remained unconvinced by, in fact scarcely interested in, Robert Goddard's pioneering rocket launches in the New Mexico desert, Nazi Germany's scientists paid closer attention, and incorporated much of his research, especially as to steering and balance, in their increasingly dangerous V-1 and V-2 rockets. A further irony: At the conclusion of World War II it was Harry Guggenheim's Aeronautical Foundation that did much to help in bringing Nazi rocket expert Wernher von Braun to America, where his U.S.-made rockets in due course became the foundation for both our defense and space programs.*

· 35 ·

THE "MAX" WHO SIGNED THE TELEGRAM was a noteworthy newspaper figure in his own right: Max Annenberg, one of the original *Chicago Tribune* tough-guy circulation warriors, who had come East to help Joe Patterson start the *Daily News*, and now, with a kind of emeritus standing, didn't mind brooking Patterson's disfavor by helping his little daughter scout newspaper properties. What he'd found was not so much a newspaper as a defunct auto-dealership, in the small Long Island town of Hempstead, in whose garage a little Newhouse shopping sheet had just ceased publication after only eight days in business: Samuel Newhouse, owner of an upstate chain of papers already burdened by labor strikes, apparently hadn't thought the location worth the trouble, even though he'd already moved in some old presses.

No sooner returned from the New Mexico desert to the Norman grandeur of Falaise than Harry and Alicia made the drive from Sands Point, away from the green lawns of the North Shore, out across the drab no-man's-land of mid-Island, past car repair shops, billboards, sunbaked acres of potato fields, down Hempstead's Main Street, with its sleepy small-town look, to the empty, plate-glass-windowed car dealership. What Harry noticed was the length of the drive: twenty-eight minutes, which he'd precisely timed with a stopwatch he'd brought along for the purpose; as he declared, a manageable commute. What Alicia noticed was that Harry, her about-to-be copublisher, didn't seem to have registered that the two presses were not only old but weren't at all suited to a tabloid format; that there was no space for a proper city room; that the setup seemed to limit them to a smaller-than-five-thousand print run, in other words one of those then-fashionable, cute little country weeklies she wouldn't be caught dead publishing.

According to reports, the Guggenheims had their first sizable fight that night, by no means Alicia's first evening at Falaise but her first as the new wife, both of them seated together in evening clothes on the double divan, itself perfectly positioned on the incomparable Falaise veranda, looking out over Long Island Sound and the distant lights of Connecticut. Just finished was a superb dinner, prepared by Harry's great French chef, appearing as if out of nowhere; in due course a silver tray of liqueurs passed by Harry's butler of many years, Walter Moulton, or rather "Walter," whom Alicia normally liked; this was followed by the ritual of Harry's cigars: the proffered little cedar box of Cuban Upmanns, the process of selecting just the right one, then Walter, at his side again, to snip off the end of it with what seemed to be a gold-plated cigar snipper. Whenever Alicia felt threatened or anxious, she had a habit of tucking her knees underneath her, as if she were a cat considering her prey. "Tell me, Harry," she remembered saying, or something like it, doubtless in the teasy, husky voice she often adopted at these moments, and then proceeded to inquire blandly as to whether Harry was harboring any thoughts, any thoughts at all, about a future role for her in the running of Falaise? Or perhaps instead she was supposed to be content as a sort of Daphne du Maurier heroine (*Rebecca* was a current best-seller), as the charmingly copeless and self-effacing wife of the lord of the manor, whom the staff might casually ignore as they chose?

As Harry remembered what came next, he told her that if she actually wanted not merely to own a newspaper but to run one, she would have her work more than cut out for her. Or was she just another *Social Register* dilettante, mainly concerned about dinner menus? Throughout their stormy life together, Guggenheim, with his irritatingly precise memory, especially of occasions when he turned out to be in the right, never failed to remind Alicia that *she* was the one looking for negatives, looking for reasons to walk away from the little newspaper they didn't even own yet. After their first night at Falaise as husband and wife, seemingly spent in separate bedrooms, the next morning she reached him by telephone, already in his Wall Street office, and told him, more or less contritely, that she very much wanted the newspaper. Harry told her that he had already set the signing in motion and had in fact hired a business consultant, which of course infuriated her, although as she wrote a friend, "One thing about Harry, he's not a man who lets himself be pushed around."

· 36 ·

WHEN ALICIA STARTED TO TELL her New York friends about her newspaper plans, some listened (as friends do) without listening, but many others, especially those in the media, all too quickly rejoined, "Oh, just like the *Connecticut Nutmeg*," referring to the urbanely amusing, sophisticated little Lakeville, Connecticut, weekly published by the famous columnist Heywood Broun and his wife, featuring poems by Dorothy Parker and assorted contributions by the Algonquin set. But this was exactly, precisely not the direction she intended to go: a top-down, self-conscious, writerly, and inevitably money-losing entertainment for exurbanites. Even her usually savvy friend Neysa McMein thought that, when it came to naming the new paper, a cute title like "The County Irritant" would be such a giggle. Fortunately Alicia had burly, no-nonsense Max Annenberg to keep her head in the right direction, besides advising her on mundane details of circulation and machinery. She also had Harry Guggenheim's business skills on her side, something of a mixed blessing then and evermore. On the one hand he could be good with numbers, which she knew were important, for example right at the beginning cleverly arranging (through his lawyers) to fix a purchase price with Newhouse of a modest fifty thousand dollars "for all plant and equipment"; at the same time he often drove her crazy by his preoccupation with feasibility studies, surveys of one kind and another, his "spreadsheet mania," as she called it.

Mostly, though, she had her own instincts and impulses. At a time when the term "market research" did not yet exist, whatever someone could figure out by nosing around, checking out stuff that made sense to check out, Alicia Guggenheim was already doing; walking the streets of Hempstead, driving the country roads, trying to figure out her potential readers: small-business owners, housewives, scallop fishermen, potato farmers. For staff, Harry had already installed the research consultant Bill Mapel as business manager; Mapel in turn had hired a personable, talkative, young ex–Foreign Service aide, Stan Peckham, whom Alicia took a liking to and made her assistant. Bit by bit things began falling into place. The seemingly intractable problem of how to get a newspaper to readers in an area where there were no newsstands and no delivery boys was solved by hiring three former newsboys from Brooklyn and Queens to come out and teach local kids the fine points of home delivery—for example, how not to just toss the paper onto the front lawn, where rain or dew would ruin it, but to walk it all the way to the front door. The more fundamental question of the actual form of the new paper, and how to print it on the old presses, took a little longer to resolve. From the start she had wanted a tabloid and asked Max Annenberg for advice; Annenberg in turn went to the horse's mouth, to her father, who now communicating only through Annenberg, tersely advised that a tabloid could only succeed in a big city besides being entirely wrong for that part of Long Island. Still she wanted it as a tabloid, though of course the presses were a problem, designed for a conventional format. But maybe they could be rejiggered to print sideways? They could, but they would have to be taken completely apart, cleaned, repaired, rebuilt. Months went by in this fashion. Since the ancient presses were being retooled, why not the equally ancient Linotype machines? Harry huffed about all the money going out, no money coming in. Alicia commissioned the art-designer husband of a friend to come up with both a fresh typeface and a new design, aiming at something cleaner and clearer than the standard tabloid clutter of, say, the *Daily News*; a page with a more inviting horizontal look, wider photos, and no more "rules," those black vertical lines between columns. Ten days from publication the new paper was still without a name, despite Stan Peckham's countywide "Name Your Newspaper" contest; back from lunch, Bill Mapel walked into Alicia's small makeshift office, just off the press room, and wrote one word on her memo pad: "Newsday." "Yes, that's it," she said.

THE DAY AFTER LABOR DAY, September 3, 1940, so many of the new young staff, their friends, family members, various well-wishers, assorted onlookers, and so on, had all pushed their way into the new paper's offices (which still had the look of a car

AP starts the first *Newsday* press run, September 1940.

dealership, without the cars) that the press foreman had to blow a whistle to clear out inessential people from the tiny composing room, where compositors were trying to set the last lines of type. "Why can't I stay?" asked Alicia, who was wearing a new dress for the occasion. "Are you going to make up the paper?" the foreman asked her. "I don't know how," Alicia admitted, and backed out into the crowded newsroom. At last she was allowed in again, officially pushed the start button for the two old (and now briefly clean) Goss presses, which forthwith clanged and rumbled into action.

"It was just a horror," one of the original staffers recalled in Robert F. Keeler's fine book, *Newsday*. In a newspaper of only thirty pages, all too many came out ink stained and muddy. Worse still, on the very first page, two photos were printed with their captions transposed. With the presses still running, many of the staff wandered down Hempstead's Main Street to the Anchor Inn where they had too many drinks and took bets as to whether or not the newspaper would last out the week. On Alicia's instructions, but without really looking at the paper, Stan Peckham had taken one of the very first copies straight into New York, hand-delivering it to Joseph Patterson's office; unfortunately it was a copy with numerous pages barely legible, except of course for one clear headline about President Roosevelt's decision to send fifty destroyers to Britain, a subject that Patterson had been fiercely editorializing against in recent weeks. Whatever the reason, Patterson's response to his daughter's first newspaper was minimal, perfunctory: "Thank you for the paper, JMP." Alicia herself owned up to a sloppy debut. "I'm afraid it looks like hell," she said of her just-born *Newsday*. Then she took a page from an editorial her father had once written, after the first error-strewn issue of the *Daily News*, and published an apology in the next day's paper, an edition happily containing only two or three small errors. She compared *Newsday* to a badly behaved child at its first public appearance, promising to make it up to her readers, and concluded with a rough paraphrase of her favorite heroine's parting words in *Gone With the Wind*: "Tomorrow will be another *Newsday*."

· 37 ·

HERE'S ANOTHER OLD PHOTOGRAPH, not quite so antique as some of the others, neither crumbly or much faded, a five-by-seven black-and-white glossy: four people standing in front of a plate-glass window, two men, two women, none looking too happy or unhappy for that matter. On the back of the photo, there's a typewritten caption on a strip of paper: "Visitors to Newsday, Sept. 27, 1940: J. M. Patterson, Editor, N.Y. Daily News; Mrs. J. M. Patterson; Harry Guggenheim, Alicia P. Guggenheim, co-Publishers, Newsday." At the left of the quartet, almost as if trying to wander out of the frame, stands Joe Patterson, wearing a serious dark suit, though one that looks as if he had slept in it, which somewhat offsets the seriousness. He's still tall, but his shoulders are stooped, and his face is rumpled like his clothes. Hard to read his expression, maybe just the expression of a busy man who never did like being photographed. Beside him is his long-suffering second wife, Mary King, tall for a woman of her time, quite fine in a simple dress, also dark, an appropriate hat perched atop her head. Unlike her husband, who seems to think that if he looks away from the camera he won't be noticed, Mary King, a resolute Catholic girl from Oak Park, Illinois, stares right into the lens.

Somewhere close to the middle of the picture, although also seeming to wish she were somewhere else, is copublisher Alicia P. Guggenheim, arms crossed in front of her, clutching a handbag as if for dear life, wearing what must have started out that morning as a nice print dress, perhaps even a designer dress, something by Claire McCardell, her then-favorite designer. (Harry Guggenheim, unlike previous husbands, took an interest in what she wore, liked her to dress well, which she wasn't opposed to doing, circumstances permitting.) And then, more or less on her left but in fact somewhat to the rear of the group, stands copublisher Harry F. Guggenheim himself, definitely as tall as his father-in-law, in fact just then probably taller without the slumping shoulders. No dark business suit for him, he's wearing maybe beige or light gray, with one of his signature bow ties, and a tight seigneurial smile, the only one in the group with one of those on his face. There's no record of what anyone said at this conclave; it certainly didn't last very long, an hour and a half perhaps, time for the foursome to wander through the cramped offices, make small talk with staffers. Patterson was persuaded to pose beside one of the presses, which he did, looking as if he'd never seen one before. Alicia had spent weeks on the phone with her father's secretary trying to arrange this visit; in a way she knew better, she was all too conscious of his almost palpable lack of support for her venture, the nearly total absence of encouragement, the uncomfortable gulf that had arisen between them. On the other hand he was the one she'd done all this for: how could he not know that? Alicia's friend Janet Hauck (wife of the art designer), remembered that some well-meaning staff person asked Patterson if he wasn't pleased, or thrilled, or something, that his daughter was following in his footsteps, at which point Patterson turned to his wife and said they should be going. It might have been right after that exchange, or lack of it, that the photograph on the sidewalk outside was taken.

· 38 ·

A NOTE ABOUT Joe Patterson's evolving (or devolving) politics: While Alicia (and Harry) were launching their little Hempstead daily, the wider world, especially the world across the Atlantic, was in an awful mess, and a mess that was only getting worse. Earlier, in June, France had fallen to Hitler's armies; by late summer the Battle of Britain was taking place in the skies over southern England, with Edward R. Murrow broadcasting his rallying, sympathetic radio commentaries, which began "This is London," back to a mostly East coast audience. Joe Patterson, alas, was not a fan of Murrow or his broadcasts. "The man employs a fine, upperclass, baritone voice, trying his best to persuade farmers, factory workers, ordinary Americans to come and fight Great Britain's war," read one of his increasingly sour *Daily News* editorials, perhaps not actually written by the editor but certainly approved by him.

Patterson was even less a fan of the man he had once, and even lately, admired: President Franklin D. Roosevelt, who was campaigning in the fall of 1940 for an unprecedented fourth term, and campaigning to a great extent on his repeated promise to "keep us out of war." Patterson couldn't stand it that the president, whom he had done so much to support with his enormous *Daily News* readership (and early, too, when he needed it, before his popularity hardened into iconic statuary) was obviously bent on taking the country once more into a European war. Worse still, as Patterson saw it—one Old Grotonian critiquing another for not "playing fair"—he wasn't being straight about it but trying to sneak the country into war under the cover of unavoidably antineutralist policies, such as the proposed Lend-Lease agreements with Britain. As he continued to berate the president in print throughout the 1940 campaign, Patterson seems to have assumed that his own patriotic credentials were unassailable: he was a combat veteran of the Great War, widely referred to as Captain Patterson, someone whom FDR himself, as recently as 1938, had briefly talked with as to his becoming secretary of the Navy, an offer Patterson had politely declined. That was one mistake; another was less understandable: Patterson seems also to have assumed that his long-standing political differences with, and editorial independence from, his ultraconservative cousin, Robert McCormick, publisher of the *Chicago Tribune*, along with his own self-described seriousness about foreign policy, somehow immunized him from being lumped together by an embattled and angry White House with McCormick—often derisively referred to by the president as "Colonel McCosmic"—and the rest of the isolationist horde.

IN THE COURSE of that same 1940 presidential campaign, it turned out that Alicia and her new husband were having their own political differences. Her deputy Stan Peckham described a meeting one afternoon in her "library" at Falaise, a little downstairs room she had been allowed by Harry to decorate as she pleased, in this instance nothing medieval, mostly comfortable chintz. He and Alicia had been working on a forthcoming *Newsday* editorial, one strongly endorsing FDR, when Harry Guggenheim appeared. "I think he was surprised to see me there," Peckham remembered, "as if I belonged in Hempstead and not at Falaise. But then he started reading the editorial, and you could see there was a problem. I forget exactly what was said, and I tried at first to leave seeing there was going to be a row. I think she reminded him they had an agreement. What agreement? he might have said. It was one of those times. But it was true, she was Editor and so she had the right to set editorial policy. Newspaper people know that, but Harry wasn't a newspaper person, then or ever. He figured he was the owner, it was his money, really his paper, and it would reflect his views. In they end, they worked something out. I think it was something her father had devised when he and McCormick were disagreeing in the *Tribune* years ago. She and Harry wrote "His" and "Hers" editorials, running side by side. That was for the 1940 election. She really wanted Roosevelt, Harry hated him and wanted Wendell Wilkie [*sic*]. I guess we all know how that worked out."

· 39 ·

ALICIA'S FIRST YEAR OF MARRIAGE to Harry Guggenheim coincided more or less with her first year running *Newsday*, both activities that might be loosely grouped under the well-worn heading, works in progress. With Harry she soon figured out what was, and perhaps especially what wasn't, expected of her in the managing of households. He (and thus they) had a big apartment at the Savoy-Plaza Hotel in Manhattan, Falaise on Long Island's North Shore, and Cain Hoy in South Carolina, and Harry as always took care of all the major stuff, certainly hiring staff and paying bills; which in some ways was a relief after the Joe Brooks years, when it was never clear who was doing what (with the answer being usually nobody, unless it was her father), although sometimes Harry's obsessiveness (his attention to detail, as he would phrase it) could make things pretty weird. Alicia was supposed to be Mrs. Guggenheim, his wife, his hostess, and on the whole she rather liked that; she liked people, she liked going out or staying in, and got on well with all the staff. She also deployed her natural friendliness, her connective skills, on Harry's family, with fairly satisfying results; she had good relations with Harry's widowed mother, Gertrude, a sometimes-difficult old lady who lived half a mile or so from Falaise in a quasi-Irish castle of her own, and also with two of his grown children from his first marriage.

With *Newsday* for perhaps the first time in her life she settled in, or perhaps settled down, making a serious attempt to master processes, details, the nuts and bolts of the newspaper business. Most days she rose at six to get from Sands Point to Hempstead by seven, and even earlier when she was coming from Manhattan. At the paper she fidgeted for a while over her office, where it should be; at first she found it hard to be confined to the windowless executive cubicle she'd either chosen or accepted; instead (as she knew her father had once done) she moved her chair into the newsroom, where she preferred to hang out, sometimes into the press room where she knew she got in the way, and sometimes she'd get in her car and spend whole days following advertising salesmen on their calls, trying to get an understanding of what their routines were like, what they were up against. She also made an effort to stay close to her growing gang of newsboys, the paper's visible point of contact with subscribers; she praised them, organized contests, handed out special *Newsday* T-shirts, this before the world had generally come to appreciate the marketing appeal of the humble T-shirt.

Her private life was also showing signs of normalcy. She was back on speaking terms with sister Josephine. She had repaired friendships with such of her New York friends who had been down on her for leaving Joe Brooks, although some still drove her a bit crazy, telling her how they missed Good Old Joe, providing unhelpful sightings of her ex-husband at some teary or beery occasion. All things considered, it was not a bad time; even her mother, the newly minted Mrs. A. H. Patterson, while never exactly cozy with her middle daughter, seemed reassured, perhaps soothed, by the all-too-evident rightness (at least in certain respects) of Mr. Harry Frank Guggenheim, a man who obviously knew his linen and china. What remained a sad, sore point, however, were her relations with her father; or rather, her notable lack of relations. When in April 1941, Max Annenberg, one of his oldest friends in the world, died in a car accident, she sent him numerous messages of sympathy and consolation but never heard back, save for another brief, impersonal acknowledgment, via secretary. Granted, with FDR's reelection, she knew from reading the *Daily News* each morning that he'd taken his strange, somehow personal (without of course his seeming to know or acknowledge how personal it was) battle against Roosevelt to new levels of animosity. When the president unsurprisingly (perhaps to anyone except Patterson) signed the Lend-Lease Bill, delivering his famous "garden hose" speech, likening his action to those of a neighbor helping another neighbor put out a fire by lending him a garden hose, Patterson was in a fury, accusing the president of "assuming dictatorial powers," writing that the Lend-Lease Bill should "rightly be called the Dictatorship Bill." In September 1941, when Roosevelt bent the facts of an encounter between a U.S. Navy destroyer and a German U-boat to justify his order that navy ships "shoot on sight" at any perceived threat, Patterson wrote an editorial making matters even worse (were that possible) between himself and the White House: "Perhaps a great leader, inspired with a cause he thinks to be sacred, can consciously distort truth in hopes of making his people see things that way," declared the *Daily News* on September 17, "but we are afraid the record shows that President Roosevelt has not an overwhelming respect for truth." One morning, spotting a *Daily News* headline, "Figures Don't Lie!" above a story championing one of its own straw polls, which asserted that a majority of Americans opposed intervention in the worsening European war, Alicia wrote a rebuttal editorial of her own, cheekily titled it "Liars Sometimes Figure!" and sent it off to him; mindful that *Newsday*, with its fifteen thousand circulation, was not in much of a position to banter with the big boys, but somehow hoping that at least on a personal level she might draw her father out of his lair (or wherever he was hiding out) and back into a well-remembered, more playful relationship. When she still got no response, not even a scolding, she composed herself and wrote a dutiful, daughterly letter, addressed to Mr. and Mrs. J. M. Patterson in Ossining, New York, inviting her father and Mary King to Cain Hoy on the first weekend in December. Back came an acceptance, promptly, correctly, on Mrs. J. M. Patterson's stationery, in her small, neat hand, proposing an arrival date of December 5.

· 40 ·

FIRST, A NOTE ABOUT CAIN HOY. In the mid-1930s, after he'd returned from four years in Havana, as U.S. ambassador to Cuba, Harry Guggenheim began buying acreage in Berkeley County, South Carolina, twenty miles north of Charleston, and by the end of the decade he had a landholding of roughly eleven thousand acres, which he called Cain Hoy Plantation ("Cainhoy" being an old Gullah name for the region, probably having to do with sugarcane, although nobody was quite sure or could remember if or when sugarcane had been grown there). This was a time when land in the South was especially cheap, and many large estates were being bought up or created, often primarily for show. Harry Guggenheim, grandson of the industrious Meyer Guggenheim, was determined to be a different type of plantation owner, and from the start he devoted much of his acreage to moneymaking enterprises, notably yellow-pine timber production and raising Hereford cattle. Even so, there was plenty of room for luxury. Harry left standing the old planter's house, which he used as a business headquarters, but then built a far grander, white columned and porticoed mansion, which stood at the end of an imposing tree-lined *allée*, paved with crushed oyster shells instead of gravel; and he turned the surrounding woods into a preserve for shooting quail and wild turkey, accompanied by all the necessary infrastructure: stables for the horses, kennels for the hunting dogs, and housing for the staff.

Joe Patterson and Mary King took the train down from Washington, where he'd spent a couple of days conferring with the *Daily News* Washington bureau staff, arriving at the Charleston railroad station on the afternoon of Friday, December 5. Alicia and Harry were on hand to meet them, prepared for the worst, hoping for the best, and were relieved to find their guests in more-or-less normal family-visitation mode, Mary King as always a bit hard to take with her businesslike briskness, but all the same not trying to

Harry Guggenheim's Cain Hoy Plantation, Charleston, South Carolina.

make any trouble, and Patterson for whatever reason more friendly, less gruff than usual. It probably helped that Cain Hoy itself was especially inviting just then, an island of soft Southern comfort in a trouble-strewn world, with its wide lawns, its great trees hung with Spanish moss, in the pewter sky a gently setting sun, and fires blazing in the many fireplaces. In her later recollections of that historic weekend, Alicia sometimes spoke of the at-least-temporary conversational rapprochement at the dinner table between her father and Harry Guggenheim, mainly on the subject of the war in Europe, both men concerned over the imminent fall of Stalingrad to the Germans; however, it couldn't have been Stalingrad they were worried about (which wasn't attacked until much later) but Moscow itself, which in early December 1941 was seemingly encircled by Hitler's rampaging armies. If anyone there was worried about rising tensions in the Far East, between Japan and the United States (which by then had become almost a newspaper cliché), they kept it to themselves. At some point Mary King asked, or said, something about radio—was there news on the radio?—which made an opening for

Harry Guggenheim to give his little speech about Cain Hoy and its closeness to nature, about its soul-improving virtues of solitude, tranquillity, reflection, all surely enhanced by an absence of such man-made interferences as radio (a déclassé invention he privately despised) and even telephones, of which there was only one at Cain Hoy, some distance away in the business office.

On Saturday, December 6, Alicia and her father went out in the woods to shoot some quail, accompanied by dogs and a gamekeeper, the soft damp ground beginning to steam in the morning sunlight as the hunters trod over it. Joe Patterson was an excellent shot, had been hunting all his life, and enjoyed the sport, as did his sportswoman daughter. So also did Harry Guggenheim, who had surely bagged his share of game birds, and in some of the world's best shooting venues—the Venetian marshes, the moors of Scotland—but that morning, out of his odd mix of gallantry and diffidence, had chosen to stay back in the main house, making small talk with Mrs. Patterson. Alicia and her father were probably at their best together outdoors, where they could each concentrate on externals—birds, guns, dogs. They stayed out for hours, walking about, standing around, taking their shots, talking to the dogs, conferring with Clyde, the gamekeeper, who had worked for the Vanderbilts in the next county and thought that Mr. V.'s dogs could use a little more training. The afternoon and evening went well, too; another fine dinner (including some grilled quail the hunters had shot earlier) around Harry's impressive Georgian dinner table, where nobody (that is to say father or daughter) drank too much or got into unpleasant arguments.

The next day, December 7, began unremarkably, with a cool mist outside drifting through the hanging moss on the live oak trees; while inside Harry, Alicia, and her father (Mary King took her breakfast on a tray upstairs) grazed peacefully through an impressive early-morning meal of grits, biscuits, and smoked turkey before the hunting party made ready to go out again. With Harry joining his wife and father-in-law, there were three of them walking the woods that day, with their hunting vests, boots, khakis, treading the soft, leafy ground, each of them focused on the business at hand, happily mindless of what was happening thousands of miles to the east, in the Pacific, where the first waves of Japanese airplanes were coming in over the coast of Hawaii. Hours later, close to two in the afternoon, they stopped for lunch, a typical Cain Hoy hunters' picnic, with hampers, a cookstove, good wine, proper china, silverware, canvas chairs, and numerous attendants trucked in from the big house. What did they eat? It was something Alicia thought she should remember, an identifying marker, but never could; fried chicken would have been obvious, but Harry never liked being obvious. But she did recall they were all sitting around on the canvas chairs, legs stretched out, almost hot in the sun, when they heard a new sound, a car being driven hard down a bumpy dirt road. Then they saw the Cain Hoy station wagon, with its bleached wood panels ("Cain Hoy Plantation" elegantly lettered on the doors), saw it stop, and out of it step the tweed-suited figure of Mary King Patterson, now coming toward them almost at a run, quick long strides, trying not to stumble.

It seems that despite Harry Guggenheim's prohibition of radio on the premises, there was in fact such a device, the secret property of the cook who kept it out of sight in the kitchen and took a listen whenever the boss was off somewhere else. All that morning the airwaves—pretty much every station, most of them usually devoted to Bible readings and hymn singings on Sunday—had been so loud, even clamorous, with talk of an imminent speech by President Roosevelt himself, that the old cook had decided to walk himself into the front of the house and tell whoever was there something about it. Thus it happened that Mary King and Mr. Walter Tyree, both of them seated at the enamel kitchen table, listened together to President Franklin Roosevelt's famous "Date of Infamy" speech before a hastily assembled and hushed joint session of Congress; and she was now there before her husband and the Guggenheims—this normally trim, tidy, gray-haired lady, currently hatless, still out of breath—to tell them, "The Japanese bombed Pearl Harbor," and, "We're at war."

· 41 ·

AND SO: THREE PUBLISHERS, one of them of a most important newspaper, stuck in the South Carolina woods, with a lot of dead quail at their feet and the country suddenly at war. What to do next? On their way back to the house, Harry Guggenheim, no stranger to executive decisions, proposed that he charter a plane to fly them all from Charleston back to New York. But Joe Patterson, not for the first time in a longish life, was already listening to his own different drummer. The man who had been preaching, indeed bellowing, in print for the past two years against the country being drawn into war seemed now to be taking the Japanese attack personally, and produced a characteristically personal response. On the primitive telephone in Cain Hoy's business office, waiting to be connected to an operator in Charleston, herself obviously new to national emergencies, trying in turn to connect to other operators up the long line to New York, Patterson finally reached his deputies at the *Daily News*, who confirmed the disaster in Hawaii and Roosevelt's declaration of war.

At that point, Alicia recalled, everyone present expected to hear him arrange an immediate return to his office in New York. Instead he asked for a plane to fly him to Washington, also for a message to be sent to Fred Pasley (the paper's Washington bureau chief) telling him that he wanted an appointment "right at the top," so that he could offer his services to the army. If anyone then, such as the normally commonsensical, even prudent, Mary King, thought to second-guess this plan, no one apparently spoke up; besides, despite his self-proclaimed, regular-guy mannerisms, Joe Patterson was someone who rarely invited disagreement, least of all from family. His daughter Alicia, in fact, despite what happened, always remembered the odd sweetness of that moment, saw it as another of Poppa's romantic gestures: Captain Patterson of Battery D, who at thirty-eight had proudly volunteered for World War I, now at sixty-one an even older soldier, but once again patriotic, positive, showing up to defend his country when attacked. They said their good-byes at the little Charleston airfield, she and Harry taking Mary King back with them to New York; Joe Patterson standing tall and rumpled beside his old leather valise, waiting for the *Daily News* plane to fly in and take him on to Washington.

JOE PATTERSON'S LAST RIDE (if we may call it that) was surely a sad and sorry affair, one whose outcome in retrospect, and even at the time, mightn't have been all that hard to predict. We present it here as part of Alicia's story, because that's what it was too, a wildly ill-considered venture that he seems to have allowed, or perhaps willed, to define his final years, his relations with life, with the world at large, the world in small, and certainly with Alicia; and also, because as part of the public record, many of the details are still accessible.

Patterson apparently landed in Washington on the afternoon of December 9, with Fred Pasley on hand to meet him. Pasley wasn't one of the *Daily News* isolationists; he was a World War I veteran, smart, hardworking, and he and Patterson got on well together. According to Pasley's recollections, Patterson's preoccupation from the start was "his desire to get back on active duty, no matter the rank, no matter the posting." Pasley more or less had to interrupt his boss's patriotic outpourings, saying that he'd "already spoken with Steve" (Steve Early, President Roosevelt's press secretary), who told him that the president would see Patterson on December 10—in fact, the next morning. Such a quick response from Roosevelt might not be totally unexpected; over the years of FDR's presidency the *Daily News* editor had been a frequent visitor at the White House, an honored guest at numerous official dinners, a summertime guest at Hyde Park as well as on the presidential yacht; Patterson had personally raised the funds to build a swimming pool in the basement of the White House, where Roosevelt could exercise his crippled limbs. However, it was also true that, for at least the past year and a half, Patterson and the president had been publicly and often angrily at odds, on what might superficially be called the war issue, on foreign policy, but which in fact reflected a deeper argument: isolationism versus internationalism, Roosevelt trying to save the world (or at least the European world), Patterson combatively challenging him for, as he saw it, betraying American interests. Perhaps momentarily conscious that he would be taking up the time of a president suddenly at war, Patterson pressed Fred Pasley, did the president really wish to see him? Pasley said that he had confirmed the meeting with Steve Early: the president wanted to see him.

Patterson spent the night with his sister, Cissy, at her house on Dupont Circle: in fact the same grand, white-marble mansion that his mother, Nellie, had built as soon as she had come into her *Chicago Tribune* inheritance, where Henry Adams and Henry James had come to tea and which President Calvin Coolidge had used as a substitute White House when the real one was being repaired. Over the years Joe Patterson and Cissy had weathered a long, bumpy relationship: as she saw it, he was the sometimes overbearing though adored older brother, who could mainly do no wrong; for him she was the glamorous, provocative, often too-smart-for-her-own-good younger sister who couldn't seem to help making trouble for others as well as for herself.

That evening, with the nation only three days into war, with no reason for anyone to be confident about the outcome, or where or when some new attack might next occur, Cissy, with too much to drink as usual, and with her fondness for conspiracy theories, launched into her own anti-Roosevelt tirades, accusing the president of dishonesty, deception, having advance knowledge of the Pearl Harbor attack, and much else besides. Her brother, himself no stranger to alcohol-fueled outbursts, commonly reacted to Cissy's harangues, indeed to most female displays of emotion, by retreating into his own alternate universe of almost prim, pained withdrawal. Later that night he sat at his desk in the guest room composing a letter to the director of recruitment at the War Department: "I have the current rank of Major in the U.S. Army Reserves, although I would serve at any rank. . . . My preference would be for active service with the troops. . . . I am sixty-two years of age, am in good health, and am licensed to operate a motor vehicle."

Fred Pasley showed up at 15 Dupont Circle at nine thirty the next morning, and the two men set off on the short walk down Connecticut Avenue to the White House. Pasley noted that Patterson's suit was smartly pressed for a change, his white shirt crisp, his shoes shined. From the light traffic on the broad avenue, the usual flow of men and women walking to work, it was hard to see that anything much was different from any other Wednesday, though as they drew closer to the White House it was clear there were more police in place, more activity near the entrance. Pasley steered Patterson around to a side door, away from possible reporters, prying eyes (a maneuver Patterson noticed noncommittally), where the president's press secretary, Steve Early, stood waiting for them. Early shook hands warmly with Patterson, while Pasley took his leave; then Early led Patterson into the White House, down a narrow corridor, opening the door to an antechamber just outside the Oval Office and left him there in the empty room.

Joe Patterson had been inside that room many times before (first when Theodore Roosevelt had been president), with its stiff-backed chairs, blue carpeting, Olivet landscapes on the walls, but he had usually not been kept waiting, at least not for long. This time the minutes ticked by slowly—ten minutes, twenty minutes, maybe longer. He lit a cigarette, tried not to look at his watch, shifted his weight in the small chair, and as he was wont to do, bounced his legs up and down, hands on his knees. Should he get to his feet? Should he assume the president was understandably too busy to see him, make a tactful exit? Just then the wood-paneled door in front of him opened; Grace Tully, the president's private secretary, stood in the doorway. "Captain Patterson?" she said crisply, something between a question and a statement. "The president will see you now." Joe Patterson put out his cigarette, pushed himself to his feet, tried to throw back his congenitally slumping shoulders, and marched briskly into the big room.

As expected, the president was behind his desk, the large presidential desk covered from end to end with folders and papers; he was seated somewhat at an angle, his crippled legs extended to the side, in the act of reading something, a paper, a document, periodically making notations with a pencil, his signature cigarette holder (with cigarette) between his lips, tilted upward at its familiar angle. Grace Tully stayed in the room but was now seated at her own small desk in the back. Patterson remained where he had stopped, standing erect, more or less in a soldier's posture, on the blue-and-green carpet near the center of the room. The president continued working at his papers, turning over some, making notes on others, seemingly unaware of Patterson standing there, ten feet away. Finally, after about ten or so very long minutes, Franklin Roosevelt raised his large head, his face still reddened with windburn from a recent outing on the Potomac, squinting through the smoke from his cigarette, and as if surprised that Patterson should be in the room, said: "Well, Joe, what brings you here?"

Most certainly this was not the question Patterson expected to be asked. Hadn't reliable Fred Pasley assured him, then reassured him, that the president wished to see him? Only thirty minutes before, hadn't Steve Early, the president's own man, welcomed him as an expected guest?

"I am here to offer my services, Mr. President," is what Patterson said. No matter how often Roosevelt had urged him to call him "Frank," Patterson knew better; a president was always "Mr. President." There were two empty chairs nearby, between where he was standing and the president's desk, but Roosevelt didn't ask Patterson to sit down; in fact, his quizzical squint seemed to be turning hard. "You're offering me your services, Joe?" he asked.

"Yes, Mr. President."

What Joe Patterson had no way of knowing, standing there, an old man trying to keep a military bearing, literally on the carpet in the Oval Office, was that just then he was at the center of a disastrous sequence of miscommunications. Whatever Fred Pasley may have thought he'd originally communicated to Steve Early, as to his boss's desire to pay a patriotic call on the president, offering his military services, the actual memo that Early sent to Roosevelt's appointments secretary for the president's review, clearly stated: "Captain Joe Patterson, publisher of the *Daily News*, will be in town for the day, Dec. 10. Patterson is coming to town, Fred Pasley tells me, with the hope of seeing the President, for the purpose of saying that he has been wrong in his isolationist policy and wishes to admit his error to the President." Grace Tully's office then replied: "Tell Early to inform Pasley that the President is standing by." But no one had passed the word to Patterson that the president was expecting an apology, and that the mere act of Patterson offering his services would be nowhere near enough for Franklin Roosevelt, still smarting from vicious attacks only a week before in Robert McCormick's *Chicago Tribune*, also in Cissy Patterson's *Washington Times-Herald*, and who was not likely to disassociate the *Daily News* editor from the hostility and opinions of the family's other newspapers.

The president's voice began to rise. "Do you know how your newspapers have held back our war effort? Do you know how much harm you've caused, what trouble you've made?" He called out to Grace Tully: "Grace, bring me some of those editorials!" But even before she could come over with the folders, already lying on her desk, the president started to recite from memory, one after another, the latest sharply worded criticisms from the *Chicago Tribune*, the *Times-Herald*, and then finally from Patterson's own editorial, earlier in the year, telling the nearly two million readers of the *Daily News* that the president of the United States was himself no better than a dictator, trying to push the country into a European war. When Roosevelt was finally done with his recitation (Grace Tully in her memoir wrote that she had never heard the president "lay it on the line" as he did with Patterson that morning), far from offering Patterson some role, active or inactive, in the armed forces, he coldly asked: "What do you have to say for yourself, Joe?"

"What I wrote was published in peacetime, Mr. President," Patterson replied. "Now it's wartime and I should like to serve my country."

"I'll tell you what you can do, Joe," said the president. "You can go back home, and you can read over your editorials. That's what you can do." Then Roosevelt turned back to his work, the interview was over, leaving Patterson to make his way out of the room with as much bearing as he could manage; and while in fact the editor outlived the president by a little more than two years, in some core, crucial sense, it would turn out that Joseph Patterson's life was never the same after that meeting.

NOTE: *Accounts of Patterson's December 10, 1941, meeting with President Roosevelt appear in Fred Pasley's papers; in Grace Tully's memoir,* Grateful to Serve; *and in Steve Early's memoir,* With the President. *Patterson himself, no slouch as a reporter, wrote out a detailed, verbatim report of the interview as soon as he got back to Dupont Circle.*

· 42 ·

WELL BEFORE THE PEARL HARBOR ATTACK, Alicia Patterson's sympathies had been internationalist, even interventionist, when it came to the war in Europe. How she escaped the pull of isolationism, with her mostly beloved father regularly preaching it from the pulpit of the *Daily News*, her uncle and aunt declaiming it on the pages of the *Chicago Tribune* and *Washington Times-Herald* (itself a deceptively complex belief system, with elements of both nativism and pacifism, that for a while even sucked in sister Josephine, a spirited, freethinking young woman who nonetheless was active in the isolationist America First movement) can be somewhat explained by her earlier decision to leave the landlocked, conservative Midwest, the nativist heartland, where isolationism was especially entrenched, for New York, a city with its toes in the Atlantic, its mind attuned to Europe.

True, Joe Patterson also lived in New York, had been living there for twenty years or so, and published an astonishingly successful newspaper for New Yorkers. But Joe Patterson's New York was an odd blend of that older, still-mainstream, mostly WASP establishment of boardrooms, law firms, private clubs (a world defined and defended by the dominant "culture" of Ivy League colleges and private schools) which he'd grown up with, and at the lower end, his blue-collar circulation base, the "little guys" who filled the seats at the *Daily News*'s Golden Gloves boxing tournaments, the "little women" who eagerly sought out the *Daily News*'s "Helpful Hints for Housewives," one of Mary King's contributions. In contrast, Alicia's version of New York, pretty much from the time she moved there, a refugee from Lake Forest, had increasingly been the "new" Manhattan: smart people, talky people, talented people, many of them part of that emerging amalgam (mostly men, though quite a few women) that would later be known as the media; perhaps above all "cosmopolitan" people, which is to say Jewish people, such as her close friends Heywood and Gertrude Broun, Bennett and Phyllis Cerf, to say nothing of the new world of the Guggenheims (which in some ways was deeply Jewish, in other ways barely Jewish at all). As much as anything, though, what probably freed Alicia from her father, from the tidal tug of his "political philosophy," was something emerging, solidifying, in her nature: what might be described as a growing (if largely unexamined) sense of who she was and what she wasn't. On the one hand she was curious, quick-witted, direct, responsive, prone to surface likes and dislikes; what she wasn't was a deep thinker, an intellectual. Joe Patterson was also a quick study, impulsive, intuitive, indeed owed much of his success to his flying-by-the-seat-of-his-pants proclivities; but at the same time, in another corner of his brain, so to speak, he lived what might be called another life, a parallel vocation: that of a determinedly, earnestly, sometimes obsessively deep thinker, but with the quotes around it: a "deep thinker," caught up in theories and abstractions, sometimes seemingly for their own sake. To a great extent, isolationism was an abstraction, a worldview based on the interplay of abstract forces. His daughter Alicia, however, who once wished so much to mimic him, traveled lighter, with little propensity for abstraction. What she saw was what she saw, her instincts unimpeded by theory. Pundits might describe her response as internationalism or interventionism; what she would probably have called it (if asked) was common sense.

· 43 ·

ALICIA'S FIRST ATTEMPT to "do her bit," as people called it in the English manner, came in 1940, with the Battle of Britain under way. At the time, in the close-knit world of women's aviation, the dominant, larger-than-life figure (since the disappearance of Amelia Earhart) was Jacqueline Cochran. As was the case with Alicia (and perhaps fewer than one hundred other women), Jackie Cochran had earned her transport pilot's license in the early 1930s, and had then gone on not only to fly the mail but, as she described it, to "fly as far and fast and often as I could," setting women's speed and distance records across the country.

After the fall of France, with Britain's survival hanging in the balance, a small group of volunteer (male) American pilots migrated to England, to help out flying transport planes for the hard-pressed, undermanned British air services, under a program called Wings for Britain. Jackie Cochran proposed forming a squadron of qualified women pilots, an adjunct to Wings for Britain, also to go to England and assist the American men, who already had more work than they could handle. One of the first American women pilots Cochran contacted was Alicia, who was thrilled to be asked. They exchanged letters; then she and Cochran met several times, once in Washington with one of Alicia's old flying mentors, now Gen. Jimmy Doolittle. Alicia also took herself out to her old training grounds, Curtiss Field, not that far from Falaise, where she signed on for some brush-up instruction, familiarizing herself with new instruments and larger aircraft. Needless to say, all too soon there were obstacles put in the way of this fine, potentially dangerous, potentially useful adventure; not least by Harry Guggenheim, who one evening, at one of his Aeronautical Foundation conferences, was accosted by General Doolittle, who warmly congratulated Harry on his wife's "spunk and spirit," this regarding a project Guggenheim himself knew virtually nothing about. He promptly put his foot down, both as husband and copublisher, not only giving a sharp no to her notion of decamping to British airfields, even for the purpose of flying tinned beef to troops in Cornwall, but also pointing out the obvious, that as editor and copublisher of *Newsday*, she had an obligation, in his words, "to stay home and mind the store," not least for the 130 employees who might need their paychecks. She was sore about Harry's husbandly disapproval—the magisterial, voice-of-reason tone he took with her, a girl only trying to do her bit—but she also knew he was right, at least about *Newsday*, which didn't make her any less sore. In any event, Jackie Cochran's "Women's Wings for Britain" never did get off the ground, not even after Pearl Harbor. When Alicia ran into Jimmy Doolitle later in the war, he told her, "Wait a few years." For female pilots in the U.S. military, the wait would be about fifty years.

ANOTHER AREA in which Alicia tried to contribute something useful, with little result to show for it, was the politically charged one of Jewish immigration. Back in 1939, the worse-than-sad, truly horrible journey of the SS *St. Louis* had demonstrated, at least to those of a mind to look, that something was seriously wrong with U.S. immigration policy for European Jews. In brief, the *St. Louis* had departed Hamburg with nine hundred Jewish passengers, not steerage passengers either but passengers paying full fare, trying to escape from Hitler's Germany. Once at sea, however, it turned out that no country would receive them; not Britain, not France, Spain, Portugal; not the United States, and so on, down the list. Possibly Cuba? The *St. Louis* slowly traversed the Atlantic, entered Havana's harbor, but none of the passengers was permitted to disembark. One man tried to commit suicide by jumping overboard, and was taken under guard to a Cuban hospital. Only eighty miles from the United States, impassioned cables were sent by the *St. Louis* to American authorities, in effect to the Roosevelt administration's State Department; but entry was still denied, with the ship then forced to return across the ocean, redepositing en route the remaining 899 Jews in Allied ports. With little public outcry, or even passing notice being taken of this debacle, a private committee was formed in May 1940, to "promote expanded immigration quotas for Jews," in which Alicia Patterson Guggenheim took a prominent part, along with fellow publisher Marshall Field 3d, specifically calling for the rapid admission to the country of thousands of orphaned, destitute Jewish children from various parts of Europe. Alicia persuaded her mother-in-law, Mrs. Daniel Guggenheim, to turn over a large section of her nearby North Shore mansion for use as an orphanage, and work was begun transforming the Guggenheim Castle (as it was known) into a home for soon-to-be-appearing Jewish children. But none appeared. The reason eventually given was "political realities," which in rough translation referred to the unwillingness of Congress to pass, or the Roosevelt administration to push the Wagner-Rogers Child Refugee Bill for increased Jewish immigration.

NOTE: *After old Mrs. Guggenheim died, two years later, during the war, her vast, empty, splendidly turreted and crenellated castle was deeded to the U.S. Navy, to which it still belongs.*

IN THE END, Alicia did find two children to take in, certainly Jewish and assuredly refugees, though far from typical victims of the period. Back when she had first spoken to her husband about wanting to do something for Jewish refugee children, her thought had been to take in some of them at Falaise, but Harry opposed the idea: Ordinary Jewish children, he said—that is, children from typical backgrounds—after spending any time in Falaise, would only look on their postwar post-Falaise lives as a dreadful comedown. Soon after that odd conversation, while at a cocktail party in Washington in June 1940, she heard from the British ambassador of two young Jewish children who seemed to need a safer home, and whose background could hardly fail to pass muster with Harry Guggenheim. The children, Patrick and Janka de Koenigswarter, aged five and three, were described as currently living with elderly grandparents just outside London, where bombs were falling and a German invasion was anticipated any month. Their father, a brave and glamorous young Frenchman, Baron de Koenigswarter, was away fighting with Free French forces in North Africa; their mother, the baroness, apparently also brave and glamorous, perhaps a spy or not a spy, after dropping off the children, was also on her way to North Africa, to join the Baron and fight the Germans. And who were these elderly grandparents? Their name was Rothschild, they were the English branch of the Rothschild family, whose residence, if you could call it that, close by London, where bombs were falling, was known for its 120 rooms, its five thousand acres, and its fine gallery of Titians and Rembrandts. Alicia quickly said yes to the ambassador, who set the paperwork in motion, confident that Harry would or could make no objection. Later that summer, when the two children arrived at Falaise (accompanied by their nanny, the formidable Miss Davenport), little Patrick de Koenigswarter was heard to remark politely, in his high, British schoolboy's voice, "Oh, what a nice little house."

Patrick and Janka de Koenigswarter, two Rothschild grandchildren, war refugees of a kind, at Falaise, Long Island.

· 44 ·

AND THEN HARRY GUGGENHEIM decided to go to war.

He was fifty-one years old, an age at which no man was required to serve; besides which, he had just signed on as coguardian of the little Koenigswarter children; besides which, not that long ago (at least as wifely memories ran) he'd sternly and rather stuffily reproved the latest Mrs. Guggenheim for even thinking about flying off with Jackie Cochran's putative air force, telling her to "stay home and mind the store." Even so, these were heady, enervating months in wartime America, especially for men, who were the ones (for better or ill) who were mostly and visibly in motion, enlisting, being drafted, sent here and there for training. Back in 1917 Harry Guggenheim, then twenty-seven, had volunteered his services in World War I as part of the First Yale Aviation Unit, and was sent to France as a U.S. Navy pilot; he flew escort and bombing missions on the western front and at the end of the war was discharged as a lieutenant commander.

Now, in early 1942, he was allowed to reactivate his commission, and was first assigned as executive officer at Floyd Bennett Field in Brooklyn before being promoted to full commander and placed in charge of operations at Mercer Field, near Trenton, New Jersey. There's no doubt that Cmdr. Harry Guggenheim made a solid contribution to the war effort. His responsibility at Mercer Field was to receive Avenger fighter-bombers, coming off the assembly line at the nearby General Motors plant in Rahway, then make sure they were properly tested and equipped before being flown to California and their eventual destination on the aircraft carriers of the U.S. Pacific Fleet. But there's also little doubt that his eagerly managed deployment, proceeding from some then fairly common mixed motives of patriotism, male competitiveness, and who knows what else, posed a number of challenges for the Wife He Left Behind.

Granted, Guggenheim was not deployed very far, not overseas

but in New Jersey. Even so, Trenton in those days was far less accessible to New York and Long Island than it is today. While Harry was on duty, which appeared to be much of the time, he lived in officer's quarters near Mercer Field, sometimes on weekends came in to the Savoy-Plaza apartment, rarely to Falaise. At first Alicia seems to have found herself in a novel position; during her years married to the genial Joe Brooks she had often complained, to him and others, that he never did much of anything, had no ambition. Her current husband was indeed doing something, doing his bit, perhaps more than his bit, and there was a strong part of her that liked men to come up to the mark, respected them for doing so; and so she respected Harry, while at the same time feeling, as she so often had when it came to the vast gulf between men and women, How come you and not me?

For a while, with Harry off fighting the war from New Jersey, she considered that she now had two responsibilities, the newly arrived Koenigswarter children, and of course *Newsday*. At first, she tried hard to be if not a mother, at least a mother figure (whatever that

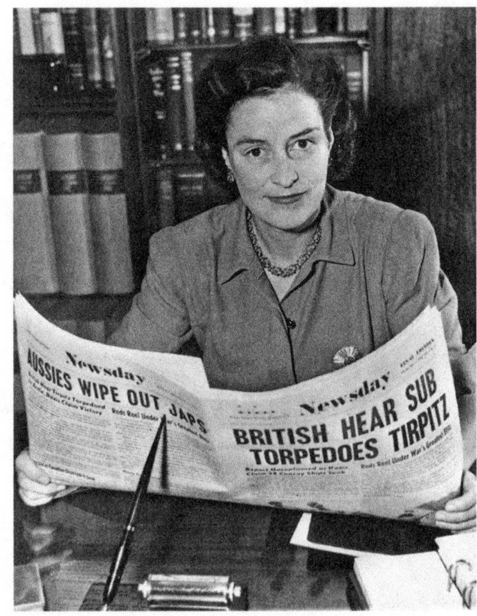

Copublishers in wartime: while Lieutenant Commander Guggenheim was running things at Mercer Field, Alicia was running things at *Newsday*.

might mean), to little Patrick and Janka. True, Alicia's notions of mothering derived from her own cool, minimalist mother, but it wasn't as if Alice Higinbotham Patterson had never read her children a story, tried to chat with them over bowls of macaroni. However, whenever Alicia entered the new "nursery," in what was now the "children's wing," uncertainly clutching a copy of Kipling's *Just-So Stories*, prepared to do what surely mother figures did, to read aloud from Kipling, magically appearing from nowhere, or somewhere, was the inevitable, impassable presence of Miss Davenport, neither large or physically imposing, in fact short, slight, with a burry Scots accent, seemingly determined to stop mother figures in their tracks. The children were either napping or about to "go down" for their naps; the books proposed were unsuitable, the board games too old, too young. With the growing fatalism of a native in one of Kipling's "lesser tribes," repeatedly throwing himself on the lances of the occupying power, Alicia eventually gave up trying to get around Nanny Davenport, trying to be someone she probably wasn't. Besides, the children seemed happy enough, whenever she glimpsed them, usually at a distance, trotting behind Miss Davenport on their way to or from mysterious errands, briefly between naps; also, as the butler, Moulton, sagely observed, they had arrived with perfect manners, Madam. Why spoil a good thing?

THUS CIRCUMSTANCES SEEMED to be pointing Alicia toward taking a firmer, or at least a more focused, role at her little Hempstead paper, something she should probably have been doing sooner; in its second year of publication, circulation hadn't moved much above fifteen thousand, advertising remained scrawny, editorial content was still noticeably amateurish, produced mostly by inexperienced young women hired to replace not-very-experienced young men disappearing into military conscription. *Newsday* wasn't exactly sinking, but it certainly wasn't swimming, at least not with sufficient vigor to offer much contrast to local competitors, even the stodgy *Nassau Review-Star*. Alicia didn't think she could do much to improve the quality of her young staff, in fact she knew she was lucky to have them. But she felt stymied by her managing editor, a man named Al Davis, a fiftyish, low-key, old-style newsman (who literally wore a green eyeshade to work) and who had been recommended to her by none other than Max Annenberg, Joe Patterson's old friend, her mentor in the business, so to speak. Davis was pale, expressionless, aloof, carried himself with what might be termed a scholarly air, did his work but no more than his work, then went home to Queens where he wrote pulp-fiction crime stories in his spare time.

By outward appearances she and Davis got on well enough, but in fact she and he didn't really get on at all; whenever she dropped by his desk he was usually too busy, or pretended she wasn't there until she went away. For a time the tactic worked; Alicia was conscious of being an owner, privileged, a woman in a man's world; she had absorbed what she thought were the lessons of her father: respect the professionals, the men on the floor, pay attention to the guys who do the work. While it wasn't her nature to accept brush-offs, she could almost accept one from her managing editor if it were part of some personal learning curve; what increasingly frustrated her was Davis's habit of equal-opportunity disengagement, not merely with his boss and with the newspaper's staff, but perhaps especially with the community on the other side of the plate-glass windows: Hempstead, Nassau County, *Newsday*'s potential readers.

By coincidence, as it were, not far from Al Davis's office, in the back of *Newsday*'s makeshift newsroom, was the desk of a man who might well be described as Davis's opposite. This was Alan Hathway, the paper's city editor, younger at thirty-five, also recommended by Max Annenberg; but where Davis was aggravatingly withdrawn, noncommunicative, the man who wasn't there, Hathway was decidedly, often obnoxiously, present. He had trained, if that was the word for it, on Chicago tabloids, with their rough-and-tumble approach to news as well as newsrooms; he was blunt, profane with everyone, drank too much (though as people pointed out, he didn't have to be drunk to get in a fight), and persisted in what was even then a retrograde habit of pinching women, literally pinching them, coming up on female staffers of all ages and administering a sharp squeeze to their behinds. On the other hand, as Alicia observed, he was shrewd, energetic, and involved in the community to the point where Harry's business manager had more than once wondered aloud to her if

Alan now and then might not be crossing a few lines, blurring some professional distinctions, as in his habit, for instance, of assigning favorable write-ups to restaurants or businesses in which he had a little interest on the side. Unsurprisingly Harry Guggenheim had pretty much detested Hathway from the start; the man dressed as if he'd slept in his clothes (which was sometimes the case), smelled of liquor in the middle of the day, and addressed the copublisher, on the happily few occasions when the copublisher and the city editor found themselves in the same room, with a slangy languor bordering on lèse-majesté.

But Harry Guggenheim was no longer around, he was off imposing his punctilious sense of order on Avenger fighter-bombers at Mercer Field. However, Alicia Patterson Guggenheim was much around; and while it took her a few months to stare down the ghost of Max Annenberg, and any other all-knowledgeable male figures who took up space in her cerebellum, the day came when she decided, if she was to mind the store, she'd better mind it her own way, and sent Al Davis, with his green eyeshade and bloodless manner, back to writing pulp fiction in Queens. She thought of calling in Hathway to her office to tell him of his promotion, but there wasn't really room for two in her office; and so she went to find him, guessing right (it being four in the afternoon), at the Anchor Inn down the street. When Hathway saw her, five feet three, in her trim little Hattie Carnegie suit, coming across the floor toward him, he cussed her loudly, picturesquely, for disturbing his peace; but she knew all the same words, knew how to use them, cussed him right back; they sealed the new arrangement with old-fashioneds, it being by then the cocktail hour.

· 45 ·

THERE'S A SAYING, possibly Irish (though it would sound as true in Persian) that there is no good season for old men; not that Joseph Patterson, in his early sixties, was truly old, even by the actuarial tables of the day; nonetheless, the war years for him were a terrible season, the proverbial downward spiral; doubtless his own fault, too, which surely made it worse. Long gone from the premises was the Renegade Heir of yesteryear, "Joe Pat," that all-too-spirited lad, friend (or at least passing acquaintance) of Butch Cassidy, youthful news gatherer at the Boxer Rebellion, the 1905 uprising in St. Petersburg, the Great Battle for Veracruz, at so many other excitements of the passing parade.

Vanished, too, in the mists of time, or as some would say in the fumes of bourbon, was the original Captain Patterson, doughty commander of Battery D, resolute warrior of the western front, sometime novelist, would-be playwright, impresario of New York tabloid journalism, truly an action figure (like the comics he popularized) of protean grasp and reach, above all a man on the right side of history, now supplanted (if you could call it that) in the early 1940s by this dark, despondent, hollowed-out, shadow of his former self, still referred to (even by his numerous detractors) as Captain Patterson, but so much sadder, madder too, seemingly no wiser, and with the passing of each day ever more on the wrong side of history. Still in command of a hugely successful paper, he had money, heft, certain kinds of power, he remained a Big Cheese. But most days he seldom left his once-moderne, now merely strange, house up on the Hudson, which he had painted in army camouflage colors after Pearl Harbor, and in whose basement he now maintained an up-to-date "war room," its walls covered with maps of military theaters, and a table (painted blue) on which he kept his eye on sea battles in the Pacific.

Patterson's decline was both surprising and unsurprising. For a man who had been such a smart guy, not always but often, and about some of the more important, worldly matters of his day: one of the dismayingly few who wasn't fooled by Hitler in the 1930s, who never thought (as did so many in the Anglo-American elite) that the German chancellor was someone one could "do business with"; a man who knew early that Joe Stalin was a bum, that the USSR was a bust, when once again so many of the knowing class—for instance, Franklin Roosevelt and his ambassador to Moscow, Joe Davies—seemed to be giving serious credence to the idea that Soviet "social justice" might represent the dawning of a new era. He had been on the whole a savvy, forward-looking fellow, who took a shine to aviation well before it became an industry, whose *Daily News* anticipated the discoveries of modern media (with its emphasis on visuals, its embrace of sports, its offhand, noir approach to crime, and its cheerful consumerism). And perhaps above all as someone who had both the nerve and common sense to strongly back FDR and his New Deal when so many in his own crowd were dead set against him; how very odd, how most unfortunate, how so strangely dumb it was that this same man couldn't then see that, first, attacking Roosevelt for wanting to save Europe and fight the Nazis was an idea best let alone; and second, given the unwisdom of the first idea, that criticizing a wartime president, in the months and years after Pearl Harbor, for errors of omission and commission in the waging of the war, was bound to get a person absolutely nowhere, worse than nowhere: painted into a dark and lonely corner, in a camouflaged house above the Hudson.

Patterson's grown children, for the most part, didn't know what to make of their once-charismatic, center-of-the-universe sire. Actually Elinor, transfigured into a fading country club beauty (gardening on her Greenwich estate after dark, to avoid the sun's glare on her still-lovely face) remained fairly consistent; as her mother's favorite, she long had avoided him, stayed away, and didn't come any closer now. Josephine, the youngest, who as a child had "had" him least, was still in thrall to some extent; she visited Patterson in his Ossining house, brought her young children, was puzzled by his depressions, silences, random eruptions, on the whole found it all too easy to blame the ever-present Mary King for the negative changes. Alicia, his scrappy middle daughter, the un-Elinor, with the cuts, bruises, and hair falling all over her face, swung between a newfound grown-upness, someone finally with her place in the road, and the child who was never far beneath the surface. Though she was never someone who went in for diaries, journals, or saving things in general, three scraps of paper survived from this period, stuffed in a manila envelope, with "father" written on the front. One is a clipping of her *Newsday* editorial of June 12, 1942, apparently in response to yet-another hammering (this one by Connecticut Democratic congressman Hugo Mill) of her politically obdurate father: "Joseph Medill Patterson is my father," she wrote. "I know him perhaps better than most daughters know their fathers. It is true that my father has from time to time criticized the Administration. Does that make him a traitor? Then anyone who criticizes policies laid down in Washington is likewise treasonous, and we have lost our democracy before we have begun to fight for it."

The second is the carbon copy of a letter, undated, but presumably written after the editorial: "Dear Father, First you cancel Neysa's drawings without warning, then you won't even acknowledge the editorial I sent you. I know it's not much, but it's meant well and a sight better than the kicks in the pants you have favored me with over the years. I still remember as a kid, when you and I had a bet that I'd never jump 5′6″, and I worked and worked and made the jump, and you never noticed, never said a thing. And then making me marry Jim Simpson, when you knew it was the last thing I wanted. And that trip to Panama when you said I was a quitter but I was sick as a dog. I've never been a quitter. And when I married Harry you wouldn't see him for a year and made those horrid mean jokes. And when I started *Newsday* I thought you'd finally be proud but you weren't. I could barely get you to come and look at the plant, and when you finally did, you and MK wanted to leave the whole time. Now I guess after this you won't want to see me again. Your affectionate daughter, Alicia. P.S. Please don't show this to *anyone*." The third is a note, handwritten on a *Daily News* memo page: "Dear Alicia, I think I am too old to quarrel with you and hope we may make up. Love, Father."

· 46 ·

THE LONG YEARS OF WAR placed strains on many marriages, bringing loneliness in its various manifestations to those away and those at home. While he was at Mercer Field, Harry Guggenheim by several accounts had an ongoing liaison with a young woman at the base (some said she was his driver), Kathleen Sullivan; "someone to go out dancing with" was how people phrased it at the time. If Alicia likewise had someone to dance with, there is no record of it, though the opportunities were surely all around her; among her numerous public escorts, it seemed evident to friends that she was attracted to Marquis Childs, the handsome, articulate (and married) columnist for the *Washington Post*, and he to her; but nothing seems to have come of it, beyond the fact that they were often in each other's company; years later he ruefully (and perhaps awkwardly) wrote her that, had he better known her interest, he might have "tried to do something about it."

Then in May 1945, in the final months of the war, with Germany already defeated and the United States now well in control of the Pacific, newly promoted Captain Guggenheim prepared to leave Mercer Field. However, instead of heading directly home to Alicia at Falaise, in the spirit of Odysseus he apparently decided to take the long way back, pulling strings in Washington to have himself transferred as an "observer" to the aircraft carrier USS *Nehenta Bay*, at the time on patrol duty near the Japanese-held Ryukyu Islands, two hundred miles from the Japanese mainland. Aboard the *Nehenta Bay* he was allowed to fly several sorties in the machine-gun seat of one of his Mercer Field Avenger fighter-bombers, engaged in strafing runs on Japanese ground defenses, thereby becoming the only member of the U.S. Navy to fly combat missions in both world wars. With time on his hands, in the officers' wardroom, Captain Harry wrote several letters back to Alicia from the far Pacific, still extant with their slanted, unexpectedly boyish pencil scrawl and little blacked-out deletions by the navy's censors; often many pages long, they're companionable, discursive, amiably impersonal, speaking to a relationship neither deep nor shallow, neither antagonistic nor especially affectionate, and written in that perhaps universal, dissociative language of men trying to talk to women about the stuff of war without seeming to like it too much. Thus: "Calisthenics on the deck this morning, officers and men. My back's not too hot but I'm learning how to stretch and W/O Symonds says it will improve. . . . Later on we had gunnery practice, with and without tracers. The racket from the .50s is amazing, terrible, I think I'd be deaf without earplugs. Our 'wing' scored highest with the towed targets. . . . As for what happens on deck when the planes launch, you could not imagine the sheer noise from the catapults, plus the roaring of the engines. . . . Frankly, it's just something that has to be seen to be believed, and I wouldn't have missed it for the world. Okay, general quarters has sounded, I don't think it's serious but I must sign off. Love, Harry."

Harry's long road home didn't appreciably speed up, even after Hiroshima and the rapid Japanese surrender; he meandered back across the Pacific on the *Nehenta Bay* to Hawaii, from where he presumably could have returned to New York fairly directly had he so wished; months seemed to go by, with a detour to San Francisco where important persons were buzzing about, putting the finishing touches (so to speak) on what would become the United Nations. Doubtless he enjoyed the company of important persons; doubtless too he liked being a U.S. Navy captain, with his dress uniform and war record; and perhaps (though there is no telling, from the mostly bland, sightseer's letters he wrote to Alicia from California) he had a premonition that civilian life might require adjustments from the relative harmony of being married to the U.S. Navy to being married (once more) to Alicia Patterson Guggenheim.

On her side, if Alicia was in any greater hurry for Harry to come home than he was to get there, she seems to have kept it pretty much to herself. Across the country it was a time for hundreds of thousands of sundered and separated couples to see what happened when you put both parts back together again, and with the Guggenheims there was perhaps more than the usual disconnect. On the one hand Harry Guggenheim saw himself as a returning warrior, selflessly having given his time, even risking his life above the Ryukyu Islands, and if he didn't actually expect a band to greet his return he probably expected something more than what he got. Not that she was exactly cool to him; on the contrary, he was her husband, she was his wife, there were pleasures and benefits to be had from his reappearance. All the same, while he had been happily off in what he never would have called his own world, rather the one of serving his country, Alicia had been in her world, also more or less happily, not merely minding the store at *Newsday* but in the process substantially improving it: The newspaper's circulation, around fifteen thousand at Harry's departure, was now close to seventy-five thousand; advertising had greatly increased, both in terms of linage as well as in better-quality accounts; and editorially, thanks to Alan Hathway and his young staff, the all-important "reading look" of the paper was finally getting somewhere, growing up, less and less relying on canned wire-service bulletins and circulation stunts, more and more generating its own professional, community-related stories.

With good reason Alicia expected praise from her returning copublisher. Unfortunately Harry's capacity for self-importance, which chronically ranged from routinely high to occasionally imperious, seemed lately stuck in the latter zone, a result perhaps of the deference he'd become used to as a navy captain, a rank he was now pleased to be known by in civilian life. Also, as Alicia's right-hand person, Stan Peckham observed, waspishly and astutely, Harry had become accustomed not only to the hierarchy of rank but even more so to "four years immersion in the happy world of men only." Whatever the reasons, his first postwar order of business was to get down to 120 Broadway and assert control over the family firm, Guggenheim Brothers, the giant mining concern that had been vastly profitable during the war and had been running more or less on automatic pilot under the chairmanship of his elderly uncle Solomon. Harry first persuaded Uncle Solomon to cede him the chairmanship, then went to work each morning in the large, hushed oak-paneled office, summoning reports, lawyers, accountants, and so on to bring him up to speed on the firm's myriad far-flung investments. He also found time to move his horse-breeding and -racing operations from Falaise to Cain Hoy, where he bought six thousand more acres; to successfully lobby the Truman administration into recruiting the former Nazi rocket expert, Wernher von Braun, to run the U.S. Army's new missile program; to serve on the planning committee for the proposed new Idlewild (later JFK) Airport; and somewhere in there he also asked his team of downtown financial analysts to take a look at his investment in *Newsday*.

It shouldn't have been much of a surprise to anyone that the Guggenheim accountants didn't altogether like what they saw, weren't exactly thrilled, when they peered into *Newsday*'s ledgers. Start-ups in any business commonly present an ugly array of numbers during their first years' outlays and losses where accountants would always prefer to see income and profits. But it was an unpleasant surprise to Alicia that her husband, walking back in the door after his moment in the military sun, his views largely shaped by Wall Street analysts, should express such sharp disapproval of the way she'd been running the business side of the paper, barely acknowledging the progress she'd made in transforming an amateurish local newssheet into "the strongest editorial voice in Nassau County," as the respected trade journal *Editor & Publisher* described it earlier in the year.

At first proudly, then defensively, then with increasing anger, she tried to focus Harry's attention on what she considered the important growth signs in the paper, leaving copies of the *E&P* article (with its forthright acknowledgment of "Editor Patterson's strong guidance") on his bedside table, at his breakfast setting, on the seat of his car. But Harry's eyes were only on the red ink in the accounting ledgers. In vain she reminded him that, when he wanted to, he could be commonsensically accommodating to the well-known dynamics of running a money-losing operation for a while, perhaps for a long while, in hopes of achieving personal satisfaction as well as turning a profit at the end, this being his long-standing (and current) approach to horseracing. But Harry was not in a mood to dicker with those of lesser rank. "*Newsday*'s a business, it's supposed to make money," he said blandly, magisterially. They were both such stubborn creatures, though about different things.

· 47 ·

ON MAY 17, 1946, Joe Patterson finally died; "finally" because although only sixty-six he had long been sinking, declining might be too graceful a word for it, subsiding into a misery of drink and melancholy, with a ruined liver and precious little remaining of the boisterous, restless, spirited "Joe Pat" of former times, to say nothing of the resolute, hard-driving, confidently intuitive Captain Patterson of the *Daily News* in its great years. Not that the *Daily News* wouldn't have some fine decades ahead of it, not that newspaper publishing itself wouldn't continue for a while as one of those powerful, impressive occupations, with its attendant cast of characters—the crusading editor, the ace reporter, and so on—seemingly fixed forever as part of the national theater. If only dimly visible at the end, a "shadow of his former self," as even his daughters agreed, for much of his life Joe Patterson had been one of those exceptional Americans, warts and all, as the saying goes. In fact his sometimes all-too-vivid defects were surely as much a part of his large presence as were his qualities. One senses that had Melville's Ahab somehow crossed paths, or wakes, with Patterson on the high seas, each man would have spotted a commonality in the other—that special American comingling of high purpose with high craziness.

His long-suffering wife, Mary King Patterson, with their son, Lt. James Patterson, held a small private funeral at the Roman Catholic church in Ossining, then released the body to be taken down to Washington, where Patterson's sister, Cissy, orchestrated a major funerary ritual, complete with horse-drawn, flag-draped casket, a full-dress, rifle-firing, send-off by a conveniently handy infantry platoon, and with herself in deep mourning, in picturesque widow's veil, accompanied by his three daughters, the younger two in little black hats, Elinor in something more competitive.

Soon afterward, Alicia returned to Falaise and wrote a brisk, lawyerly letter to Harry, saying that with her expected inheritance she wanted "to purchase a substantial interest in *Newsday*," in other words to become majority owner. Harry was not responsive, or perhaps was responsive in his own fashion. "As you know," he stiffly wrote back some days later, "I wish to retain a controlling interest in the enterprise . . . but I am prepared to sell you a 49% interest in *Newsday*, which on the overall value of $165,000 comes to $82,500. As I think you also know, when I acquired *Newsday* in 1940 I transferred to you a $4,000 capital interest, which due to losses in the business has been reduced to $362.52. This sum should therefore be deducted from the purchase price, leaving a net payment for you to make of $82,137.54." When Alicia eventually received her share of the Medill-Patterson inheritance, she quickly borrowed against it in order to buy the permitted 49 percent stake, a minority stake in what she (reasonably and unreasonably) always considered her own newspaper, and which she would keep trying for the rest of her life to augment by the crucial 2 percent.

• 48 •

ON HER FATHER'S DEATH, and in the months afterward, Alicia shed many tears, though none in public, which was in itself a kind of homage. Joe Patterson, who had grown up in a world where male surrender to the so-called softer (i.e., female) emotions was disapproved of to the extent of being impermissible, had made a point of passing along this manly code to his three daughters, with many fatherly reiterations of his favorite story, the fable about the Spartan boy so fiercely tightlipped that he had stayed silent, uttering not a sound, nary a squeak, as a stolen fox he was hiding beneath his tunic chomped away at the brave lad's innards. Elinor, the eldest, brief star of *The Miracle*, once the apple of his eye, had largely escaped or ignored his tidal pull, retreating into the genteel privacies of a Greenwich, Connecticut, haute-suburban lady. Josephine and especially Alicia, however, continued hearing their father's voice in their ears, in their heads, remaining lifelong acolytes, devoted aspirants to the Spartan ethic.

Thus in the months after Patterson's death, Alicia did her best to soldier on, dry eyed, uncomplaining and seemingly unemotional, despite the demise of the one person who had meant most to her in life. She also appeared to shrug off, at least on the surface, her illogical but nonetheless deep tribal disappointment at being bequeathed no ownership stake in her father's *Daily News*, although the sensible part of her knew that, as the *News* was a subsidiary of the *Chicago Tribune*, he had no ownership stake to give her. Similarly, and around the same time, she presented a "civilized," matter-of-fact response to another blow, also illogical though nonetheless strongly felt, which was the reappearance of those adventurous aristocratic Koenigswarters, also taking the long way back after the war, who finally showed up at Falaise to reclaim their children: little Patrick and Janka, in fact no longer so little, or so withdrawn, who had been living all the while at Falaise, going to school, closely managed of course by Nanny Davenport but also affectionately companionable to "Aunt Alicia," who not entirely seriously, and yet seriously enough, had led herself to think that one day she might be able to adopt them. In fact, perhaps the one exception to all this ongoing, outward display of Spartan stoicism was when her dog Dinah died, of what might be called natural causes, at which point Alicia literally collapsed in grief, as if her various layers of pain and loss were for the moment subsumed in the death of the little spaniel, whose corpus she carried down to her place in Georgia, where she buried it beneath a marble headstone, overlooking the St. Mary's River.

On her return she wandered about the house for a few days, "like a sleepwalker or a Tennessee Williams character," as Stan Peckham observed. She tried telling Harry that she could no longer get out of bed in the morning, let alone leave the house; but Harry was predictably unsympathetic, offering (maybe cunningly, or just obtusely) to send one of his "young men" from 120 Broadway to help out in her absence. And so back to work she went, back to the office, back into her routine: so much to do just then if you were running a newspaper in Nassau County, a newspaper whose circulation was now fast approaching one hundred thousand, as once sleepy Long Island began stirring under the impetus of what would become the great postwar building boom; and while she was about it, out of the blue, as people say, for no reason at all as she wrote Josephine, she decided to pay a much-postponed and -avoided visit to her mother back in Illinois.

SHE MADE THE TRIP in late July 1947. In fact sister Josephine, married young and divorced, then married again to the painter Ivan Albright was herself living in Chicago, where she'd just had her third child and was planning to spend August with her mother, out at the old family house in Libertyville. Why not a family reunion of sorts, absent of course Poppa, and Elinor, who never went anywhere and surely wouldn't show up? Of Alice Patterson's three daughters, Alicia had been least in touch over the years, few face-to-face meetings, occasional letter writing; unsurprisingly, after her marriage to Harry Guggenheim, such a hard pill for her father to swallow, it turned out once again that her mother, tiny comme-il-faut

Joe Patterson as painted by his son-in-law, Josephine's husband, the artist Ivan Albright.

Alice Patterson (who nearly always took an opposite tack from her ex-husband) got on splendidly with the beautifully mannered, augustan Mr. Guggenheim, the two of them periodically exchanging letters full of elegant mutual admiration, and fabulous little presents at Christmas. Still, Alicia had not been back to the Libertyville house for nearly twenty years, when she had been Mrs. James Simpson, one of the Lake Forest country club set.

Since then obviously much had changed. Originally Joe Patterson's Libertyville property ran to almost three hundred acres, and in addition to the main house included a large working barn, numerous outbuildings, and substantial cornfields. Before the war Josephine (in her own homage to her father's agricultural aspirations) ran a commercially successful, small pig-and-dairy operation on the farming acreage. But when she remarried and moved back to the city, the farm property had been sold off, with the result that Alice Patterson's domain was now reduced to the big house and its immediate environs. Even so, much was familiar; those stately elms, grown much taller and in full leaf, still lined the quarter-mile driveway, connecting to the wider asphalt county road. Her mother's once prizewinning garden, perhaps no longer prizewinning but still handsome, remained at the end of the long, grass allée (once tended so stalwartly by Mr. McGregor, and now surely by someone else), where the old lily pond, dormant and brackish, suffered as always in the summer heat, watched over by the same sculpted bronze deer. The thick trimmed hedges stood in their accustomed places, perhaps less closely manicured but all the same impressive, that European touch; while off behind a semicircle of shrubbery, lay, or perhaps languished, Poppa's old concrete swimming pool, once such a proud statement of up-to-date modernity in the chronically behind-the-times Midwest; and might that be the same faded, green-striped canvas awning hanging above the veranda, or at least one of its descendants?

On the whole the main house looked better from the outside: its red-brick, three-story facade presented a fine Georgian face to the world; the David Adler entrance hall remained imposing with its glistening gray marble. But farther inside, all was not so *bien*, as Alice Patterson might have put it: The chintz on the living room furniture, whose once-fashionable chic her father had been fond of protesting by repeatedly sitting on it in his wet bathing suit, looked threadbare and badly faded; carpets were frayed and worn; the library, her father's favorite part of the house, had the sad look of a room no one entered, dusty books all in a jumble. Worse still, the inner workings of the large house were in obvious disrepair, with evidence of leaks in the roof, brown water coughing out of rusty pipes, numerous warped and creaking floorboards, all clearly beyond the capacity of her mother's elderly chauffeur-handyman, John, to stay abreast of; and reminiscent of an earlier time, two also elderly Swedish farm women, thinly disguised as domestics, moved thickly in and out of the rooms, attempting to take care of Josephine and her two children, plus new baby; and now Alicia.

Josephine's children called Alice Patterson "Gaga," and tried hard (usually in vain) to behave correctly in her small, imperial presence. Alicia called her "Mother," and even at forty-one tried less consistently to behave correctly, conscious that as her father's favorite daughter she was never going to gain complete approval. Soon after arriving, in one of those forced attempts to be lightly self-deprecating, when she remarked that she still didn't know where the linen closet was in Falaise, her mother took the admission seriously, which it partly was, and pointedly observed that knowing the location of your linen closet should be "more important to a woman than working at other things" outside the home. For mutual solace, Josephine and Alicia shared the same room, with its open window, the warm air that never stirred, and often the same bed (into which the baby was periodically brought for feeding), giggling together like sisters on a sleepover, missing their father—who had been mostly absent from their childhoods and was now permanently absent—and wishing their mother might become a little easier to be around.

Then, as such things happen, with no plan, with seeming randomness, on the last weekend in August, which was also the last weekend of Alicia's visit, her mother unknowingly set in motion a sequence of casual, commonplace events that would turn out to have a marked, indeed transformative effect on the remainder of Alicia's life. The first was Alice Patterson's decision to give a cocktail party at her Libertyville house; nothing too elaborate, just cocktails and tea sandwiches: a little late-summer hospitality in honor of her daughter visiting from the east, and perhaps also a signal from Alice to old friends in the area that she herself had not vanished from the earth. The second was her notion to invite Ellen Borden Stevenson and her husband, lately moved to the area, Ellen being one of the Chicago Bordens (the Borden dairy people), a contemporary of Alicia's, both girls having made their debuts in the same year, her husband being a personable lawyer named Adlai Ewing Stevenson, from a newspaper publishing family downstate in Bloomington; then, ultimately perhaps the most consequential choice was Ellen Stevenson's, to send Adlai and not come to the party herself.

In fact Adlai Stevenson and Alicia Patterson had known each other for years, though in that mostly offhand, abstract way of young people, ships passing in the night; when she was nineteen and he twenty-five, at one of those Scott Fitzgerald–era, Chicago winter dances, they had briefly flirted, kissed in one of the hotel corridors, then gone their separate ways, he to Princeton, a social marriage, a conventional Chicago legal career, interrupted by military service in the navy. On that late August afternoon in 1947, she was forty-one, with hints of gray in her hair and faint lines on her face; he was forty-seven, with more than a slight paunch and a balding pate. Both of them were married, each with different strains, challenges, obligations. Both of them still possessed ample quantities of, call it what you will, charisma, personal magnetism, sex appeal. Sister Josephine, who was quick to notice such things, long remembered the sight of the two of them, Alicia and Ellen Stevenson's husband, standing in the lee of one of the hedges, both holding drinks, talking, two people at a cocktail party, herself not thinking much of anything about it. Then a while later, when she looked again, they were still there talking, the same two people, drinks, maybe a cigarette in somebody's hand, but now she thought. There was something, you could tell there was *something*.

What had they been talking about so intently that Labor Day afternoon, on the lawn of the old Patterson house? When Josephine asked her sister after the party, Alicia at first replied, "I don't know," which struck even Alicia as so unlikely; then she said they'd been talking about politics, specifically about Gen. Dwight Eisenhower, the wartime Allied Supreme Commander, lately everybody's favorite dark-horse candidate for the U.S. presidency, though no one yet knew which party he'd declare for. Alicia told Adlai she didn't care on whose ticket Eisenhower campaigned, as long as he ran. Adlai strongly agreed: Eisenhower had the experience, the credentials, plus a winning smile; he couldn't lose. Just then Alicia seemed to be the more confident of the two, the more firmly positioned: Alicia Patterson Guggenheim, just dropping in from New York and Long Island, Joe Patterson's daughter, herself a publisher of a growing newspaper. By contrast, Stevenson self-admittedly was floundering, at a loss about what to do, about his marriage, his unsatisfying, midlevel legal career. In fact, they had apparently talked as much, or more, about Stevenson's future as about presidential politics. He told her he was working hard to put together a consortium to buy the *Chicago Daily News*, hoping to get back into newspapers, say good-bye to the law; should he, shouldn't he? For a woman such as Alicia Patterson, perpetually surrounded by know-it-all fathers, husbands, editors, pretty much all men, there was surely something appealing, novel, intriguing, in this interesting, intelligent, clearly capable man, with an engaging, almost malleable manner, seemingly so willing to listen. As she later recalled the conversation, she told him "to take the bit in his teeth," which is what people said in the days before they could more simply urge, "Just go for it." Long afterward Josephine would still remember the look of those two figures on her mother's lawn that day: "Alicia wearing a silk print dress, some kind of hat, Adlai in one of those seersucker suits like all the other men, but with a bald head and a big grin, and she with her head cocked, looking up at him, as if he were tall."

· 49 ·

A NOTE ABOUT *Newsday* and Long Island's building boom: In hindsight it might look as if the great "population explosion" that spread like a tsunami over Long Island's Nassau County after the war had an inevitability about it that only required the people and institutions already on the ground to sit back and ride the wave. But whereas postwar population growth might have been a good bet to make, almost a sure thing, the specific areas to benefit were not so obvious to predict. Back in the middle of the war, with victory still far away, Alicia had written a nervily prescient editorial: "During the postwar period, we will undoubtedly see a big increase in our population. Men coming home from the war to new wives and new babies will want to settle down in the country, so that their children may play on the grass instead of the pavements of New York." In many ways, certainly viewed from today, this might be considered a normal, even plausible assumption. However, in May 1943, the date of the editorial, the economics and basic practices of the real estate market were quite different from what they became. As far as anyone knew, the war had only interrupted the Great Depression, when only the well-off lived in suburbs, when attractive land close by the city was expensive, and more significantly: Should you have land and wish to build on it, there were still the time-honored constraints of homebuilding, which is to say, houses were built of usually expensive materials, and always, as if by law, one at a time.

Alicia had missed or skipped college, depending on one's point of view; perhaps because of this seeming lack of higher learning (as it was termed) or perhaps in spite of it, she liked to worry at matters she found interesting, poke around them, try to find a way in with improvisation, common sense, the wit God gave a flea, as she sometimes put it. Thus it was with her intuitive notion about the upcoming need for postwar housing, for new communities where young parents of what much later would be called "the baby boom" could hatch and rear those babies. As it happened, she sometimes played tennis with a Long Island neighbor, a man named Albert Wood, a semiretired architect, who before the war had designed some of the first mass-produced worker housing for the Ford Motor Company out in Michigan. Wood was proud of his designs, and happily told her about the even newer modular, concrete-block construction coming into use during the war; economic building techniques, he said, that might potentially be combined with New Deal federal housing programs already on the books, thereby bringing home-buying costs within the range of ordinary citizens. Armed with Al Wood's insights and information, Alicia persuaded her reluctant managing editor, Alan Hathway, to assign one of the paper's fledgling women reporters to put together an ambitious five-part series on the unglamorous subject of the postwar possibilities for affordable housing in Nassau County. On the surface hard-boiled, skeptical of his boss's "do-gooding" projects and even ornery about following them up, Hathway was nonetheless a quick study, with an eye for opportunities great and small. He not only published *Newsday*'s anticipatory housing series (in September 1944, when the war finally seemed winnable), but was probably one of the few who read it attentively enough to be on the lookout for how to do something about it when the time came.

Thus evolved *Newsday*'s venturesome "collaboration" with the maverick homebuilder Bill Levitt: during the war a builder of barracks for the navy, after war's end an ambitious and visionary prophet of affordable mass housing, an industry that didn't really yet exist, an idea that still conjured up a vista of shacks, tenements, and the impecunious tenants who usually went with them. Levitt, however, was both salesman and a serious student of the new house-building technologies. His plan was to build simple, sturdy, wood-frame houses out of prefabricated modular components; then, with new techniques of pouring cement, fasten them to standardized cement-floor slabs, thus no basements but with all the new electric appliances. Moreover, he could build them by the hundreds, by the thousands; in theory the more houses he built the cheaper they would be to construct and purchase. The problem was, where to build them? Traditional communities were aghast; mass-produced housing seemed crass, lacking in the aesthetics of homeyness, almost un-American. Levitt found opposition nearly everywhere, from zoning boards, newspapers, all the usual guardians of value. Out in quiescent, semiverdant Nassau County, however, Patterson and Hathway saw in their own backyard both an appetite for new houses, as well as what might be called an oversupply of small farms and potato fields, few of them doing much better than breaking even in the postwar world of agribusiness. It seemed an easy call, having *Newsday* in its editorials support Levitt, who in turn would fill the underpopulated region with up-to-date affordable houses, not tenements, not apartment blocks, but individual homes, which would in turn attract families, all potential *Newsday* subscribers.

Patterson and Hathway pushed hard for Levitt; others pushed back just as hard against the interloper, with his newfangled ideas, wanting to bring crowds of new people from who knows where into places that had done quite well without them, thank you very much. The elite, culture-conscious New York papers, the *Herald Tribune* and *Times*, outdid themselves in decrying the threat of "urban sprawl" in Nassau County, an area presumably sanctified to potato fields and moribund communities. *Newsday*'s copublisher, Harry Guggenheim, also joined the opposition, at least in the privacy of Falaise, his tastebuds in recoil at the notion of dozens, if not hundreds, if not thousands, of new houses, all in a row, all alike, his sense of authority repeatedly affronted by his scrappy, culturally insensitive wife, to say nothing of her appalling, insufficiently subordinate managing editor Hathway, whom he tried to persuade her to fire numerous times, without success. In the end, by June 1947, ground was being broken for Levitt's first development, the first of his many Levittowns, which helped usher in a new era of homebuilding and home ownership across the country. Nassau County started filling up, coming alive. By 1949 *Newsday*'s circulation had reached 125,000, no small potatoes, and showed few signs of slowing.

· 50 ·

SOON AFTER SISTER JOSEPHINE married the artist Ivan Albright, in the summer of 1946, the Albrights moved into a larger house on Chicago's Near North side, though they still kept the smaller apartment they had been renting on State Street—one floor in an old brownstone, which Ivan now used as his studio and which Alicia began to borrow for her romantic liaisons with Adlai Stevenson. Albright kept several easels plus various painting materials tumultuously deployed about the living room (where he was in the process of painting his *Self-Portrait with Easel*, now part of the permanent collection of the Art Institute of Chicago), but this was the phase of Alicia and Adlai's long relationship when they least had need of a living room, being more than content to spend afternoons in the bedroom at the back of the house.

This was a time when Stevenson seemed almost immobilized by both professional and marital indecision. True, Patterson herself was increasingly at odds with Harry Guggenheim, often fighting with him, sometimes noisily, sometimes silently, mostly over *Newsday*, although doubtless there were plenty of other bones of contention; also, according to various observers, for reasons never made explicit, he and she were in a period of being sexually "off" each other, to the extent of keeping separate bedrooms, certainly one reason she was happy to have a physical connection with someone she found as appealing as Adlai Stevenson. Even so, she was by no means at the point of flying the coop, leaving *Newsday*, Falaise, her marriage, perhaps all the more so given her paramour's apparent lack of direction, traction, something solid at his base.

Not that he lacked for ideas, or ambition for that matter, which was surely one of his early attractions for Patterson, an ambitious woman who prized ambition in others. Back on her mother's lawn in Libertyville, he'd spoken of wanting to break away from his stodgy lawyer's job in Chicago, with no real financial rewards to speak of, above all little sense of larger purpose. At the time he had talked of partnering with a group of liberal Chicago businessmen to buy the struggling *Chicago Daily News*; then, as plans for the newspaper consortium foundered, he switched aspirations, first toward a job in the State Department, which at least would return him to Washington, where he'd worked during the war; next, to Illinois politics, specifically to one of the state's Senate seats coming up for contest in next year's elections, perhaps a more visible way of getting back to Washington and the national stage. He'd made it clear to Patterson that he wanted a place in national politics, also that he was being blocked by two powerful forces: one being his wife, Ellen, a forceful and volatile woman, from a still-important Chicago family, who made no secret of her dislike for politics and unwillingness to return to Washington; the second being the Illinois Democratic Party, under the thumb of its chairman, Col. Jake Arvey, which was open to him as candidate for governor, a job he didn't want, but opposed to him running for the Senate.

Stevenson and Patterson probably managed no more than two or three rendezvous in Albright's studio during the fall of 1947, but corresponded frequently, with Stevenson unburdening himself as to career insecurities, marital guilt, all-around ambivalence, and with Patterson affectionately and commonsensically supplying the direction and confidence he seemed to expect her to provide. More than once she wrote him, "If you want to play an important role you have to make up your mind." More than once he wrote her back, "Of course I know how right you are," and then once again declared himself unable to make a decision. In November 1947 Jake Arvey renewed his call for Stevenson to run for governor, setting an end-of-the-year deadline for his acceptance, and took the unusual step of paying a personal call on Ellen Stevenson to gain her approval, which she gave with reluctance, finding the relative quiet of nearby Springfield, Illinois, slightly more palatable than the noise and wickedness of Washington. Stevenson passed all this along in letters to Alicia, accompanied with expressions of eternal love ("I dream of when we can be together always"), also paragraphs of reasons as to why he couldn't possibly run for governor, or if he ran why he couldn't win, or should he win, why he couldn't conceivably spend

Alicia, sister Josephine, and Janet Hauck try to push their speedboat away from the bank of the St. Mary's River, Georgia.

six years in Springfield. In December, the week before Christmas, Alicia reappeared in Chicago, ostensibly to see her mother and Josephine's family, though in the process managing a brief meeting with Stevenson. Make sure you go to see Arvey before the deadline, she told her waffling friend (who also wanted advice on Christmas presents for his children) before herself returning East. On December 30 Stevenson, bundled in overcoat and snow boots, made his way to Colonel Arvey's office in the Loop and agreed to have his name entered as Democratic Party candidate for governor in the 1948 elections.

As a dark-horse reform candidate, Adlai Stevenson won the Democratic gubernatorial primary in March 1948, helped by voter backlash against an unpopular president, Harry Truman, and stories of "Washington corruption." Then, before resuming his campaign in earnest he made a quick trip south, ostensibly to visit his sister, Buffie Ives, in North Carolina, but with a tacked-on three-day detour to the little airport in Jacksonville, Florida: There he was met by Patterson's Georgia estate manager, Nub Colson, and driven north thirty miles, past piney woods and hand-lettered billboards advertising pecan pies and alligator exhibits, across the state line into Georgia; then another dozen miles deeper into the backwoods, past scrubland, scrawny trees, primitive shacks, and finally up a sandy, dirt road to Patterson's riverside retreat: a one-story, soft-spoken, gray cypress main house, not too small, not too grand, with expressive shrimp-pink shutters looking out on the black, fast-flowing St.

Mary's River, a tennis court was hidden behind thick bamboo, a little boathouse at the river's edge; in front of the house, along the riverbank, stretched a rough wide lawn, with three magnolia trees and a huge live oak, Spanish moss hanging from its branches.

Adlai Stevenson was an interesting man of his time, indeed more interesting than most, on the whole easier with women than with men, though even with the women he favored he could be variously and unpredictably charming or obtuse. In the course of their long friendship, he and Alicia were all too often out of step with each other, driving each other crazy. But over that long weekend, in the warm, moist air of southern Georgia, they appeared to have been truly close, in sync, simply happy together, as they all too rarely managed to be afterward. It probably helped that she was in a position and mood to be the strong one, reassuring, confident, seemingly invulnerable. And for her it doubtless added to a sense of the rightness of the moment that Stevenson was so tribally familiar, another Midwesterner, but not like all the others, the hardheaded, stuffy narrow-minded businessmen she wanted to leave behind when she came East so many years ago. Stevenson had a sense of humor, he had read the right books, he knew how to talk, he was both sexy and comfortable, unlike, for example, the cosmopolitan exotic she was married to, Harry Guggenheim.

She and Adlai took long walks together in the surrounding woods, went bird-watching (which she was good at), shot some quail (which she was even better at, certainly better than Stevenson, who was "loose" with his gun). One long afternoon she took out her speedy little Chris-Craft from the boathouse and drove him upriver, skimming over the surprisingly deep, mostly coffee-colored (from the tannic acid in the leaves) water; egrets and cormorants along the banks; also alligators and water moccasins; not a house or human in sight for endless miles. Later they sat together in front of the great brick fireplace, drinking corn liquor (made from a still on the premises), with ice from the icehouse in the woods, followed by a dinner of quail (feathers and buckshot removed) and pecan pie; and on the evidence of subsequent correspondence exchanged, swept along by the romantic conspiratorial haze of the moment, they seemed to have talked of a future that looked to be unfolding for both of them, she with her newspaper, he with his as-yet-indeterminate career in politics; a future admittedly full of problems but also possibilities.

On his return flight to Chicago, Stevenson wrote a letter to Patterson, already back at Falaise, full of the boyish enthusiasm of a not-altogether-worldly man, who clearly had not had such a good time in years, or ever: "I hope you don't mind my happy idiocy . . . or the abandoned way I shed my shackles and float away half conscious, dreaming dreams and seeing visions, and like a wraith you're always dancing in front of me, beckoning me on. . . . How I enjoyed my little walk hand-in-hand down Tobacco Road. I can still see you, striding in that solid straight-legged way along the bank and through the pines. . . . For the moment I'll have to resist the awful temptation to sweep you up into a soft white ball, that magically unfolds into a sharp savage little tigress . . . at least until I'm very much alone, and the hour is late and the night is still." And finally: "I hope you will come out to Libertyville this summer. I want you to know the boys, I want them to grow to love you like their father does. (Of course I also want you to know Ellen better). You can probably help me a lot in that direction, not that you are good but because you are wise."

SOME WEEKS LATER a stream of letters began arriving at Falaise, postmarked from stops along the less-than-glamorous campaign trail of a little-known candidate crisscrossing the Illinois hinterland. From Urbana: "I wonder what the hell I'm doing and why, and then I think of you and that you think it's good and worthwhile and wouldn't love me if I didn't make this effort." From Champaign: "Surely there's nothing we can't do if we want to enough and are wise enough. . . . Each night, all night I'm tormented by memories and moonlight. I'll hope for a letter from you soon, an adolescent letter if you are still feeling adolescent." And from Galesburg: "Just to say good night, my sweet. Tonight like all nights I miss you, and wonder what you are doing. How you look, what you are thinking. Sometimes this whole Gov business seems a bit of a dream to me, but I suppose it's real enough and I should keep at it. . . . Have I told you that I love you more than yesterday, though less than I will tomorrow."

· 51 ·

IN EARLY JUNE 1948, Patterson returned to her mother's old house in Libertyville, not quite one year since her lawn-party meeting with Adlai Stevenson. This time the occasion was more muted, an end of something not a beginning: Alice Patterson in fact was giving away the family house, donating it to a Catholic convent as a way of escaping heavy postwar taxes. Alicia made the trip ostensibly to show support, also to choose some of her parents' old English furniture for herself, but there were other compensations; after much fussing and back-and-forthing, Stevenson had arranged to take a weekend break from his campaign, and the two were able to spend some time together in his own conveniently empty house, ten minutes' drive down the old county road from her mother's. By Sunday night, when she was gone, on her way back East, and he was temporarily alone, seated on the little balcony outside his (and of course Ellen's) bedroom, he wrote her another of his effusive, lovelorn letters; "My dear, I'm still dreaming of Saturday, when you were sitting right here, your back to the sunset, never more beautiful, your lovely hair piled high on your trim little head, pouring out your heart. . . . This week I've been speaking to grandstands at county fairs and I wish, wish, wish this ordeal was finished and we could be together. . . . When are you coming here again? Why do you always drive reason away?"

That month, June 1948, seemed to mark the low point in Adlai Stevenson's quixotic bid for a mainstream political career; for on June 22, incumbent president Harry S. Truman, visiting Chicago to shore up his own election campaign, guest of honor at a well-publicized dinner for sixty "inner-circle" Democrats, pointedly arranged, or allowed, for reform candidate Stevenson to be left off the invitation list. As it happened this downdraft in Stevenson's prospects coincided with an unexpected moment—both exhilarating and destabilizing for Patterson—when her Aunt Cissy, heaven knows for what complicated, private reasons of her own (though surely having to do with her ongoing feud with cousin Bertie McCormick), suddenly reappeared in her life, making her niece the focus of a sequence of seductive conversations and letters, impulsively promising to leave Alicia the ownership and running of the *Washington Times-Herald* in her will. Thus for a few odd weeks, while Stevenson's campaign was showing signs of incipient collapse—with the candidate, publicly snubbed by the president of his own party, again gripped by pessimism and needfulness—his romantic partner and chief cheerleader seemed to have confidence to spare, doubtless much of it stemming from her natural gumption when it came to people and causes she believed in, though probably some of it just then colored by dreams of grandeur, to say nothing of fantasies of marital emancipation, put into her head by Aunt Cissy's blandishments.

By midsummer, however, both narratives were once more on different paths. First Stevenson's campaign began to regain traction, with the voters if not the party bosses; this most unlikely of candidates, urbane, so un-Midwestern, a kind of rumpled gentleman-scholar speechifying to a state mostly filled with farmers. Then, with Stevenson drawing bigger and bigger crowds, as he eloquently distanced himself from "the mess in Washington," on July 22, the ever-unpredictable Cissy Patterson died suddenly, supposedly in her sleep, though such was the messy, operatic nature of her life that the circumstances of her death were long considered by those who knew her as mysterious if not downright suspicious. In any event Alicia's fantasies were also thereby put to rest, with the reading of Cissy's will, a 1946 document bequeathing the *Times-Herald* to seven employees, with no mention of her niece. For the remainder of the campaign Patterson's and Stevenson's roles weren't exactly reversed: Nonetheless their correspondence from that period shows Stevenson, whether knowingly or unknowingly, changing shape as it were, from self-doubting antihero (lovelorn suitor and reluctant campaigner) to a more familiar, political type: the overbusy, self-involved candidate, preoccupied with meetings, speeches, and of course "the schedule"; and on Patterson's side, she begins to appear more and more as another familiar figure, the woman in the shadow of the important man. By July 24 he writes her impatiently: "I don't see the problem, why are explanations necessary? Can't you just fly here the afternoon of the 29th, stay the night, and head west in the morning?" On August 6 she apparently met him somewhere on the campaign trail outside Springfield, but the rendezvous seems not to have been a success, with Stevenson distracted and surrounded by campaign staff. Later he sent her a rueful, ironic note: "I didn't like Saturday night either, but at least you were there and caught a little of the panorama of these great events." In mid-August he wrote her again, at Josephine's ranch in Dubois, Wyoming: "I don't like the sad note of parting and misgiving in your letter. Of course our lives are complicated, but we must look forward gaily, happily, hopefully—with thirty years to come!" In early September: "Sometimes I'd like to throw the whole damn Gov thing out the window and catch a plane to you, dream in the purple twilight, sing in the mornings." In October: "Darling, five speeches today, 200 miles of wild motoring. Why anybody should submit to this brutality I don't understand. I was desolate to miss your call in Peoria, and then in Danville, but I think I did well in Danville." And then from Springfield: "The crowds are getting bigger or am I losing my eyesight? You know, I could bite your ears off, and I will. I love you utterly. P.S. I'm really afraid I'm going to be elected."

On November 6, 1948, in the national elections that returned President Truman to the White House, though by only a narrow margin, Adlai Ewing Stevenson was elected governor of Illinois, and by a vote of such landslide proportions that it propelled him from dark horse to the very front of his party. In her role as editor of a newspaper with growing national ambitions, Patterson went out to Chicago for election day, ending up at Stevenson headquarters on the night of his triumph; though such were the crowds, and such was his victory, that she couldn't get close enough to congratulate him, and returned home the following morning, with the proverbial mixed feelings. Sometime on the same day, clearly no longer Hamlet, not quite Caesar, Stevenson sent her a message at Falaise: "I carried Illinois by 565,000 at least, probably more, 515,000 ahead of Truman. Never anything like it in history. Now, I'm really in trouble." Then adding: "I know you were here, I think I saw you amid that fantastic frenzy. Don't worry, there are years and years ahead of us." There's no question that Patterson was pleased at Stevenson's win, seeing that she'd been behind him from the beginning, trying her best to keep him in the game despite his own ambivalence and occasional downright reluctance. But she was also a fast learner able to note the shift in wind, the change in temperature; much of her life she'd been in the shadow of self-preoccupied men, and while happy for Adlai in his new role as conquering hero, she was realist enough to parse the casual words "I think I saw you" and decide it was time, if not to be moving on, at least to keep moving; who knows, maybe a bit of both.

· 52 ·

WHERE SHE WENT WAS GERMANY, or West Germany as it was then known, much in the news on account of the Berlin airlift, the latest and most dangerous confrontation between the United States and the Soviet Union in what was only recently coming to be called the Cold War. Her trip was obviously not a last-minute affair, given the need for the many visas and military permits required for travel on a European continent still rubble strewn, impoverished, and filled with occupying troops of the victorious Allied powers. In fact she had signed on for it only a few weeks before, briskly informing Harry (who seemed to be spending more and more time at Cain Hoy, at his new stables) by one of those memos with which they increasingly communicated; Harry had also replied by memo, "Good luck," and maybe something else of a similar bland, disconnected nature—who knew what he was really thinking, probably about horses. Even so, she had left any final decision about going to how Adlai's election night played out; mightn't he need her at his side in defeat, wouldn't he want her close by in victory? As it turned out, not so much, neither.

Accordingly, on the afternoon of November 6, 1948, Patterson boarded the still stately *Queen Elizabeth*, largest and fastest of the prewar Cunard fleet (finally back in service after its wartime troopship duties) for the four-and-a-half-day run across the choppy, windblown North Atlantic; she was traveling light for a Cunard passenger, only one manageable suitcase. Apparently not traveling so light was her journalistic companion, Dorothy "Dolly" Schiff, the regal, tart-tongued publisher of the then relatively influential *New York Post*, who, as Alicia remembered, "changed her clothes four times a day in keeping with First Class trans-Atlantic tradition."

BRIEFLY DESCRIBED, the Berlin airlift was the hastily improvised response by American and British forces in West Germany to Soviet leader Joseph Stalin's sudden decision to block all road and rail access to Berlin from the West, in effect to isolate West Berlin and its citizens from food and fuel supplies, something he could do because Berlin (then divided by postwar agreement into French, British, U.S., and Soviet zones) lay three hundred miles within Soviet-occupied East Germany. Stalin was essentially daring the United States and Britain to go to war in order to keep two million West Berliners, their recent enemies, supplied with food, medicine, and above all coal for the winter. It was estimated that a minimum of five thousand tons overall were needed per day; Stalin's harsh gamble had been on the impossibility of funneling such tonnage into West Berlin by air, given the lack of suitable transport aircraft, the primitive nature of both instrument flying and ground controls, and the predictably threatening and impenetrable European winter weather.

Against these odds the airlift's planes and pilots, called into service on an emergency basis, had so far been holding their own: Two hundred C-54s were flown to the U.S. Air Force base at Wiesbaden, outside Frankfurt, from bases as far away as Hawaii; recently discharged air force pilots were ordered back into uniform; and a never-before-attempted experiment in massive airborne logistics was somehow set in motion, with workhorse, twin-propeller passenger aircraft, crammed with coal and foodstuffs, now flying at three-minute intervals along the narrow, three-hundred-mile-long air corridor through the Soviet zone, often buzzed and fired upon by Soviet fighter planes, before coming in, literally just above the rooftops of West Berlin, to land on the short, bumpy runway at Tempelhof Airport. By mid-November, however, the weather was becoming even more dangerous than the Soviet fighters (who seemed to be trying to intimidate rather than shoot down the airlift pilots); on a recent "Black Friday," four C-54s had crashed, either from lightning, fog, or engine failure, with all their crews killed.

Patterson and Schiff had been running into bad weather themselves since leaving the ship at Cherbourg, from where they first took a brief working detour out to Normandy, whose little towns were still in ruins from the war, and whose rainswept beaches were still littered with abandoned barriers and machinery left over from

D-day. Patterson, at least, was working, researching the first of eight articles she would eventually publish in *Newsday*; Dolly Schiff found roughing it in a no-star Normandy inn more of a challenge, but brightened up when they reached Paris. Three days later, the two women were out at Orly Airport, standing in a fog so thick that no planes were flying, or even visible on the runway; save one, a little C-47 with U.S. Air Force markings, from which a young air force captain was walking toward them. "Captain Blevins said the ceiling was down to 250 feet," Alicia reported, "and that we should leave sooner than later. I asked him if he thought he could pull it off, since 250 feet means close to flying blind. 'If we leave now,' he said. And so we did." What she didn't mention in her piece was that the "we" no longer included Dolly Schiff (who in her memoir described Alicia as "the most fearless woman" she had known), who took a taxi back to Paris and the Ritz.

After five hours in the air with Capt. Blevins, Patterson arrived in Frankfurt, literally dropping out of a hole in the omnipresent fog to land at another closed-down airfield, where she was met by a one-man welcoming committee: Larry Rue, bluff, good-natured, wisecracking, an archetypal foreign correspondent of the old school, who had been assigned to shepherd two women VIPs through the various layers of Air Force bureaucracy and briefings. On seeing only one woman coming toward him out of the misty drizzle, he told Patterson he could see she was the "kind of gal who didn't mind flying in the kind of weather when even the birds are walking." For her part, Patterson recognized in Larry Rue a kindred spirit, a fellow rule breaker, and having little patience herself for official briefings and meet-and-greets, she prevailed on him to stick close and show her the real thing, life in the occupied zone, unfiltered by official public relations. Thus, instead of regimented tours and speeches from information officers, she and Larry Rue hung out for days together, drinking with other reporters at Frankfurt bars, playing poker with airlift pilots at the Wiesbaden airbase, walking the streets of the rubble-strewn city, with its haggard, hungry citizens, housewives doubling as prostitutes. The night before she was scheduled to ride an airlift aircraft into Berlin, the weather closed in once again, and two planes crashed and burned over at Gatow field in the British zone. She let Larry Rue drive her through the backstreets to a "seedy nightclub in what seemed like the catacombs of the ruined city . . . , where Dutch musicians were playing American jazz, you could buy a bottle of something like champagne for twelve cents American, and women danced together like they meant it." She sent her mother a prewar postcard (a view of the Rhine) with a daughterly greeting, bought a card for Adlai but never got around to sending it.

When the weather finally lifted, she (with Larry Rue occupying the seat reserved for Dolly Schiff) took off from Wiesbaden on a C-54 laden with sacks of flour and coal, flying low over the gray countryside as they were handed off eastward from one control tower to another, the C-54's pilot asking Alicia with her husky, female voice to radio in the plane's position, thus getting a rise out of the air controllers. "Once in the Soviet zone," she wrote, "everyone tightened up, no more joking, as we droned slowly eastward, a few thousand feet above Soviet airfields, soldiers clearly visible at the anti-aircraft gun batteries, dozens of fighter planes lined up beside the runways." Eventually, they crossed without incident into West Berlin airspace, descending still lower, "low enough so that you could actually look into apartment rooms, see people in the windows waving," until landing with a crunch on the steel-mesh airstrip at Tempelhof.

In Berlin once again Larry Rue got Patterson away from her air force minders, who wanted to keep her in the sterile safety of the U.S. official compound, "with its award-winning, Best in Europe, recreation center, as if one had come all this way to get an American-style chocolate milkshake." Rue commandeered a car and took her on an eye-opening drive into areas of the city that few American visitors saw, a Berlin before "Berlin noir" became the name for a movie genre. "The face of the Berliner," Alicia wrote, and was in fact one of the first to write, "is the most terrible part of Berlin, even more terrible than the ruins. It is a dead face and the eyes are dead eyes." She wrote of groups of families camped out in abandoned mansions, of buildings without heat, of a city without light, since lacking coal there was not enough electricity for more than two hours each day. One afternoon, in one of those happenstances with which life abounds, she found herself standing in a part of the city that seemed dreamily familiar, almost surely one of those lovely, impressive, tree-lined streets where she had once walked as a child, clutching Poppa's hand, back in October 1910: "The buildings might have withstood time, they were built beautifully, to last. But wars, dictators, the march of armies trump good architecture . . . today block after block of those once beautiful houses, built to last beyond the imperial Kaisers, remain like disemboweled honeycombs, like ghosts, one with only a single wall standing, on which six carved marble cherubs were still dancing, holding their garlands."

Patterson didn't think of herself as a writer; the simpler skills of a reporter were what she aspired to; nonetheless, her airlift pieces had range and eloquence as well as information. She spent no more than three days in the haunted strangeness of Berlin, then rode another air force C-54 back to Frankfurt, "squeezed in with forty sacks of coal," and then home, to a more familiar though hard-to-manage planet. Months later, when she was back at Falaise, Larry Rue, then somewhere in North Africa, wrote her a long letter, many pages, single-spaced, fulsome and awkward as a schoolboy's, recalling her "rare beauty," "amazing pluck," "all-out adorableness," much else besides, concluding with the triste lament that he wished they had "been closer than a brush of fingertips at parting." In due course she sent him copies of her *Newsday* pieces, with a friendly thank-you for his help, but she never knew whether he got them or not; he was someone who always moved around so much.

· 53 ·

THAT WINTER, 1948, when she got back to Long Island, and to her little office in freezing Hempstead, her desk and nearby floor littered with the spiral notebooks from which she was trying to winnow the resulting articles, she also found waiting for her a half dozen or so letters from the new governor of Illinois, some short, some longer, all handwritten on official stationery, and each pretty much a complaint of one sort or another. Mostly about her absence: "It's been six ghastly weeks since you went away, leaving me here . . . what could be so fascinating in the ruins of the Third Reich?" Some about his new job: "What could I have been thinking of? This job is murder . . . a funereal mound of details, appointments, official appearances." Some about his marriage: "Ellen of course is no help . . . hates it here, can't say I blame her." Patterson, however, was not in a mood to take up the relationship where she had left off, as a mere sounding board for Stevenson's moods and needs. In her first reply, a mostly news-filled letter about her experiences overseas, with pointed casualness she dropped in the admission that she had "tried to fall in love" during her trip overseas. Stevenson wrote her back in immediate anguish: "I've read your letter again and again. Frankly, it makes me a little sick. Oh ye of little faith! 'I tried to fall in love in Berlin.' How can you think such things, let alone try to put them into action? I need understanding and encouragement but clearly have none."

A few weeks later, in February 1949, she made a fence-mending expedition to snowbound Springfield, spending at least part of a weekend in the Governor's Mansion itself, with apparently mixed results, owing to an all-too-predictable combination of factors. As governor, Stevenson's time was even less his own, besides which he felt aggrieved, distracted, expecting Alicia to play the role of accommodating girlfriend, not asking too much of him, in bed and elsewhere. Patterson, for her part, had issues of her own, was taking risks all over the place, and doubtless was hoping for some heat as well as talk from her supposedly lovelorn suitor. When she returned to New York, she wrote him what was supposed to be a ground-clearing letter, saying that her idea of a love affair was more "committed" than his, that since they were "cut from different cloth" they should end their relationship. "I have never loved anyone before," she wrote, "but now all I've known of love and genuine interest is *kaput.*"

Stevenson replied disconsolately: "Well, maybe we are cut from different cloth as you say. I'm not resentful, don't worry about me. Work has been my refuge for many years. My only regret is, we couldn't talk. I tried to start that first night, and the second, but that failed. You *had* drunk too much, although the hours were precious for talking wisely." He added: "I'll make no groveling effort to mend what you call this 'kaput' state. I'm not a whiner, just a fool and a little sick. Maybe we'll just be friends." One month later Patterson was back in the Midwest, ostensibly to see Josephine, though she and Stevenson managed another rendezvous in Ivan Albright's new studio on Ogden Avenue. Once again there seems to have been something missing. "Dearest," he wrote her afterward. "A charming night at the Albright studio, with an early morning walk in the first whisper of spring. So grateful for those hours, though I wish some things had been better—as always, I was too harassed and tired to make the most of it, and our time is inevitably so brief."

OF COURSE all this was going on while she was married to Harry Guggenheim. What of that? What of him? One answer is that he didn't seem to know of her affair with Stevenson. Even later, when Patterson and Stevenson saw much more of each other, though presumably by then without a romantic-sexual component, Guggenheim never seems to have thought it more than a friendship, a meeting of minds. On his side, more and more, he lived a largely separate life, compartmentalized, often in South Carolina with his horses, or downtown New York at the Guggenheim offices. In public they continued to appear as husband and wife, gave and attended dinner parties, theater parties; there's a photo from this period showing Harry, Alicia, and another couple, George and

Helen Backer, at the "21" Club after some play, everyone smiling, normal, so to speak, two happy couples. But as in the Cold War taking place in the wider world, which now and then produced social situations wherein Soviet and American diplomats might be seated together, polite, affable, even superficially friendly, the Guggenheims when not on show, more often than not in private, were stuck in a chilly standoff of their own. On Patterson's part, from her papers, from the comments of friends and family, there is a record of overt disagreements, issues, largely regarding *Newsday*, some of which would continue for the rest of the marriage. From Guggenheim there remains a similar record, in the form of memos and legal correspondence. As any psychiatrist or psychologist would have pointed out, however, these were only external signs, disturbances on the surface; and needless to say, no psychiatrists or psychologists were asked for their opinions.

At this moment, with Patterson, as she saw it, getting nowhere in her private life, stuck in a marriage to an imperious, disapproving husband who had gone cold on her—and with no better luck trying to distract herself in a romance with another important man, who seemed to have plenty of his own commitment problems—she now received a much-needed boost in what was for her perhaps the even more important area of her public life: *Time* magazine came calling, as it were, with a prominent piece about *Newsday* in its "Press" department. (Here is possibly as good a place as any to remind today's reader, accustomed to the variety, multiplicity, and splintered nature of current media, that in Patterson's time, when the word "media" didn't exist save in Latin dictionaries, newspapers were local, television news scarcely counted, and what took the place of a national stage were a handful of dominant, widely read magazines, *Life*, the *Saturday Evening Post*, *Collier's*, *Newsweek*, and most consequential of all, *Time*.) Breezily titled "Another Patterson," the *Time* piece was uniformly positive, first describing the modest origins of *Newsday* ("In a dim converted old garage in Hempstead, Long Island"), then noting approvingly its rags-to-riches success: "A jagged circulation graph last week snaked off its chart and up a wall. Circulation of Miss Patterson's chatty *Newsday* has rocketed past 100,000, a man-sized mark for any newspaper." As for Patterson herself, the normally critical magazine had only praise for "Alicia of the publishing Pattersons, now forty-one and nervously energetic," barely mentioning "her third husband Harry Guggenheim, the mining scion, who has invested 750,000 Guggenheim dollars," before continuing for the better part of a full page, spelling out Alicia's and *Newsday*'s achievements: "A journalistic jackpot . . . brightly edited . . . more ads than any competing afternoon paper in Manhattan."

Not surprisingly the publication of the *Time* piece did little to lift the chill from the Guggenheim marriage, with Alicia so much the focus of its spotlight, and Harry (with his moneybags) relegated to a virtual footnote, a disparity she pretended not to notice and in any case considered essentially fair. Thrilled with her new signs of acceptance by the great world, she sent off a tearsheet of the *Time* article to Stevenson (should he have somehow missed it), along with a warm, fond note, in which she made the mistake of sharing with him the latest of her private fantasies: that of turning *Newsday* into her own publishing power base, something that might be eventually solidified and extended via Josephine's children. Stevenson acknowledged the *Time* piece with his own brand of self-regarding approval: "Dear one, I marvel at you more and more. What a success you've made in the very field where I once dreamed of working. . . . I wonder, can love and envy meet?" Then he chided her, or so it would seem, for letting him see her larger ambitions. "But why this Napoleonic tone, 'I'll found an empire?' Why must Caesar forever gather laurels to be happy? Surely, the stuff of greatness is goodness not more conquests. You may think you want to be a hard little empire-builder, but as to me I love a gentle, wise compassionate woman, not a mighty, ruthless determined conqueror." And then adding, with his customary ambivalence: "Or do I?"

Doubtless emboldened by the *Time* piece (surely read by everyone who mattered to her), she resumed her never really kaput affair with Stevenson, thereby continuing an energetically complicated life, as editor and copublisher of *Newsday*, as Harry Guggenheim's wife, and when the opportunity presented, finding the time and place to meet with her harried epistolary lover, although more and more of those meetings had been turning into near-misses. For instance, in

April, at the National Correspondents' Dinner in Washington, she and Stevenson had taken rooms at the same hotel, the Hay-Statler, but they scarcely saw each other, were never alone for more than an hour, with Stevenson on the phone for most it; much of the time he was both surrounded by staff and waiting for a summons to the White House and a private meeting with President Truman, who was briskly encouraging to the new governor, and whom Stevenson then infuriated with his talky unwillingness to declare himself an outright candidate for the presidential race in 1952.

In mid-July, Adlai and Alicia were both briefly in the same city, this time Chicago, but once again they somehow couldn't manage a rendezvous, with her waiting at Josephine's for a summons, with him always running late in his official duties, finally sending an aide with a note of apology that he was "unavoidably committed" to visiting a National Guard camp in Wisconsin. She sent word back, calling him "an egotistical stinker," to which he replied, "If I was, forgive me. I do so love you, my wild bird." No better luck awaited her, and them, in the matter of a proposed reunion out in Wyoming around Labor Day. She was scheduled to visit Josephine at her ranch near Dubois; he was planning a trip with his three sons to Jackson Hole. They had exchanged several letters on the subject, with Stevenson telling her he would get out there early, a few days before his boys' arrival; accordingly she went early herself, not to Josephine's but by prearrangement, so she thought, to a guest ranch near Jackson, where she waited in vain for him to show. Days later, back at Josephine's, she got another apology, full of cheery fondness, saying he had "no gift for Rocky Mountain geography," which she figured might almost be true.

· 54 ·

NOT THAT THE GUGGENHEIMS could never agree on anything. Theirs was a not-insubstantial ménage, after all, and much had to be agreed on, day by day, one way or another, the easy way or the hard way. Take *Newsday*'s move into its new building: a definitely substantial, thirty-thousand-square-foot, all-white rectilinear structure built largely of concrete blocks, situated roughly two miles from the original Hempstead car dealership showroom in the town of Garden City. The need for a larger building had existed pretty much from the beginning, or soon afterward, as new hiring and lack of office space quickly resulted in reporters and editors being pushed out of the newsroom and squeezed into the nearby composing room, elbow to elbow with the compositors and type trays. Patterson had long argued for something roomier, more like a real newspaper, but Harry Guggenheim was both mindful of the paper's losses and less confident of its future than his wife, and argued just as forcefully against what he called "premature expansion" and construction costs. The "new building" thus remained for years a subject of abstract yearning and frustration on Alicia's part, while with Harry it was one of the many aspects of "sound business principles" on which he felt impelled to hold the line. Both parties knew their own positions were flawed, that the opposing arguments had merit, but each spouse (or copublisher) was stubborn, liked to be right, hated to be wrong, thus the problem kept being pushed into the future.

What changed the situation was another casual conversation between Patterson and the architect Albert Wood, the man who during the war had clued her in on the new technology of affordable housing, which in turn had resulted in *Newsday* being an early responder to Long Island's postwar building and population boom. In the intervening years Patterson and Wood became friends, at least tennis friends, with Wood one of the regulars who dropped by late Sunday mornings, in good weather, when the Guggenheims took to their court, not far from the water's edge, above the seawall. (A sidebar note about tennis, a sport both Guggenheims enjoyed, at least in their own fashion: Harry of course had played since boyhood, schooled by the best instructors; indeed he had been good enough at college to earn a coveted "blue" at Cambridge, and played conscientiously ever since, even during the war at Mercer Field. Alicia had come later to the game, taking it up only after marriage to Joe Brooks, himself a star in college, and while never a natural on the court, she made up for her lack of style with plenty of unladylike hustle, and the determination never to lose a point she didn't have to. In the romantic early days of her marriage to Guggenheim, they often played singles together, but she got tired of losing and he grew bored with winning; they then switched to doubles, at first on the same side of the net, husband and wife as partners, requiring teamwork and no muttering at each other, which proved challenging; then across the net from each other, husband and wife as opponents—though that was difficult too, sometimes dangerous.) Over time it became more or less understood that, while Mr. and Mrs. Guggenheim enjoyed a few sets of tennis on a Sunday morning, their preferred mode of play was neither side by side nor across the net from each other, but at different times and with other partners, or as now and then happened, at different times with the same partner. That was the case with easygoing Al Wood, not quite as good as Harry, a little better than Alicia, who enjoyed dropping by on a Sunday and playing with either one. It was after one such workout, he and Alicia sitting together at one of the courtside tables, that Wood mentioned that construction was nearly finished on the new office he was building for his architecture firm in nearby Port Washington: a new kind of concrete-block structure: simple, stylish, and surprisingly inexpensive.

She had him drive her there that afternoon for a look, and decided it was exactly what she wanted for *Newsday*. She went home and told Harry, who automatically vetoed the idea: Not necessary, bound to cost too much, Al Wood was a visionary, visionaries rarely paid attention to the bottom line. But Patterson persisted, though avoiding the spoken word, which usually led to arguments, frustration, and defeat. Instead she communicated with her self-described eminently rational husband entirely through memos, sent to him at his Wall Street office. Among other things, she reminded him that their current building had so little heat in winter that pressmen were forced to wear overcoats and hats indoors; that summer's warmth required installing lawn sprinklers on the roof, resulting in leaks and little cooling. She sent him lengthy, single-spaced, cost estimates on the economics of concrete-block construction, on real estate values, heating oil consumption, newsprint trucking, and so on; sometimes she sent the same memos more than once. For a while Harry successfully defended his hold-the-line position with his own memos, austere and impenetrable. But then, as the paper started to cut its losses, in fact turned profitable, his tone shifted, becoming more conciliatory, less automatically negative, until one day a memo from 120 Broadway arrived at Patterson's *Newsday* office suggesting that his copublisher begin looking around for a building site.

As it happened, she had already found one, with the assistance of the helpful Wood: ten acres just outside the nearby town of Garden City, right next to a railroad spur, which could be used for offloading rolls of newsprint. After a flurry of still more businesslike-sounding memos from Hempstead to 120 Broadway, Harry gave another qualified assent, provided half the ten-acre site could be sold right away to defray the cost of purchase. Patterson soon bought the ten acres, sold off five, submitted plans for the new building. But Harry grew cautious once again, fired off a Polonius-level memo on the perils of rushing; instead of constructing the new building all at once, which might in certain ways be sensible, even commonsensical, certainly convenient, but would require a sizable outlay up-front, even more Guggenheim cash to be advanced, on top of Guggenheim money already advanced, the majority owner proposed, or rather insisted, that the new *Newsday* building be constructed sequentially, piecemeal, in three stages, each stage to be financed from current operations.

And so it was. Patterson and her staff described the resulting, mostly cheerful, chaos as their Pony Express era: Since the first stage of construction included the pressroom, this meant that *Newsday*'s presses were now in Garden City, two miles from the main office, which was still in Hempstead; thus, the Hempstead staff first had to write and edit each day's copy, set it in type, make a cardboard mat from the type tray, roll up the mat, place it in a special cylindrical container, and frantically drive with each container in the back of a beat-up, army-surplus jeep, two miles through the placid tree-lined streets of Garden City, in time to make the press-run deadline. This eccentric system persisted for eighteen months, and was only somewhat improved when the composing-room section of the new building was allowed to be built; by then all the so-called mechanical parts of the newspaper were in Garden City, but of course everything and everyone else—reporters, editors, and advertising people—were still in Hempstead. At last, three years later, the go-ahead for building the last stage, *Newsday*'s newsroom and editorial offices, was authorized by Mr. Guggenheim from 120 Broadway; which meant that Mrs. Guggenheim and her staff were finally once again under the same roof. Not surprisingly, when *Newsday*'s impressive modernist new Garden City building was officially opened on May 7, 1949, it was already running out of space.

· 55 ·

IT WAS AROUND THIS TIME that Alicia and Adlai's hot-and-cold romance, affair, mutual entanglement, lately much on the cool side, began once again to warm up; one factor promoting greater rapprochement was Stevenson's finally consummated divorce from Ellen, a bright, difficult woman with "mood problems," who had grown increasingly unstable and vindictive toward her soon-to-be-ex-husband, among other things making unfounded charges of homosexuality that his political enemies would feed on for years; another was Governor Stevenson's growing national prominence (as the Democratic Party's new alternative to President Truman's old-style "crony politics"), which now brought him East on a regular basis. "I do wish you wouldn't write me such sharp imperious notes," he wrote Patterson in October 1949, on his way to New York to give an important speech at the United Nations introducing the Indian prime minister, Jawaharlal Nehru. "I can't get out of the Rockford bridge dedication here until 4 pm on Friday, then I must be in Conn. by noon Saturday, getting to NY on Sunday, maybe by early afternoon. Where will you be? Where do I go from LaGuardia? Will you be able to meet me, and wouldn't it be better on Long Island where we could spend some of Monday in the autumn sun?"

As it turned out, this potentially overcomplicated rendezvous turned into one of their more satisfactory reunions, combining moments of intimacy with a breezy, almost reckless disregard for appearances. Not only did Patterson take her friend, the governor of Illinois, on a public tour of the new *Newsday* building, but with Harry Guggenheim down at Cain Hoy, she invited Stevenson to spend the night at Falaise, the next day took him into New York in her car to the UN, where she sat in the gallery listening to his speech, after which she joined him at a big lunch in the UN dining room. "I enjoyed our Monday very specially," he wrote her when he was back in Springfield. "Wasn't it fun having lunch at the U.N. and all the rest? I thought we were more relaxed and natural. Also, I'm marveling over *Newsday* and what you've done there in just a few years. You're certainly a remarkable young lady. How can you be so many things at once, lovely and feminine, brisk and businesslike—wise and strong and *mine*? I am praying that my visit to Falaise did not aggravate your situation in any way. By the way I took your suggestion and went to Brooks Brothers for a new homburg and if it looks like Hell it's your fault—but now I'm dreaming of what we had, and of you my love."

Three weeks later Stevenson tried to persuade Patterson to visit him in Illinois, closer to home, though preferably not in such close, familial quarters as her brother-in-law Ivan Albright's studio. "Besides, I'm thinking that a long evening with Ivan is a bit hard when we have so little time, then sneaking off to the Ogden studio seems so brazenly conspicuous . . . also the mechanics of the rendezvous, all that business with the car or cars in the morning, etc. Instead, couldn't we just drive out to my place in Libertyville, which would be deserted since the gardener and his wife will be away for the day. Or then again, if you'd rather, we could just go to the Ogden studio, keep Libertyville for another time, please think about it."

Such dithering and fussing apparently cooled off Alicia's travel plans; thus another letter from Springfield: "Do you want me half as much as I miss and want you? What happened to your plan to come out here for a rendezvous? I've been waiting expectantly, forlornly." In mid-November she flew to Chicago, took a little plane to Springfield, and spent one night with him in the Governor's Mansion, which later evoked a somewhat-mixed-signal letter from the governor, combining Stevensonian misspeak ("I wonder, are you back on the job at *Newsweek*?"), romantic effusion ("You were so sweet to me, so special, and I am still laughing and smiling"), with perhaps an unexpected dollop of antiromantic admonition ("*Please* don't leave that strong scent behind, the place reeked the next morning, the maids must have been more than a little confused") and the newfound caution of a politician with still-larger ambitions ("Frankly, I'm beginning to worry about how secure these letters are.")

· 56 ·

IT'S HARD ENOUGH TO GUESS, let alone know, just where Patterson thought her romance with Stevenson was eventually going to take her. She wasn't a woman with much natural temperament for long-term planning, someone who often factored "eventually" into her decisions, least of all those of the heart. Moreover, while the first phase of the relationship was definitely physical, sexual, it also seems clear from what remains of their long correspondence, mostly in the form of Stevenson's "collected letters" at Princeton University Library, that even when their affair was most heated, its temperature was seldom that of a Grand Passion; Patterson's friend, Dolly Schiff, in a memoir, cattily though doubtless accurately recalled Alicia telling her that "in the bedroom Adlai lacked urgency," which is perhaps not the worst way of putting it.

Most likely, Patterson more or less stumbled into the affair, beginning with that first sexy, talky *rencontre* on the lawn at Libertyville, because it was there to be stumbled into, because she was no longer young and not yet old, because she was childless, because Harry Guggenheim, once rich and charming, was now only rich and distant, because her father was dead, and the war was over, and was that all there was going to be of life and love? Then Adlai himself, though in many ways an unlikely love object, was definitely appealing, a growing source of attraction to numerous women; mostly bald, somewhat pudgy, by no means a youngster, nonetheless he was a new type of man for the mid-twentieth century, brainy, humorous, warm, attentive, at least when the needs of his own ego permitted it; and while his own romantic impulses may have tilted more to words than actions, at least there *were* words, words aplenty, both written and spoken, in contrast to the manly, tight-lipped, lockjaw habits of the day. Sometimes he dithered too much, sometimes he didn't seem to know what he was saying, as in his periodic, clumsy-puppy references to Patterson as "my half-man, half-woman"; but mostly one has the feeling, reading their letters, and between the lines in their letters, that he was a man who could make her feel womanly, certainly as womanly as she had felt in a long time.

At any rate, by midsummer 1950, given the challenging circumstances of their separate lives, she and Stevenson seemed to have what might be called a nice thing going; even to the point of having droll nicknames for each other: "Dear Rat" is how she often addresses him in her letters (which his secretary remembered him rushing off to read in the privacy of the governor's bathroom in Springfield), to which he would fondly reply, "Dear Cockroach"—as in, "the rat and the cockroach will meet in the Ambassador East, July 28, to discuss matters of mutual interest to predators of all sizes and shapes."

For the time being, in fact, the two sometime lovers, sometime pals, seemed to have found what might be called a working balance between their public and private lives. Patterson remained fully engaged with *Newsday*, her spirits revitalized by her special friendship with Stevenson, her marriage to the geographically and emotionally distant Harry Guggenheim seemingly one of those facts of life to be lived with, not especially gratifying and yet not worth the sizable problems that would inevitably come with trying to exit it. Stevenson, for his part, while no longer married, thus single and visibly available ("eligible," as people said), seemed content to stick close to the Governor's Mansion in Springfield, "learning the ropes as a novice Gov needs to do," as he told Patterson, all the while keeping a circumspect social profile, with his sister, Buffie Ives, acting as hostess at official functions. When anyone raised the question of larger, presidential ambitions, as when a *Newsday* reporter asked him, during his earlier tour of the building, if he was considering throwing his obviously new hat (bought the day before with Patterson) into the ring, "the Governor laughed heartily and called the idea absurd."

By then it was widely expected that hugely popular Dwight D. Eisenhower was going to run and prove unbeatable. Patterson herself had been an Eisenhower fan as far back as her 1946 Libertyville meeting with Stevenson, when she and Adlai had talked about General Ike as an almost ideal candidate; on her trip to Europe for the Berlin airlift, the only piece of clothing she'd bought overseas, and brought back with her, was an army-issue "Eisenhower" jacket.

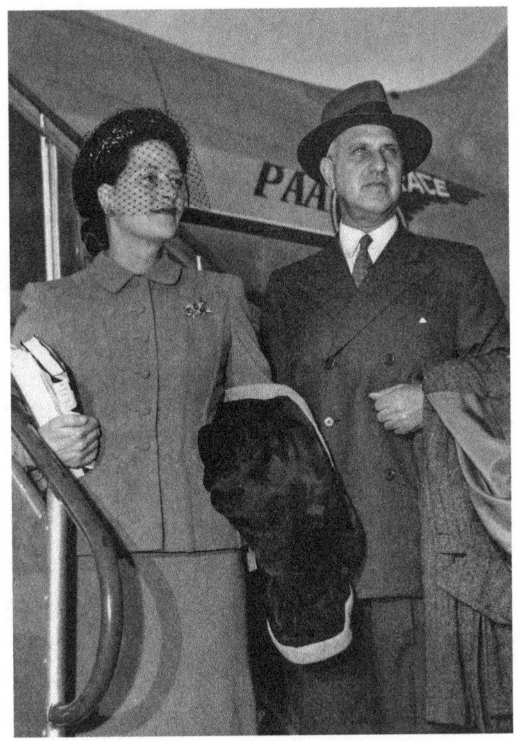

Alicia as Company Wife, with Harry on the 1951 tour of Guggenheim copper mines in Chile.

What might be wrong with this picture, with this happy balancing act, with this more or less agreeable status quo? Of course, the immediate answer is that there's no such thing in nature as a status quo; neither Patterson nor Stevenson were exactly stationary figures, either in their own lives or in relation to each other. While Stevenson repeatedly insisted, and with what was becoming his signature, eloquent humility, that he didn't want to run for the presidency, had no larger ambitions than continuing to serve his constituents as governor, as it turned out, and as his posthumous papers make eminently clear, what he really meant was that he didn't want to run for the presidency in 1952, against a war-hero general, although he had every intention of running in 1956. In other words, while Governor Stevenson, in lovelorn-suitor mode, might talk and write to Patterson of love and kisses and the hope of years together (and in some part of him might actually mean it), with each passing month, his alter ego, Adlai Stevenson, aspiring Democratic presidential candidate, though still largely under wraps, was making it ever less likely that such dreams might be delivered on. As for Patterson, her own command of the status quo was no better; no matter what temporary calm, ease, moments of accommodation might descend on the Guggenheim marriage, no matter how a commonsense, logical, businesslike view of *Newsday*'s provenance might suggest that Alicia's glass, with a 49 percent ownership stake, was if not precisely half full, then full enough to warrant giving the issue a rest, this seemed to be the very thing she just couldn't do. Thus, with Harry's pride and self-regard still smarting from the dismissive, almost condescending way he'd been treated in *Time*'s piece on *Newsday*, with no contradiction from his wife, either in print or in private, Patterson seemed to double down on showing the world who really ran the show at their jointly owned paper. She not only signed on for a major profile about herself in the widely read, mass-circulation *Saturday Evening Post*, but invited the writer, veteran *Post* journalist Charles Wertenbaker, down to her place in Georgia, where for several days she charmed and dazzled him; with the predictable result that when the lengthy, vivid, entertaining *Post* profile ("The Case of the Hot-Tempered Publisher") appeared, it was mostly a three-thousand-word rave on the subject of Alicia Patterson (accompanied by numerous glamorous photos of Alicia and her friends), barely mentioned Harry at all, and drove him to fury.

The Guggenheims had fought before, about all kinds of matters, but the heated arguments, as well as the cold hard feelings, especially on Harry Guggenheim's part, provoked by the *Post* piece, seemed this time to reach a new level. For weeks that summer they battled over the ownership issue, that crucial 2 percent majority, which Harry now was less than ever of a mind to hand over to his wife, for all her angry insistence that she was doing all the work, that it was her paper in every important way but legal. One afternoon in late August, as her deputy Stan Peckham remembered it, she was in her office at *Newsday* finishing things up for the week; that evening, she was supposed to be giving a dinner party for some of Harry's business associates at Falaise. Instead, telling no one (save Peckham) what she was doing or where she was going, she simply left, flew the coop, literally, in a series of planes, to the relative sanctuary of Josephine's ranch in Dubois, Wyoming. From there, she wrote Stevenson that she'd left Harry, was willing to give up *Newsday*, and would be waiting there to hear from him.

36

The Case of the Hot-Tempered Publisher

By CHARLES WERTENBAKER

Spoiled child of a doting father, kicked out of some of America's best schools, Alicia Patterson grew up to be a success in her own right. Now they're calling her paper one of the brightest ideas in a decade.

ALICIA PATTERSON, publisher of a unique and phenomenally successful Long Island daily paper called Newsday, is the daughter of a famous and forceful father, a handicap she has overcome at the cost of considerable effort. The effort shows in a drawing down of the corners of her mouth, which has kept her from being quite a beauty and, ironically, increases her resemblance to the late Capt. Joseph Medill Patterson, founder of the New York Daily News. Patterson taught his girl to be many things he himself would have liked to be—an athlete, rider, hunter, aviator—but when she talked him into giving her a job as cub reporter on his paper, he fired her within a year. The publisher of Newsday is a frustrated cub reporter.

Of the various ways to break into the newspaper business, the one most often recommended is to start at the bottom. Prevented by paternal ukase from getting on with this method, the captain's daughter had to start at the top, which is a good deal harder, as the record of unsuccessful publishing ventures shows. Alicia Patterson was pretty well fixed financially by her father before his death, but she didn't have the kind of money it takes to get a new paper going. Her husband, Harry F. Guggenheim, put up $750,000, by his own conservative estimate, to carry Newsday through six lean years, and took charge of the business side of the paper to protect his investment. For the last four years it has looked more and more like one of the best investments a Guggenheim ever made.

While New York papers have been growing fewer, New Yorkers have moved to Long Island in droves, and stores and small industries have moved with them. "Miss Patterson," as she is known around the office, has given these transplanted city people a newspaper that is a cross between the tabloids they had been reading in the city and the small-town paper they hoped to find with community life and a garden. In doing so, she has found an outlet for a burning energy that often got her into trouble, as well as for her cub reporter's frustrations.

Her paper has few inhibitions. It is bustling, nosy, gay, lively and fresh. But it is also well groomed and essentially serious-minded, after the fashion of present-day cubs. It doesn't often play up sex unless there is some useful aim in sight. It featured, for instance, the case of a psychoneurotic pharmacist's mate accused of wartime seduction in Italy, but persuaded the Navy that the proper place for one of its heroes was the hospital. It has the cub's fondness for a campaign, and has campaigned against illegal gambling, high-school immorality, wrecks on the Long Island Rail Road, water pollution and excessive annihilation of misplaced dogs.

Last fall Newsday jumped head-first into the congressional campaign of a dignified but obscure Democrat named Ernest Greenwood for the seat held by Rep. W. Kingsland Macy, Republican boss of Suffolk County. Alicia Patterson, whose usually calm brown eyes can burn with indignation, espoused the slogan, GOOD REPUBLICANS DON'T WANT MACY. She was aided by a song that was blared from loudspeakers all over the district: "We don't want him; you can have him; he's no good for us." Macy lost by a few score votes, and one of the Macy papers paid Publisher Patterson the tribute of calling Newsday "a sneering, snarling sheet that represents the dregs of the newspaper profession." Managing Editor Alan Hathway sent her the editorial with the note, "From one of your dregs," and she thumbtacked it to the bulletin board, next to a statement by another candidate the paper had opposed that ended, "I wish they were supporting me."

Newsday, which started in 1940 with a press run of 11,000, now has a circulation of 130,000. It has only to keep up its current rate of growth to reach within a very few years a circulation of a quarter million, confining itself, as it does now, to Nassau and Suffolk counties. But Long Island also bears the weight of two New York City boroughs, Brooklyn and Queens, the latter adjacent to Nassau County and an inviting territory for expansion. And on the northern side of Manhattan sprawls the Bronx. Newsday, which keeps its local news local by delivering four different editions to different parts of the island, is in an excellent position to experiment with the same technique in the city itself.

Its publisher, at forty-four, has plenty of time in which to think about employing against the mighty News the tactic used at Cannae and the Ruhr. She doesn't have to commit all her forces at once, and for the present she is occupied with building up her strength. From having to fly airplanes and shoot big game to work off her excess vigor, she has made herself a job so exhausting that now and then she goes off to rest in a Georgia hide-out. Sitting in her smallish office in a corner of a white, one-story building in Garden City, she usually looks like a

In her chintzy Garden City, Long Island, office, Alicia Patterson instructs her editorial writer, Stanton Peckham, and her cartoonist, Cliff Rogerson.

Alan Hathway is the present managing editor of Newsday. His boss, who prefers to be called "Miss Patterson," was once a reporter herself.

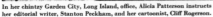

National recognition for AP and *Newsday*; Harry was none too thrilled.

· 57 ·

JOSEPHINE AND IVAN ALBRIGHT'S RANCH was up in the Wind River valley of western Wyoming, eleven hundred high-country acres, at an elevation of 7,800 feet, wedged against the national forest: simple Western cabins, a dozen horses with a handsome, working barn, corrals, pastureland, cottonwoods, also much sagebrush and semidesert, with a little creek running down through the property, feeding into the trout-happy Wind River three miles below. Alicia had been visiting her younger sister in Wyoming since Josephine bought the ranch in 1946, just before she married Ivan Albright, and it had quickly become her second-favorite destination to escape to, after her place on the St. Mary's in Georgia, which while appealingly remote and wild, grew oppressively hot and humid in summer. By contrast, western Wyoming, up in the Wind River Range, near the tiny horse-and-cow town of Dubois, was dry, dusty, blazing with sun and also wild. (It might be said that both sisters identified with their father's affinity for the raw, rough-and-tumble extremes of nature.) At the Albrights' Three Spear Ranch (the name referred to their cattle brand) Patterson had her own cabin ("Alicia's cabin") out in back, right up against the forest, facing a steep, narrow canyon, home to mountain lions, lynx, huge owls, and much else. She and Josephine were both light-handed, confident riders, skilled on Western terrain, and daily went for long rides together, wearing matching black Stetsons, across the dry, rolling hills above the ranch. She also kept a fly rod at the ranch, and when she tired of the tumult of Josephine's four children she took herself down to the river and rarely came back without a catch.

And for all those weeks of bright, dry, high summer in the mountains, she waited to hear from Stevenson.

AS IT TURNED OUT, the first of the several disappointments that Adlai visited on Alicia that August was one she never knew about; for while at the time she was still the special object of Stevenson's affections, she was no longer the only object. As his political star began rising, both in Illinois and the East, he soon became the willing recipient of attentions from politicians as well as many women, some of them no more than would-be party givers, campaign donors; others, such as Dorothy Fosdick, a well born political consultant, unmarried, in her thirties, who began visiting Stevenson in the Governor's Mansion, showing up with him at events in place of Buffie Ives; also "close," definitely on the inside track, was Jane Dick (wife of Edison Dick, an important Chicago businessman and Stevenson supporter), who seems to have moved into the role of leading, on-the-spot confidante to the ever-needful governor; in fact she was the person he immediately rushed to with Patterson's letter, unexpectedly announcing her decision to leave Harry Guggenheim.

Dick seems to have been equal to the task. "The more I think about the letter from A the more I think you'll have to be very wary and more forthright than is your natural wont," she quickly replied to Stevenson. "I like her as a friend, I like her loyalty (to everyone but her husband!). I admire her incisive mind and her point of view about many things, but to say that she is temperamentally unstable, self-centered and demanding puts it very mildly. Qualities that may be interesting, amusing, even appealing in a friend are not those which work out in a more intimate relationship. Anyway, just remember: Beware and Be Firm!"

Granted that a Stevenson-Patterson union of any serious kind was almost surely a terrible idea, as likely as not to self-combust in moments, or certainly in months, given the egos and temperamental differences of the principals; granted, too, that Alicia Patterson Guggenheim, surely no lovelorn, star-crossed ingenue herself, could scarcely have picked a more unlikely rescuer, a man less prone to swift, life-changing decisions, to leaping tall buildings and all the rest of it, than the portly, meditative, preternaturally ambivalent Adlai Ewing Stevenson. All the same, with Patterson, his all-too-recent object of all manner of endearments, affections, protestations of eternal love, and the like, sitting out there on a figurative rock in Wyoming, day after day after day, waiting for a sign, Governor Stevenson's painfully slow-in-arriving reply, itself a textbook mixture of faux astonishment, huffy-puffy concern, and classic male downshifting, came as severe disappointment. "Your message from Wyoming is much to my surprise," he finally wrote her, in a letter that took ten days to get to Dubois, "and I am sorely distressed by the turn of events. I was under the impression that things were going better with you and Harry. . . . I understand the Sat. Eve Post blowup was difficult but it sounded like a not too abnormal fit of jealousy on HG's part. What I suggest is deliberation, moderation. Certainly to seek a divorce impetuously would be, I believe, a great mistake and should be your last resort." And so on, and so on. "Remember," he added, in case she might have forgotten, "you have your child to think about . . . *Newsday*."

As it happened, the one person in Alicia's life who stepped up to the mark just then was Harry Guggenheim. He didn't know about the Stevenson romance, and he may well have been imperially clueless as to the extent of Alicia's alienation. But he knew his wife had flown the coop, and he knew where she'd gone, and so when time passed and she didn't return, he took a commercial flight to Denver, then chartered a little single-engine Cessna, flew north over the mountains, and up the Wind River valley until he found Dubois (pop: 650), and the alkali flats outside town that served as a landing strip. A cowboy who worked for Josephine, Georgie Conwell, and Josephine's ten-year-old daughter (a coauthor of this narrative) were on hand to meet Mr. Guggenheim when he clambered out of the little plane, in an elegant summer suit and Panama hat, peering up into the blazing Wyoming sun. But Harry seemed in good humor from the flight, cheerfully unfazed by Conwell's down-home greeting: "I never met a Jew before, but you look okay to me." Up at the Albright ranch his runaway wife met him with the brisk suggestion that he unpack the fly rod he'd brought with him, get into some real clothes, and come down to the river with her and do some fishing, which he did. The Guggenheims stayed another two days at the ranch, both of them squeezed into "Alicia's cabin," and then flew back East together, back to the substantial and surely complicated coop she'd tried—though perhaps not all that hard—to fly away from.

· 58 ·

NOW, IF THIS BIOGRAPHICAL NARRATIVE, about an actual person, were instead one of those novels that people rightly love to read, populated by characters who plausibly dot their i's, reassuringly hit their marks, whose comings together (and flyings apart) are accompanied by satisfying, resonant, make-no-mistake-about-it chords, then this might be one of those moments, an inflection point where, for example, our heroine's recent travails lead to a timely spurt of self-knowledge and shall we say personal growth, with the additional happy possibility that these two lives, husband and wife, that had been sadly, even pointlessly diverging, will slide back together like tectonic plates, to a comfortable, earthquake-free resting place. In other words, how satisfying it would be to write that at this time Alicia Patterson and Harry Guggenheim returned together, from the clarity of blue, cloudless, Western skies, with restored intimacy, revived fondness, a renewed sense of shared purpose, four shoulders to the wheel. But this was, alas, real life, and Alicia P. and Harry G. by then were pretty much who and what they were; no worse than, but certainly no better than, their own, albeit remarkable, quite particular natures; which is probably why, on their return, as soon as they practicably could, each went off to his (or her) own office, back to her (and his) own bedroom.

Alicia Patterson had lived her life thus far (as so many did in those days) determinedly not admitting hurt, whether emotional or physical, either to herself or to anyone else. Sadness, loss, pain and so on—these were all grouped under the derisive catchphrase, "hurty feelings," and were to be laughed away or not admitted to in the first instance. One upside to all this stoicism or denial or sadness aversion was that recovery from reverses often took place, or seemed to take place, with amazing rapidity. Didn't Patterson grieve, a little or a lot, over her failed "elopement" with Stevenson? Wasn't she sad or furious, or both, that he had responded so feebly, so minimally, had left her standing alone at the bus stop? Surely all of the above; and yet life moved on, new days began, there was always so much to do.

But there was also an obvious downside to this bravura tactic of getting on with it, of not boring other people with one's problems. Ever since her long-ago "air cruise" expedition with Poppa to the Caribbean, with its problematic, physically demanding, fishing adventure on the Chagres dam, Patterson had been bothered by abdominal pains, which is to say she was sometimes made uncomfortable, sometimes severely stricken. For most of her life she had the temperament, or fierceness, to shake off pain, by an act of will it seems, especially these kinds of pain: female pain, a woman's body's pain—another sign of women's weakness. But then there were the moments, more and more lately, and perhaps it was just a mark of age that she took them seriously at all, when she hurt enough to finally get herself to a doctor: in this case to kindly, avuncular Dr. Harold Meeker (once her father's physician, one of the best) who had treated her years before, and who now, on her return from Wyoming, examined her the way doctors did in those days before scans and imaging; in other words with naked eye, with one hand in a rubber glove, and found nothing. Probably ulcers, he told her (and so noted in his file), and sent her off with a handwritten diet that advised against "ham, pork, bacon, raw fruit or vegetables," instead recommending "chicken, lamb, beef (no more than twice a week), well-cooked vegetables and vanilla ice cream."

With no letters arriving from Stevenson, Patterson broke the ice late in September, writing him that she was back with Harry, though "lying low, feeling under the weather, missing more days at work than I'd like to." He wrote back quickly, first blithely congratulating her on the restoration of the domestic status quo: "I like to think your home life is now obviously more tranquil. . . . Maybe Harry was secretly proud of the Saturday Evening Post piece after all." Then he addressed her mostly implicit, certainly nonspecific, admission of ill health with the faux heartiness of a football coach, as if speaking to her from a distant planet: "What collapse? I want more and exact and honest details, and at once! What were you doing, working too hard? Why would you do that? You've been worried?

Worried about what? And what's this talk about dieting? Since when have you become one of these women who diet? Of course I'm full of sympathy if you're feeling poorly, but—excuse me—there is no harm in learning to act one's age, so maybe some good will come from all this. Anyway, feel better! I'm off to speak to 300 'Business Professionals' at the Gettysburg battlefield, wish me victory."

· 59 ·

TRY AS SHE MIGHT TO GET BETTER, forcing herself to eat cooked vegetables that bored her, and vanilla ice cream ditto, the next few months were a rocky period for Patterson, who stayed haplessly under the weather, feeling tired much of the time, a new experience for her, requiring a real effort to get herself to her *Newsday* office, then having to leave early. As usual, Harry was largely away, once for three weeks to Chile on mining business, otherwise down at Cain Hoy tending to horse matters; when he was home (although perhaps "home" wasn't quite the word for it: he and Alicia moved in and out of various residences, sometimes finding themselves in the same one at the same time), in his good-natured though abstracted fashion he too would urge her to get better, feel better, get needed rest and so on, and even presented her with a new diet book that was all the rage, advocating red wine and plenty of red meat.

By the turn of the New Year, however, by January 1952, it looked as if she was on the mend, beginning to feel more like her old self. Dr. Meeker complimented her on her dietary discipline, the only known cure if only people would take it seriously, while Harry took much of the credit for her recovery, on account of the red wine, red meat diet book he'd given her, which she hadn't read or certainly followed. With a return of energy, Patterson not only took back the reins of *Newsday* from Alan Hathway but also resumed a more active correspondence with Adlai Stevenson, who seemed to be approaching that year's presidential race with his by-now-customary ambivalence, finding new rationales for not running wherever he looked. Thus: "Ike would of course be a very strong candidate, extremely strong, probably unbeatable. . . . As for me, I honestly don't want any part of that national business." And: "I've been in a fiendish travail trying to decide what to do. Commonsense and duty tell me to stick in Springfield." And: "Every day I hear a different line as to when Ike will declare, or even *if* he will declare. . . . I feel I must keep out of this thing! Besides, politics is the way to the poorhouse and I have to think about earning some money."

In early February, Stevenson called a press conference at the Governor's Mansion to announce definitively that he was not then, and was not about to be, a candidate for president in 1952. But a few days later the columnist Marquis Childs reported that Governor Stevenson had recently held three secret meetings with President Truman, with the predictable result that Stevenson's face was soon on the covers of both *Time* and *Newsweek*. Alicia wrote him that he should now "forthrightly put himself forward and declare," and soon afterward published an editorial in *Newsday*, stating that "General Eisenhower and Governor Stevenson are both great men. If the Republicans nominate Eisenhower and the Democrats choose Stevenson, either way it will be a blessing for the nation." Two weeks later, at the Jefferson-Jackson Day dinner in Washington, President Truman surprised everyone with his announcement that he would not seek reelection, which caused Stevenson, a prominent and visible guest at the dinner, to put his head in his hands in theatrical dismay. "I'm desperately worried about my future, have no plans, need cash in the bank" he wrote Patterson afterward, "but I'm now more than ever convinced I should stay in the Illinois job. . . . Besides, I don't think I have the stamina for a national campaign."

Patterson accepted her friend's disavowals, resigned herself to the fact of his not running, and went off to Europe to seek an interview with General Eisenhower, then in charge of NATO in Paris. She was cooling her heels in Athens, at the Hotel Grande Bretagne, waiting for a summons from Eisenhower, when Stevenson reached her with still another message of indecision: "Of course, they may want to draft me, but how can I tell them that if the Republicans nominate Taft, then yes I'll do it, but if it's Ike then no. That would be a deadly thing to say politically, wouldn't it? Please advise me, promptly, promptly—Shall I say no again and more decisively? Should I keep quiet? Shall I indicate that I would accept a genuine draft? Help me, my little bird, my Maid of Athens."

Patterson wrote him back, advising Stevenson not to shut any doors, at least none too firmly, in the matter of the upcoming race, which was apparently what he wanted to hear. "Your advice makes me feel so much better," he replied. "You're sweet to me, wise and understanding. I still don't want to run but I hate to say something that will make it sound as if I deprecate the office or the duty or whatever it is." When her summons to NATO headquarters came through, she flew back to Paris for her interview with General Eisenhower, a busy man who spent a couple of hours with the lady editor from Long Island, and about whom she wrote in *Newsday*: "I came away most impressed with his honesty. Here is a man incapable of double-dealing. . . . It is such a blessed relief to see someone above the slime of our present-day politics."

PATTERSON WENT TO BOTH national conventions in that summer of 1952, both held in Chicago, one after the other in sweltering July heat, both tumultuous, full-throated, in the old pretelevision mode, full of sweaty men, endless speeches, cardboard placards, bunting, straw hats, and cigars. The Republicans came first, on July 17, with their Midwestern true believers still wanly hoping for the anointing of virtuous, uncharismatic Sen. Robert Taft of Ohio, though in the end glad enough to nominate the immensely popular General Ike. The Democrats assembled on July 24, with Chicago never hotter, the stench from the neighboring stockyards mingling with thick smoke from the lakeshore steel mills. Patterson, accompanied by a staff of three from *Newsday*, two reporters and a photographer, stayed with the rest of the press in the Blackstone Hotel, whose lobby and outside sidewalks were nearly always jammed with cheerful, chanting ("Madly for Adlai!") Stevenson Volunteers, an expanding, mostly youthful cohort, which by now included academics, society women, and movie stars such as Lauren Bacall and Joanne Woodward. Governor Stevenson himself opened the convention with an address welcoming the delegates, who all rose to their feet the moment he appeared at the podium, cheering him noisily for close to ten minutes, so that he was forced to cut short his speech. He was nominated unanimously on the third ballot and—for a man who up to the last minute kept insisting he didn't want the nomination—had a stirringly eloquent acceptance speech in his pocket. Patterson watched the triumphant proceedings from a folding chair in the press section in the back of the hall, but chose to skip the overcrowded reception afterward, at his friend and campaign manager William Blair's house on Astor Street. Next morning she flew East, where two days later a semiplaintive note reached her from the new Democratic candidate: "Why didn't you come to Bill's house for the party? Where were you? I hoped so much for a final glimpse and word, but you were gone. . . . Do you suppose I want this? I still refuse to believe my life is over."

In the aftermath of both conventions, Patterson was occupied in gearing up *Newsday*'s political coverage, hoping that the paper with its wider circulation and heftier presence might begin to play a more serious journalistic role in the national campaign, also in trying to resolve a more personal, though nonetheless political dilemma. Some months before, she had pledged her word to Harry Guggenheim that she would join him on *Newsday*'s editorial page in publicly endorsing General Eisenhower as the newspaper's candidate for president; earlier, in Paris, she had also personally assured Eisenhower of her paper's support in the important crossover demographic of eastern Long Island, and while General Ike sometimes gave the impression that he was above noticing or remembering such details, Patterson was fairly sure he both noticed and remembered. The fact was that, even after Stevenson's nomination, she still favored Eisenhower for president, though mainly because she strongly believed that after twenty years of unbroken Democratic governance the country needed a change; a change in the ranks, a change at the top. As such, she wore an "I Like Ike" button to the office, authored and authorized pro-Eisenhower editorials. But increasingly her private preferences were shifting to Stevenson, so humane, eloquent, accessible; and while surely the governor was not bathed in as heroic an aura as the great war commander, she was coming to think that even the general's bright glow had been diminished lately by his halfhearted and muddled responses to Republican witch-hunting.

Accordingly, as the end of summer unrolled, she made two personal political decisions. First she made plans to give a campaign-launching dinner for Governor Stevenson, a politician still not solidly known in the East, often brushed off as a regional, farm-state candidate; the dinner would be held at the impeccable River Club, with the guest list not limited to politicians and wealthy donors but also including that new social class of media people, prominent women as well as men. The second decision snuck up on her from the side so to speak. In mid-August a local weekly television show she was then appearing on as a panelist, *Meet the Editors*, began running into some of the anti-Communist, witch-hunt headwinds that just then were blowing hard across the country. One of the program's other panelists, it turned out, an esteemed young editor named James Wechsler, had briefly joined a Communist youth organization while at college, although resigning soon afterward. As soon as this Communist taint became known, the program's chief sponsor, a locally powerful supermarket chain, Grand Union, threatened to cancel the show and demanded Wechsler's dismissal. Patterson requested airtime for a rebuttal, itself a spunky thing to do, given the frightened, hostile "Red Scare" temper of the times to say nothing of the fact that Grand Union was a substantial advertiser in *Newsday*. On the air herself, she vigorously argued against the "hasty, unexamined decision" of the censorious sponsors, describing their call for Wechsler's dismissal as "a dreadful mistake," thereby keeping the little program alive and setting at the time a much-admired and all-too-rare example of a publisher with something to lose, standing firm against witch-hunt hysteria.

September 21 was the date set for the Stevenson dinner at the River Club, a much anticipated event in that early autumn's social schedule, certainly by Stevenson himself, who came to town with a growing entourage, already in full campaign mode yet not too busy with world affairs to try to fuss with dinner-party seating arrangements, how much time for the passing of cocktails, and whether hot or cold canapés, given the Indian summer heat. But Patterson by then more than knew how to handle such social theatrics, and what she didn't know the River Club did. So far none of the eighty-some guests had declined, unless you counted Harry Guggenheim, who had begged off long ago, alleging pressing business in Cain Hoy, still unaware of his wife's romantic liaison with the Illinois governor, but as a stout Republican not wishing to advance the interests of yet another talky liberal Democrat. The weather was fine, balmy, not too warm and not yet chill; everything was in readiness, the large but not too large wood-paneled dining-room, with its windows looking out on the East River, rarely more inviting, well-appointed, elegant. But Alicia Patterson now had a problem, a private difficulty. That morning in the bathroom she could see signs of bleeding, internal bleeding. She more or less willed the signs away, and for a while they seemed to disappear, but then later in the afternoon they were back, unmistakable. Even for someone who was not so closely keyed to her own body, she could tell something was wrong. But she had a dinner to give for Adlai, who needed it, who needed her to give it, to take care of him at least in this way, and so she did.

As dinners go, it was a noted dinner for its time: the big black cars turning off Fifty-Second Street into the River Club's private courtyard; the splendid guests, rich men, heads of banks and department stores, smart powerful men from the *Times* and *Herald Tribune*, *Time*, the emerging television networks; smart, glamorous women, Babe Paley, Marietta Tree, Clare Luce. Stevenson was at his best, people said: eloquent in his formal remarks, personable and appealing as he made the rounds of the tables, for his hostess had cleverly left an empty chair at each table for him to drop by and visit. Patterson herself, in a grainy news photo of the evening, looked quite splendid, at least to the camera lens, in her new Mainbocher dress, those bright dark eyes, swept-back dark hair, that familiar, faintly quizzical expression on her face, whose unnatural paleness would have been hidden behind not a little makeup. Then, early next morning, without a word to anyone, she walked herself into Doctors Hospital.

· 60 ·

WHEN DOCTORS HOSPITAL originally opened its doors in 1929, it was the first of a new kind of hospital, designed specifically for the growing population of well-to-do New Yorkers who up to then were accustomed to receiving medical care at home or in small private clinics, away from the dangerously unsanitary conditions and minimal services of most hospitals for the general public. A fourteen-story, clean-lined, white brick building on fashionable East End Avenue at Eighty-Eighth Street (overlooking the mayor's residence at Gracie Mansion and beyond that the East River), "Doctors" was known for its spacious private rooms (furnished and decorated at the level of a good hotel), its restaurant-grade kitchen and accommodating menus, and its staff of mostly Harvard-trained medical men, attended by a battalion of brisk, no-nonsense nurses, in turn supported by an army of virtual domestics who, in addition to the usual dirty work, unpacked the suitcases of patients as well as arranged meal tables with the linen cloths and silverware that patients sometimes brought with them.

Patterson, however, was in no shape to be thinking much about whether or not her room had a river view (it had) by the time she was admitted around ten in the morning; later than she intended, since despite a high fever, bleeding, and continued pain, she had insisted on personally handing to her private secretary, Dottie Holdsworth, first the key to a locked cabinet containing all her private correspondence from Stevenson and then a "last letter" she had written to him that night after the dinner, both to be hand-delivered to Stevenson in the event of her death. "When you read this," the letter read, "I will be residing in spirit by the banks of the Black River. One day perhaps you will pass and I will turn into a breeze and kiss your nose. I'm enclosing the letters you wrote me. I think they are beautiful letters and I hope you will not destroy them. Perhaps you would consider turning them over to the Illinois Historical Society to be opened a hundred years hence when all your family have died. How wonderful it would have been if Lincoln had written Ann Rutledge and those letters had been preserved. With your sense of history please think it over. I love you so much, Alicia."

Hospital records show that Mrs. Alicia P. Guggenheim, age forty-six, was admitted on September 22, 1952 (assigned room 1005), with a temperature of 104 degrees. The attending physician, Dr. William Rawls, noted: "Patient reports moderate to severe pain in left lower abdomen, also bleeding for 4–5 days. Patient complains when abdomen is palpitated by hand. Probable cause is inflammation of diverticulum." But that was no more than a guess since doctors had no way of knowing what was going on inside a patient without opening them up. Well, actually, there was another way: a barium enema, which coated the insides with barium and thus could reveal anomalies on an X-ray plate. Doctor Rawls ordered a barium enema for the next day, which however didn't work, since "patient's colon did not retain fluid." He ordered another for the day after, which also didn't work, presumably for the same reason, and called in Dr. Albert Aldridge.

Dr. Aldridge, a surgeon of some experience, first checked her earlier hospital records, then tried to talk to Patterson, whose fever was still at a high 102 degrees and was only intermittently communicative. Aldridge noted that, "In 1930 patient had an operation for an ectopic pregnancy and subsequently two more operations relating probably to tubular problems." More significantly, he also noted that, "Eight years prior patient received an insertion of radium to relieve difficulties of menstruation on account of dysmenorrhea." Aldridge prescribed heavy doses of a new antibiotic, Aureomycin, to lower her fever; two days later, on September 27, he performed a "diagnostic dilation and curettage." In his notes he reported: "With great difficulty the cervical canal was dilated enough to curette the uterus, removing a large amount of soft necrotic tissue which had the typical appearance adenocarcinoma of the uterus corpus."

Patterson was returned to her room on the tenth floor, with its view of the East River and its Manet prints. Her temperature was now back to normal, her pain was less. Sister Josephine had flown in from Chicago, and now sat in the room with Alicia as she recovered, both of them drinking the luscious eggnogs for which the Doctors Hospital kitchen was famous, both under the impression that Alicia's problems had been largely resolved; Dr. Rawls, the only visible physician on the case, stopped in once to take Patterson's pulse, pronounced it "a fine pulse," and suggested she order the eggs Benedict, another favorite from the hospital kitchen.

But Patterson herself was not fine. Unfortunately Doctors Hospital, while strong in the kitchen, didn't have its own diagnostic laboratory, at least not an up-to-date lab for cancer cell diagnosis; thus several days elapsed before the results came back from Dr. Aldridge's D & C procedure. In fact Aldridge already suspected that eight years before, when Patterson had been given radium treatment for "female abdominal problems" (her insides packed with radium isotopes, as was then the practice), the doctors might have packed in too much, or in the wrong place. On October 1 he noted, "Tissue removed from the uterus appear mixed with fragments from the bowel wall." And: "In view of these findings there is some suspicion that the patient has a carcinogenic involvement of the sigmoid." While Alicia and Josephine watched television, special-ordered from the menu, and passed the time waiting for clearance to leave, Dr. Aldridge in the meantime called in a second surgeon, Dr. Henry Cave, to assist him on the case.

On the morning of October 3, Patterson was taken down to the fourth floor and another operating room. Once again Aldridge was in charge, though with Cave assisting; Aldridge started things off by making a six-inch incision on the lower abdomen. "When the abdomen was opened," Dr. Aldridge noted, "it was found that this patient had an extensive carcinoma of the sigmoid, furthermore the sigmoid was firmly adherent to the left lateral wall of the uterus. There was apparently some thinning of the wall and in doing a curettage on Sept. 27 it was obvious that the curette had passed through the thin uterine wall and removed some of the tissue from the bowel itself." Cave then stepped in and "mobilized the sigmoid . . . following this, the entire uterus and left ovary were removed by Dr. Aldridge, employing the Aldridge modification of the Worrell technique." Much stitching was then done ("No. 2 chromic catgut for the mucosa and musculature"); also some minor patching ("No. 4 chromic catgut to attach the bladder flap of the peritoneum"); and then some decidedly not-so-minor repairs: "Following the hysterectomy," the careful notes read, "Dr. Cave did a Mickulicz type of bowel resection, bringing the loop of bowel out through the lower angle of the wound." Apparently a further look into Alicia's abdomen had revealed intestines abnormally twisted together, a section of lower intestine actually stuck to the colon, with "a large cancerous tumor completely encircling the sigmoid," which was removed, along with her uterus for good measure, after which she was returned to room 1005, semiconscious, with a colostomy bag attached to her stomach for the emptying of fecal waste.

Surgery is seldom easy on a patient, even nowadays, when medicine is so much more evolved than in the middle of the last century. Back then, in 1952 (a time when medical techniques in the better American hospitals were regarded as the most advanced in the world) pretty much every aspect of an operation was assaultive to the body: Incisions were longer, instruments were larger and clumsier, stitching material was thicker, needles of all sorts were wider, and the anesthetic of choice, sodium pentothal, had the kind of sledgehammer effect that often took days of headaches and nausea to dissipate. And then, for Patterson, there was the ghastly surprise on waking up of the colostomy bag (which fortunately could be removed in six weeks or so when the "bowel resection" healed). In addition there were all the tubes: tubes down the throat, tubes up the nose: rubber tubes (there being no plastic), relatively thick and minimally pliable, which a parade of nurses were regularly inserting, then removing, then sticking and poking back in. Patterson was now in real pain again, mainly from her insides healing, but she seemed to hate the business with the tubes most of all; her throat was narrow, as were her nasal passages, which added the pangs of claustrophobia to the duress of the whole situation. Granted she hadn't died; in fact the surgeons appeared to have found and excised a threatening cancer; but for many days she despaired, and told Josephine she felt like dying.

Josephine, the good sister, kept a constant vigil, seated day after day in room 1005, sometimes on the sofa, sometimes in the armchair with its view of the gray river, and its barge traffic, reading aloud from the cornucopia of the city's newspapers, whether Alicia could hear her or not; also listening, with dismay and some surprise, as her older, tough-guy, tomboy sister, the one who was never scared of anything, who was always quickest to "get back on the horse," lay abed, complaining about the tubes and the pain and just wanting to die; until one afternoon Josephine, having heard enough, in a voice loud enough to get the patient's attention, told her sister she was sounding "like a yellow-belly quitter," there being no greater insult one could give to one of Joe Patterson's children, after which Alicia reportedly settled down somewhat and let the healing process take its course.

Another feature of medical care in those days was the length of time that people were kept in hospitals; for example, one week for a routine appendectomy, which is now usually treated as an outpatient procedure. Patterson remained in Doctors Hospital almost a month, and as she recovered her strength and spirits a small number of visitors were logged in on the nurses' records. Her older sister, Elinor, wasn't one of them, staying close to her garden in nearby Greenwich; her mother, too, stayed away in Chicago, her mother whose shamefaced approach to her own hospitalizations caused her to undergo them in grim, determined secrecy. Harry Guggenheim, noted on the record as "husband," visited four times, although not right away, taking his time getting back from Cain Hoy. Other names in the visitors' book were Dorothy Holdsworth, Virginia Pasley, also big old Joe Brooks, currently a little the worse for wear but apparently as moony over his former wife as ever. One afternoon, in fact just before one of Harry Guggenheim's planned visits, Governor Stevenson showed up between campaign stops, seated briefly at her bedside, alternately tongue-tied and overtalkative, before Josephine pushed him unceremoniously out the service door to avoid the arrival of the "husband." Doubtless Alicia could have received many more visitors, certainly toward the end of her stay, when she was feeling much better, reading, watching television, dining on the hospital's famous rib-eye steak and baked potato, washed down with Johnnie Walker. But this was an era when cancer was still, by and large an unmentionable illness, something close to leprosy, an ill omen, a black mark of a disease; in fact the word "cancer" almost never appeared in obituaries at the time, being replaced by the euphemism "died of a long illness." Patterson herself, forthright in so many other matters, seemed no more eager to advertise herself to the world as a cancer patient than she was to acknowledge that cancer was the cause of her hospitalization, rather than some more generalized, abstracted "internal problem."

She was discharged on the morning of October 25, not quite four weeks after the Stevenson dinner, and was advised to go directly home, continue resting. But she'd been away from *Newsday* a long time, an important month, and so, instead of going back to Falaise, she had herself driven out to Garden City in time for the daily editorial meeting, at which she dictated the concluding editorial on the presidential campaign, thus keeping an earlier promise to Harry, while doing the best she could by Stevenson. "Both General Eisenhower and Governor Stevenson have turned out to be good, hard-working campaigners," the editorial declared. "But the major issue today is the need for a change. Because of this, and not because one man is more able than the other, we give our continued backing to General Eisenhower. Stevenson is a Democrat and, despite his skill and devotion, the corruption of the Truman administration, with all its waste, bungling and toleration of Communism, would be so much harder for him to deal with than for Eisenhower. In reaffirming our support of General Eisenhower we also reaffirm our high esteem for Governor Stevenson, who deserves much honor and a high place in government." And then she went home.

· 61 ·

JUST BEFORE PATTERSON entered the hospital, with a health issue she rightly suspected might turn into something serious, the one person most in her thoughts, and to whom it turned out she had written a kind of deathbed letter for posthumous delivery, was her old friend and sometime lover, Adlai Stevenson, in whose honor she had been giving that big River Club party; and yet at no time in the course of that evening had she told him how sick she was feeling, that anything was wrong, that she was entering the hospital. In fact, only ten days after entering the hospital did she allow Josephine to get word about her to the traveling candidate, and then no more than a brief note in the mail, with a deliberately nonspecific, almost evasive message as to the actual situation. Even then, although still weak and miserable in her hospital bed, she explained to Josephine that she didn't want to burden Stevenson, didn't want to distract him from what was proving to be an uphill campaign.

Not that Josephine really needed an explanation, for both sisters shared the same idiosyncratic brand of feminism—what might be called Pattersonian feminism—whereby you brooked no nonsense, took no guff, considered yourself fully equal to the ordinary male. With the extraordinary male, however, the special man, the gifted man, you stepped aside when needed, you always tried to make the path of genius easier, smoother. Adlai Stevenson, very much a man of his time (despite a tendency on occasion to confuse both himself and others with the new language of the-man-who-cares-about-women), took all too easily to the role of this special man, for whom women naturally fetched and carried, did the scut work, for whom they even pushed their inconvenient illnesses out of sight. When Stevenson belatedly had showed up at Doctors Hospital one afternoon—hurried, distracted, shy to the point of awkwardness—Patterson never once talked about her condition, and Stevenson (the man who ten months before had written her, "I want details!" about her supposed ulcer) didn't ask. By mutual consent, seemingly, they talked about the campaign, then entering its final days, with Stevenson trailing badly in most of the polls. History, of course, shows that Ike won big on November 2; also, that Stevenson, despite a large loss in the Electoral College, emerged with enough popular votes to assure himself a major presence in the Democratic Party. What there's no record of, either in letters, reminiscences, or the recollections of the few people she confided in, is what Alicia Patterson thought at that point about the roller-coaster ride she'd been on the past few years.

Once upon a time, six long years earlier, on her mother's lawn in Libertyville, Patterson had been the solid one; *placée*, as the French say, not merely established but empowered, as Harry Guggenheim's wife, as editor and copublisher of *Newsday*, and with Stevenson not exactly on the outside but definitely not *placé*, a Chicago salaryman with a bad marriage and muddled prospects, with dreams of this and that, and no strong sense or confidence of how to move forward. Back then, the easy part for her had been providing confidence: spurring his ambition to match her own, urging him forward when he wanted to stay put or back off, telling him to commit, to get out there, when he so sincerely (or so it seemed) wished to achieve some private state of grace by hanging back. Four years before, there had been the narrative of the reluctant candidate for governor, the man who had eyes only for Washington, where nobody wanted him, who was ready to turn down Springfield where he *was* wanted. Once ensconced in the statehouse, then came the multiyear drama of the governor who couldn't or wouldn't quit the Governor's Mansion to run for president, even to please the sitting president, the head of his own party; soon followed by the "Let this cup pass from my lips!" national candidate. Patterson had seen him through so much of his unlikely adventure, sometimes from the distractingly close perspective of the bedroom, for the most part from the perhaps-truer intimacy of all those letters, messages, notes, with their handwritten pen-or-pencil scrawls, their potpourri of romantic effusions and scheduling details. But for a woman who prided herself on the sharpness of her intuition, on her quickness on the uptake, she had been slow to read the signals. Had she really thought he would be content to stick on as governor, as he kept insisting? Hadn't she somehow guessed that already he was massing his battalions, planning his strategy, somewhere out of sight, in his own head, a politician who was bound to be keeping secrets from himself as well as others? Only a year earlier, give or take, when she'd launched herself out to Wyoming, hadn't she known that something was off, something was up?

Now, in the aftermath of the great election, far from letting the cup pass from his lips, it seemed that Stevenson had grabbed it, drunk deeply, and was in no hurry to give it back. He might have lost the race to Eisenhower, and by a sizable margin, but it turned out that Hamlet loved the stage. "Did you see that Salisbury in the *Times* called me the 'Democratic Party's standard-bearer?' I don't mind that at all, I quite like it," he told Patterson in mid-November, in the first of a sequence of letters he wrote her as he traveled the world on a grand consolation tour. From London: "Please not to worry too greatly on my account. Weekend at Chatsworth. . . . How warm some of the people over here are to me, warmer than some at home I could mention. . . . And you? Are you are mending rapidly?" From Barbados, in January, where he was visiting Marietta Tree and her husband, Sir Ronald Tree, at their grand Palladian beachfront villa, he wrote: "I've no regrets, I did the best I could. At least I didn't betray my principles. . . . Someday soon maybe we can talk again, who knows beside the Black River . . . get better, be well."

But she wasn't well or better; in fact she was down beside the Black River herself, on her own, recovering after yet another three weeks in the hospital, this time from an infection brought on when they'd removed her colostomy paraphernalia. She spent much of that winter, the first months of 1953, virtually hiding out in her house by the St. Mary's, "dragging herself around like an old dog," as she described it to Josephine. Harry Guggenheim urged her to move north to Cain Hoy, where he was readying a new thoroughbred for the year's racing season, but in no mood to move, least of all to Cain Hoy, she found a dozen reasons for staying put. From chilly Long Island, *Newsday* managing editor Alan Hathway spoke with her by telephone almost daily (on her end, a scratchy rural party line, with the drawly voices of Georgia neighbors cutting in and out in the background), sending his own mixed messages: one moment urging her to come back soon, the troops needed her, he needed her; the next moment telling her more or less the opposite, everything was fine, stay down there as long as you need. Her secretary and all-purpose assistant, Dottie Holdsworth, came down for a week, supposedly a working visit; Patterson had said she wanted to "get some planning done," to put her recovery time to good use. But once there, Dottie found her normally hard-charging, talkative boss dismayingly muted, almost lethargic, uninterested in work, in planning, in much of anything. Before returning North, Holdsworth reported back to Josephine that her sister was "in a funk," that dread zone somewhere between malingering and melancholy (what people in due course would learn to call depression), needless to say a state of mind or body seldom visited by Alicia Patterson.

· 62 ·

A CHANGE IN PATTERSON'S SPIRITS, or condition, or in some interior weather system of her own took a long time in coming, but when it came she seemed to turn around as on the proverbial dime. April on the banks of the St. Mary's, sunshine, soft warm winds blowing up the Florida coast, camellias beginning to bloom, egrets and cormorants in the air. Josephine came down for a post-Easter visit, to bring cheer or at least companionship to her drooping, ailing, perhaps permanently melancholic sister, also to get away from the still frozen Midwest, but instead found Alicia already on the bustle, a spring in her short steps, full of talk, plans for *Newsday*, though at the same time second-guessing herself about her strength and nerve: Did she still "have it"? Was she ready to go back and run a paper, a staff, a newsroom? One morning, after Alicia had led them on a panting, spirited hike through the woods, the two sisters were relaxing on the little dock by the river, talking of this and that, when up from the dark waters beneath them, climbing one of the support poles, appeared one of the river's many water moccasins, sleek, glistening, deadly; Josephine could see the snake, now gliding in their general direction across the gray wood planks of the dock, but didn't know if Alicia had seen it; Alicia, still talking, rose to her feet, grabbed a nearby oar, raised it, smacked the snake to snake heaven; "You're ready," Josephine told her. "Go back to work."

Two weeks later, halfway home so to speak, she joined husband Harry in Louisville for the seventy-second running of the Kentucky Derby; a day in the sun in the company of the country's horse-racing *ton*, those grimly beaming men in linen suits, their blondish wives in floral-print dresses, wide-brimmed hats, drinks in their hands, a military band playing "My Old Kentucky Home" over and over again. As it happened, this was the year Harry Guggenheim's horse won the Derby. There's a photo of the four of them in the Winner's

Circle: From left to right, Mr. Harry Frank Guggenheim, splendid in a double-breasted linen suit, sporty fedora on his head, racetrack binoculars hanging from one shoulder, proudly holding the reins of his Cain Hoy Stables thoroughbred Dark Star; the fine bay horse himself, sternly handsome as a matinee idol despite the frilly necklace of flowers around his neck; his rider, the tiny, fierce Panamanian jockey Manuel Ycaza; and then the owner's wife, Mrs. Harry F. Guggenheim, not looking too bad at all, in fact looking pretty good, all things considered seemingly happy to be where she was, at least for the time being.

Then, late Sunday morning, with the weekend winding down, with Harry, his voice hoarse from giving interviews, though still giving more interviews—on his way back to Cain Hoy, Patterson took a plane north, to New York, Falaise, and *Newsday*.

· 63 ·

A NOTE HERE about the DeKoning story, which was about to reoccupy the attentions of *Newsday*'s staff and returning editor, with such consequential results; "reoccupy" for the reason that this would be the second go-round between the newspaper and Nassau County's current hiding-in-plain-sight gangster.

In fact Nassau County, almost an hour's distance by rail or road from the fleshpots of the big city, with its population mix of residential and small business, might seem like an unlikely venue for crime and criminals of any substance, which presumably was why, in the late 1940s, William DeKoning had begun setting up shop, right there in Greater Hempstead, far from the prying eyes of the FBI and the interest of New York's newspapers; his "shop" in this instance being the rapidly growing body of union labor in the construction trades on eastern Long Island. As one of the nation's less visible labor bosses, riding the wave of the postwar boom as well as a surge in union membership, the bullet-headed, bespectacled, notoriously violent Bill DeKoning (his favored form of keeping people in line was having acid thrown at them), duly elected president of Local 138 of the International Brotherhood of Electrical Engineers, soon controlled thousands of dues-paying members in the Long Island building trades, gradually broadening his reach by taking over union labor at the popular harness-racing tracks springing up outside New York.

Newsday was well aware of DeKoning's emerging presence on the local scene, but the paper's first responses had been fairly muted, even docile, befitting a regional daily with no crime "desk," no experienced crime or labor-racketeering staff. When, in April 1949, with much municipal fanfare, DeKoning personally inaugurated a huge, newly constructed, bar-restaurant-entertainment complex, nicely called the Labor Lyceum, financed by union dues and supposedly owned by union workers, *Newsday* had cheerfully joined in the fanfare, approvingly reporting on the "labor leader's" charitable activities, and his sponsorship of community youth organizations, with a fairly straight face. One of DeKoning's leading local supporters for a while was none other than *Newsday*'s eccentric, obstreperous managing editor, Alan Hathway, among whose numerous, almost Dickensian defects was a disposition to chronic indebtedness, mainly a result of excessive drinking, leading him to gamble away his salary (usually more than his salary), leaving him continually on the lookout for a quick fix, a deal, any deal—even a deal with someone he knew to be as crooked as DeKoning, who smoothly offered him a paid position on the board of the Labor Lyceum.

Hathway was about to accept the offer, would have accepted it but for his own boss, Patterson, who said no: How could *Newsday*'s managing editor be on the board of an outfit such as the Labor Lyceum, whether legal or not, which the paper was bound to cover, supposedly dispassionately? Hathway's next move was to join a "private investing group" about to begin construction on a rival attraction, a sports arena; this edifice, the Hempstead Garden, was eventually built, but with so much interference and active obstruction by DeKoning's union troublemakers, with so much consequent loss of time, money, and personal aggravation to investor Hathway that the editor decided it was time to go after DeKoning in the paper.

In April 1950 Hathway, who normally drank his lunch late in the afternoon at the nearby Anchor Inn, asked his boss, "Miss P.," as he and many of the staff referred to her, to take a proper lunch meeting with him for a discussion of business. As described in Robert F. Keeler's fine book *Newsday*, the two met at the also nearby, more-or-less Italian restaurant Chez Nino, Alicia's favorite place in Garden City; Patterson at her usual round table in the far corner, her spaniel at her feet, eyeglasses perched atop her head, puffing on Lucky Strikes. Hathway said he wanted to go after DeKoning, run an exposé. Patterson asked him—not was it personal, since everything with Hathway was somehow personal—but how much of it was personal. A bit, but not all, not even most, Hathway replied. DeKoning was a crook, he told her, a huge crook; he cheated his own people, he cheated everyone. If he didn't get his way, his goons beat you up; if he really didn't like you, there was that acid thing. Then Hathway told her, as she remembered it: "This could be the big one for us." Patterson had the background, if not the hands-on experience, to know what he meant, that the DeKoning story, wherever it led, might have the heft, the serious journalistic dimensions to put *Newsday* on the map as a big-story newspaper. On the other hand there was no shortage of risks and caveats, not least among them that Bill DeKoning controlled most of the union labor in *Newsday*'s territory, a nest it might be unwise and actually dangerous to disturb. In the end the deciding factor was probably that both Patterson and Hathway shared the love of a good fight. "Are you tretching me?" she asked him at one point ("tretching" was one of Joe Patterson's old-timey slang words for being treacherous, a sneak, a low-down rat, and so on). Hathway said no, in fact gave her his word, literally his word; the two of them were like that. Then they shook hands on it.

Even so, *Newsday*'s investigation of DeKoning had a slow start and modest beginnings, given that Hathway's putative anticrime task force consisted of no more than a single novice reporter: Helen Dudar, a twenty-three-year-old Columbia University night-school graduate, whose journalism experience was limited to a few months covering petty crime arraignments at the nearby county courthouse. But Hathway, for all his wayward personal habits, had an old-fashioned news editor's gift for making do with what the Lord provided. In the case of earnest, hardworking young Helen Dudar, he took her seriously, encouraged her, and—more important—gave her the tip that set the coverage in motion. Go back to the courthouse, he suggested, check through the real estate title records, and see who really owns the Labor Lyceum. After many days grubbing through the haystack of the county's filing cabinets, Dudar eventually found the right needle: proof that DeKoning's grandiose Lyceum was owned, not as claimed by the members of Local 138, International Brotherhood of Engineers, but instead by one Rose Mary DeKoning, the labor boss's wife.

Dudar's first piece, which appeared on May 11, 1950, opened on a fine combative note (with doubtless a stylistic assist or two from Hathway): "From the lavish Uniondale estate he publicly dedicated to labor and privately dedicated to his wife, pugnacious Bill DeKoning rules a kingdom rich in the unnatural resources of the strong arm and the double-barreled threat." The article then went on to delineate the far-flung reach of DeKoning's empire, which controlled not only several large Long Island construction unions but also workers at the popular Roosevelt Raceway. Two weeks later a second *Newsday* piece spelled out DeKoning's ties to another notoriously corrupt and brutal labor leader, Joey Fay. This was followed by three more full-length stories, including first-person accounts by members of DeKoning's racetrack union, which told how DeKoning shortchanged and exploited his workers, had them beaten and worse when they complained. "Bill DeKoning is a hated man, but the hatred simmers in dark and silent corners," was how Dudar's five-piece series concluded, though it was a series without a byline, since (at a time when labor reporters were being set on fire, doused with acid, and blown up in their cars) Patterson and Hathway wished to protect their young reporter from retribution.

In many ways *Newsday*'s DeKoning exposé was impressive, certainly for a midmarket newspaper; it was well promoted across eastern Long Island, widely read and talked about for a while, and even prompted a number of tips to the newsroom about other DeKoning crimes and misdemeanors. But the series wasn't really a game changer for the newspaper; its impact was general, almost impressionistic. DeKoning was obviously a thug, a bully, a bad guy, but after five separate articles nothing new had been turned up that could be made to stick, nothing substantial enough to get a rise out of law enforcement; even the momentarily satisfying revelation as to the true ownership of the Labor Lyceum didn't "have legs"; it might be shady, shabby, possibly contemptible, but it wasn't illegal. The day after the series concluded, Patterson published an editorial describing it as "a preliminary series of reports that have only begun to scratch the surface of DeKoning's corroding influence," confidently announcing that "additional chapters about the public and private life of Long Island's labor czar are in preparation, and will shortly appear in early issues of this newspaper." But none did, at least not as advertised. *Newsday* continued to cover DeKoning, though mainly as a background figure in periodic labor dustups, and of course as patron of those local youth charities; there were no major news breaks, no more big crime stories, no "additional chapters." After two years of press quietude or inattention, in fact, it looked as if Long Island's tough-guy labor racketeer had managed to slip back into the shadows, or at least out of range of the only newspaper that had been trying to nail him; while *Newsday* for its part seemed to have let the DeKoning ball drop, the moment slip by.

WE'RE NOW BACK IN MAY 1953, with Patterson returned to her desk after a nearly four-month absence. By coincidence or luck, the first week she was back a piece of DeKoning-related news came in over the proverbial transom. A young investigator on the New York State Crime Commission had noticed, in the jumble of state prison visitation records, an interesting anomaly: One of the "regulars," who paid a monthly visit to the convicted gangster Joey Fay at Attica, was none other than William DeKoning, whose consistent mantra over the years had been a pious disavowal of any personal connection to organized crime. Since nobody on the State Crime Commission seemed interested in DeKoning, the investigator, Bob Greene, funneled the material over to *Newsday*, which remained the only news organization to date that had ever questioned the union boss's legitimacy. Greene's file landed on Hathway's desk, who told Patterson about it. The two of them then invited the investigator out to Garden City for a meeting, after which Greene spent three afternoons dictating the contents of his DeKoning notebooks to Patterson's secretary, Dottie Holdsworth. One week later *Newsday* broke its new DeKoning story, a carefully documented account of DeKoning's extensive, month-after-month, time-consuming, unmistakable involvement with one of the country's most notorious criminals. It was the big story Patterson had blithely promised two years before; *Newsday* then followed up with two related stories, tying DeKoning even closer to Joey Fay's operations. But then, once again as before, DeKoning seemed to slip out of the spotlight, literally escape, by announcing his retirement and relocation to Florida, just another working-class guy moving south to the sunshine, though leaving his son back home in charge of union business. On August 12, however, a classic big-city shootout took place, though not in New York but thirty miles north, far beyond the city limits, at suburban Yonkers

Raceway, another of the new trotting tracks. As first reported by the Associated Press, a hitman by the name of "Snakes" Lewis had apparently gunned down another powerful labor leader, Tommy Allen, and was then himself killed in the proverbial hail of bullets by state troopers. *Newsday* picked up the AP story and then started digging further, finding all sorts of links and parallels, in union negotiating patterns, strongarm tactics, and so on, between the faraway Yonkers track and nearby Roosevelt Raceway. At Patterson's and Hathway's instigation, *Newsday* reporter Stan Brooks began looking into the tangled and covert records of ownership of the two trotting tracks, and soon found DeKoning clearly involved with both of them, not only as union organizer but as a stockholder. On a tip Patterson herself interviewed Long Island Republican congressman J. Russell Sprague, who, after initial denials, was also revealed to be a secret shareholder in the profitable racetracks.

For much of late summer and early fall, *Newsday* pounded away at Bill DeKoning's "web of thuggery and corruption," and this time the stories seemed to have the requisite heft, the reporting finally had traction. What ultimately changed the game was that the New York newspapers woke up to the fact of their being scooped, on the kind of story they were supposed to do best, and started to pay attention. In fact, the city's big afternoon paper, the *World-Telegram* did more than pay attention; it came out with a dramatic banner headline: "$345,000 Track Extortion Mulcts Roosevelt Workers" over a story that basically recycled material from *Newsday*'s original 1951 series, adding some guesswork arithmetic of its own. *Newsday* then countered with three more freshly reported stories, which finally prompted the Nassau County district attorney to announce an investigation. On October 7, six weeks after the Snakes Lewis murder, a grand jury in Mineola indicted William DeKoning and nine of his aides for extortion and conspiracy. The next day Governor Thomas Dewey of New York announced the appointment of a special commission to investigate DeKoning, whom he described as "the wealthiest labor leader in the world."

When *Newsday* reported these satisfying developments to its Long Island readers, it also made sure to remind them, as well as the newspaper rajas over in Manhattan, that it was *Newsday* that had been first with the story. Accordingly its promotions often repeated a quote from DeKoning's own lawyer, about how the big-city papers had discovered the DeKoning scandal: "They must have read it in *Newsday*, they've been printing these things for years." But to make certain that there were no mistakes or misunderstandings on that score, in other words to prevent the late-to-the-party New York papers from grabbing the credit, Patterson asked Hathway to contact Richard Clurman, the young *Time* editor who had earlier written the "Press" piece on *Newsday*, and make sure he knew of *Newsday*'s long history with the DeKoning story. Hathway sent Clurman a three-page letter outlining in detail, and with relevant dates, *Newsday*'s four-year history of pursuing DeKoning, and *Time*'s subsequent piece was a major vindication for the Long Island paper. "*Newsday* knew what it was talking about," *Time* declared in its influential "Press" section. "Unheeded by other papers or by state officials, *Newsday* had been loudly hammering away for more than three years at corruption at the Long Island track in Nassau County. Last week *Newsday*'s long campaign finally paid off with a blaze of Page One stories in the Manhattan dailies on one of the biggest state scandals in years."

The governor's State Commission on Crime began its hearings later in the fall, and before the end of the year a grand jury had issued major criminal indictments against DeKoning, his son, and five associates. The DeKoning regime was effectively kaput, as Patterson would say. Not one to be shy about her paper's role in the affair, on January 20, 1954, Patterson signed and sent a letter to the dean of the Graduate School of Journalism at Columbia University, accompanying a massive file of *Newsday* news-clippings going all the way back to Helen Dudar's original series, submitting the paper's DeKoning coverage for a Pulitzer Prize.

· 64 ·

THE PULITZER PRIZES were announced later in the year, in May, and *Newsday* did indeed win one of the coveted awards: the Pulitzer Prize for Meritorious Public Service, one of five important journalism prizes handed out by the twelve-man jury, which included some of the nation's most august editors as well as Joseph Pulitzer's son: a jury, it might be added, operating at such a lofty level of discrimination that it didn't deign to give an award for fiction that year.

Then as now, the Pulitzers were not one of the showier ceremonies: letters went out in the mail to the winners, followed by a press release and later by a lunch at the Columbia University Faculty Club. On the other hand this was a different, decidedly quieter time in the matter of public awards ceremonies; which is to say there were precious few of them, almost none: no Emmys, Grammys, Tonys, Golden Globes, country music medalists, and so on; Hollywood's Academy Awards existed but weren't yet familiarly called the Oscars, and were usually handed out in a hotel dining room, with only West Coast television coverage, often too late to make the East Coast morning papers. Thus the Pulitzer awards made a fairly large splash in a far smaller pool. Patterson tried to be a nongrandstanding boss, sending Hathway and a handful of reporters to pick up the award at the official lunch, signing an editorial giving credit to her managing editor and "the team." But there was no hiding her unmistakable pride of place in the proceedings. Much as she thought of *Newsday* as intrinsically hers, despite Harry's owning the extra 2 percent that made it legally his, so she came to regard it as *her* Pulitzer, no matter how often she reminded herself in public to say ours, the team's, the staff's, the paper's.

Then, as if a Pulitzer Prize wasn't enough of a step up in the great world, came word from Rockefeller Center, headquarters of the Time-Life empire, that *Time* was considering her—not the team, not Harry Guggenheim with her—her, as a potential subject for a cover story. Only fifty-two covers every year, each one with an artist-commissioned, full-face portrait on the cover, and each subject—with rare exceptions such as Hitler and Stalin—an exemplar of the best and brightest in the nation or in the world. Of course almost always men: prime ministers, senators, generals, important scientists, executives who ran the big car companies, occasionally a writer, especially if he had just won a Nobel Prize. Soon came a formal letter from *Time*'s editor: Would Alicia Patterson be a consenting subject? Would she be willing to furnish a list of people who knew her, old school roommates, distant relatives, friends, acquaintances anywhere in the world, whom *Time*'s vast network of reporters and researchers could then seek out and interview? She would.

Not surprisingly the impetus for the profile had come from Dick Clurman, the twenty-nine-year-old editor of *Time*'s "Press" department, who had authored the magazine's first piece on *Newsday* and its editor, and whose help Patterson had lately sought on the DeKoning story. In those days of the great magazines, a *Time* cover story inevitably meant a full-court press for the cover subject, often lasting many months. First among the numerous *Tim*e representatives to appear in Patterson's life was a distinguished Hungarian photographer, with several assistants, who spent the better part of a week at Falaise shooting dozens of rolls of film, which were then turned into hundreds of prints, which were then sent off to the cover artist, in this case the distinguished realist Boris Chaliapin, for a portrait that might well take months to complete. As soon as the photographer left, a tall, gaunt, scholarly female researcher arrived (a graduate of both Bryn Mawr and the Sorbonne), who dogged Patterson from Falaise to Garden City and back again until she had extracted roughly sixty names of contacts for *Time*'s national and foreign correspondents to interview.

As the summer unfolded, Patterson tried not to think about the cover story she knew was in the works, but also could be endlessly postponed or cancelled. "Apparently I'm still on the *Time* cover list," she wrote her mother in July, "though I shudder to think what they may be digging up. Of course my chief fear is that Harry will somehow feel slighted." Alice Patterson might have replied, though she didn't, that if her daughter was worried about her husband's feelings, all she had to do was make sure that Dick Clurman knew not to slight them. As to worrying about what the magazine might be "digging up," Patterson was doubtless well aware (as was any savvy reader of *Time* cover stories) that the magazine's major profiles, especially of consenting subjects, were invariably positive, approving, enhancing, like the cover paintings themselves, save for the seemingly obligatory inclusion of one or two minor flaws, thrown in as if to keep the profile credible. The truth was, that with the winning of the Pulitzer and now the attentions of *Time*, Patterson was moving into a new place. It wasn't the first time she'd been in the public eye, had her photo in a magazine, but what was happening lately was on a whole different level, not only as an individual but as a woman. In mid-August she chaired a week of staff meetings in Garden City, trying to map out *Newsday*'s post-Pulitzer future. Late in the month she went out to Josephine's Wyoming ranch, hoping to relax, feel normal once again, which she did, until another *Time* photographer showed up, shooting more rolls of film: Patterson on horseback, with her sister; Patterson knee-deep in the Wind River, fly casting for trout.

· 65 ·

THE *TIME* STORY CAME OUT on September 13, with Patterson's face—handsome, self-possessed, attractively weathered—right there on the cover of two million magazines, above the terse caption, "Publisher Patterson." Inside a lengthy four-thousand-word profile was everything its subject might have wished for: "In creating her own highly successful *Newsday*, Alicia Patterson has also created a new form of U.S. journalism. It is as perfectly in step with the new trend in American life—the flight to the suburbs—as tabloids were in the 20's." *Time* described Patterson as having "a touch of the journalistic genius of her late father, Capt. Joseph Medill Patterson," and someone who, "set out to violate every canon of sedate, well-mannered and deadly dull suburban journalism." It traced her life story in attentive detail, approvingly noting her expulsions from "two of the world's fanciest finishing schools for general obstreperousness." It recounted Alicia's long, tomboyish, hot-and-cold relationship with her father, and placed her squarely in the Joseph Medill newspaper dynasty, making sure to explain that, "On national and international affairs *Newsday* smashes every Patterson-McCormick political tradition. *Newsday* is as liberal and internationalist as the family's *Chicago Tribune* is hidebound and isolationist."

Time's densely written, admiring narrative made appropriate mention of Alan Hathway ("balding former *News* staffer with a police reporter's instincts") and several other *Newsday* personnel. The name of Harry Guggenheim, however, was harder to find, not impossible; he appeared briefly, in what might be called cameo roles, as rich husband ("the mining and mineral heir") and dour, de facto owner, lacking everything but a green eyeshade, "who keeps tight control over the paper's finances." But if Patterson's presence on the cover and in the text of the hugely prestigious newsmagazine, might fairly be described as something of a star turn, then Harry

Guggenheim's role was barely a speaking part, little more than a walk-on. Patterson received an early copy of the magazine, hot off the presses, hand-delivered at ten at night, courtesy of Dick Clurman. She read and reread it for hours, falling asleep close to dawn. Then later the next day she flew off to Paris, by prearranged plan, to join her mother for a few days. Apparently one morning, the two of them were walking down the rue Saint-Honoré, and there at a newsstand kiosk was a display of *Time*, with "Publisher Patterson" on the cover; indeed it seemed to be at all the kiosks, everywhere in Paris. It often took a lot to please Alice Patterson, especially when it came to her second daughter, but as Alicia remembered, even she was pleased by this.

An even bigger splash, the 1954 *Time* cover.

· 66 ·

AS IT HAPPENED, Harry Guggenheim had once been on the cover of *Time* himself. But that was long ago, back in 1929, when he'd been ambassador to Cuba (the U.S.'s man on the spot during yet another regime change in Havana), when so much of everything was different, with him a thirty-nine-year-old, up-and-coming progressive Republican, in the seemingly solid Herbert Hoover Republican era, and *Time*, a relatively new magazine, neither widely read nor yet a significant national presence. Today, as a sixty-four-year-old, a business leader, an important voice in yet another supposedly Republican era, he was little pleased by the now widely read magazine's cover story on his wife; in his view, little more than a fawning fan letter to her, at the same time puzzlingly and deliberately dismissive of him. After its appearance across the country, all over the known world, Harry prided himself on being wise enough not to make a public row about it, doubtless also mindful that favorable publicity from *Time*'s story could only make his majority stake in *Newsday* worth more in the end.

But what Patterson did next made Guggenheim, a self-described most reasonable man and model of imperturbability, demonstrably furious. She hired Richard Clurman, *Time*'s "Press" editor, author of the "Publisher Patterson" cover story, to be *Newsday*'s "editorial director," a position that hadn't previously existed, and that Patterson more or less invented ad hoc, mostly, it seemed, as a way of getting Clurman onboard.

Why did she want Clurman so badly at *Newsday*? On the surface there were certainly some plausible reasons for the hire. As a youthful, savvy thirty-one-year-old, in addition to being a talented writer and editor, bright and well credentialed (with a master's degree from the University of Chicago), Dick Clurman was also someone who could speak the new emerging languages of media and communications, who knew his way around Madison Avenue and Rockefeller

Center. Then, too, there was the matter of *Newsday*'s own outmoded editorial infrastructure. Even after its Pulitzer, the paper still didn't have a regular copy desk, a separate department as at other serious newspapers, which received and processed raw reporting from the field, then turned it into finished stories; instead, in an informal hit-or-miss arrangement, carried over from its Hempstead garage days, reporters phoned or brought their stories in to Alan Hathway personally, if they could find him, and what happened next—and when it happened—depended greatly on Hathway's mood, sobriety, enthusiasm of the moment, and so on.

Patterson's stated ambition, to push the new post-Pulitzer *Newsday* to a higher level of professionalism, "in a new direction," as she declared to the staff, made a good deal of sense and was hard to quarrel with as an institutional goal. In fact her first "new direction" hire, some months before Clurman, was a twenty-eight-year-old North Carolinian, William McIlwaine, who was dropped cold into the day-by-day chaos of the paper's editing procedures and asked to put together a suitable copy desk for a paper now wishing to be taken seriously. Bill McIlwaine was soft-spoken, easygoing, almost professorial in manner, and while *Newsday*'s reporters hadn't taken happily to seeing their own copy rewritten, they were soon appreciative of how much the new system improved their colleagues' stories. Dick Clurman, however, was a bird of a different feather, a horse of another color: confident to the point of arrogance, impatient, not one to waste time on people who didn't matter, an emissary, as it seemed to many, from an alien and condescending Manhattan magazine culture. Also, given Patterson's stated wish to make *Newsday*'s operations more professional, it was quickly noted that Clurman himself had no newspaper experience, nor seemed to think he needed any. Indeed, some of the old hands took their griping even further, wondering if it was a case of Miss P. having decided one day that *Newsday* lacked specific capabilities, and that only Richard Clurman could provide them, which would have been odd enough; or whether there might exist a more complicated personal attraction, or at least connection, between the young interloper and their editor, which would be even more unsettling.

During the three years Clurman was employed at *Newsday*,

Patterson's relationship with him was consistently professional, observing proper boundaries, no hint of anything extraneous. At the same time she was an intensely personal, strongly ambitious woman, Clurman likewise was intensely personal, strongly ambitious; as such they hit it off on any number of levels: likes, dislikes, jokes, and perhaps above all politics. Alan Hathway was naturally a problem; his early response to Clurman's arrival had been a predictable stew of anger, jealousy, sulks, and drunken misadventures. By then Patterson had decidedly mixed feelings about her urban cowboy managing editor. She knew enough to be grateful for the old-style newsman's energy he'd brought to the operation; she also knew enough to realize that *Newsday* was outgrowing Hathway. But perhaps not right away, not just yet. Thus her first task for Clurman was to send him to Washington to set up a *Newsday* bureau in the nation's capital; everyone else was doing it, and while *Newsday* was late to the party, the party seemed only to be getting started. Clurman set up a small three-person bureau, renting the office space and making the hires, whose duties were defined as developing congressional or governmental stories with a particular relevance to Long Island readers, a mission that over time would prove easier to define than to achieve. On his return to Garden City, Patterson gave him his next assignment, editorial director, another newly minted position, which put him in charge of the edito-

Harry and Alicia with her spaniels at Cain Hoy, Thanksgiving, 1955.

rial page: the editorials themselves, plus political cartoons, columns, and op-eds.

From a number of perspectives this was a smart move. Patterson now had a kindred spirit in an important editorial role, personally sympathetic and politically astute. It also took the heat off Hathway, who had no interest in editorials and fancy-pants political columning, and could now continue running the reporting staff in his own unbuttoned fashion. But Patterson's copublisher, and needless to say husband, was very far from being on board with the new program. From the start Harry Guggenheim had been dismayed by Clurman's hiring, not even bothering to conceal his almost visceral dislike for the new arrival from Rockefeller Center. He didn't like his attitude, which he considered disrespectful to the majority owner. He didn't like his know-it-all manner on pretty much every subject. He especially didn't like it that Patterson had installed him in a big new office right next to hers. To Stan Peckham, Patterson professed surprise at Harry's opposition to Clurman, who she claimed was just the sort of confident, well-spoken, properly dressed, suitably educated young man Harry usually seemed so fond of (moreover, such an improvement over the ill-spoken, disheveled Hathway), but even such a pro-Alicia stalwart as Peckham was of the opinion that Miss P. had developed something of a blind spot when it came to her new editorial director. On one notable occasion, a dinner being given by Patterson at Falaise, Harry showed up late, took one look around the room he was about to enter, then spotted Clurman, and disappeared upstairs for the rest of the evening.

· 67 ·

HARRY GUGGENHEIM might be majority owner of *Newsday* but Patterson was clearly running things at the paper, and running them well. It had taken ten years to grow it from "a little Hempstead daily," with ten thousand readers to a county-level newspaper with a circulation of one hundred thousand and a Pulitzer Prize. Now, in a relatively few years, its circulation was bumping up against the three-hundred-thousand mark. Regular editions sometimes came in at an advertising-heavy 120 pages, heftier than New York's *Daily News*, and the Garden City building was in a constant state of expansion. Obviously some of this came with the nature of the territory, the still-surging growth of eastern Long Island. But if Nassau County's population growth had a certain inevitability, not all businesses automatically keep up, sometimes least of all newspapers, whose owners choose to hoard money at the wrong moment, whose editors don't like to change habits, patterns, ways of doing things.

The fact was that Harry Guggenheim—that most reasonable, most prudent man—made expansion, change, "new directions," as difficult as possible. He fought Alicia inch by inch, or rather dollar by dollar, and she fought him back, winning enough of the battles to keep moving things forward, and she kept hiring new people on the edit side to keep the paper just far enough ahead of its readers so they'd want more of it rather than less. Around this time she admitted to Josephine what might be guessed at anyway: that if she couldn't actually own the paper outright, in a legal, 51 percent kind of way, she was damn well going to own it in the only real way an editor owns a paper—her people, her kind of stories, her stamp on the page.

Then, in the mid-fifties, Adlai Stevenson came back into her life; not that he'd been entirely away. There were always letters, gossipy travelogues, from here and there, as he drifted across the political landscape, the "standard bearer" and "titular leader" of the Democratic Party, the opposition voice to President Eisenhower. The days of romance between the two seemed long past, with Stevenson now happily attended, in various ways, by what seemed like a touring company of geisha-like society women, Ruth Field, Marietta Tree, Jane Dick. Instead of lovers' billets-doux from "Dear Rat" to "Dear Cockroach," there remained a steady, almost businesslike friendship. Stevenson himself seemed to have put aside his congenital ambivalence and indecision about running for president, and after the congressional midterms in 1954, when the Democrats picked up more seats, he professed himself eager to take on Eisenhower in the 1956 election. "I think I can do it," he wrote Patterson in January 1955. "I know I can do it. Arthur (Schlesinger) says Ike is a hollow man and I agree." In fact Stevenson's second presidential campaign had its unofficial beginnings at a November 17, 1955, gathering at Patterson's Georgia retreat, when she hosted Governor Stevenson, his new campaign manager, the Chicagoan Willard Wirtz, and several others, for a five-day planning session, during which he wrote his first three speeches.

Three years earlier, partly from her belief in Eisenhower's potential for leadership, also partly after being pressured by Harry, she had officially committed *Newsday* to endorse Ike for president, despite her many-layered feelings for Stevenson. This time around, disappointed by what she saw as Eisenhower's muddled leadership in office, also by his reliance on his intransigent secretary of state, John Foster Dulles, she felt free to support Stevenson, both personally and with her ever-more-substantial newspaper. "Of course you can do it," she wrote him after the Georgia meeting. "This is your moment. . . . Just don't get pushed around by pols and polls. . . . To thine own self be true!"

But as the months of the presidential race began to unfold, Stevenson's moment once again proved elusive; indeed in many ways his 1956 campaign turned out to be a rockier road than 1952. For one thing, the folksy Kentucky senator Estes Kefauver made the Democratic primary race uncomfortably close, causing Stevenson to blur his own message in finally gaining the nomination. For another, while it was true that Stevenson had shed much of his personal indecisiveness, his actual campaign performance lacked focus

Alicia lunches with Adlai Stevenson, the two-time Democratic candidate for president, at the United Nations, 1956.

and consistency, and his campaign staff, burdened with academics and well-meaning intellectuals, often suffered from a disorganization and amateurishness bordering on the dysfunctional. Throughout the heated electioneering months of late summer and early fall, Patterson and her editorial writer, Clurman, watched with dismay as Stevenson's numbers fell farther behind Eisenhower's; then with greater dismay as Stevenson sought to reverse the drift by personally attacking Eisenhower on age and health issues, when the sitting president's personal popularity was still unassailably high. All the while *Newsday*'s editorials and coverage fought hard for the Democratic program and Stevenson in an important crossover market. At the end, when it came time for the paper's official endorsement, Patterson thought to play fair by instructing Clurman to write competing endorsements, one for Eisenhower, the other for Stevenson, and then choosing between them. Needless to say, when she chose the Stevenson endorsement it surprised nobody, save perhaps her husband, copublisher, majority owner, Harry Guggenheim, who hadn't been consulted in the matter, and who as an active and loyal Republican assumed that his paper would once again support Eisenhower.

· 68 ·

THE STEVENSON 1956 ENDORSEMENT caused a huge ruckus between the Guggenheims. Not that *Newsday*'s support made an appreciable difference one way or the other: Eisenhower easily won a second term, by a wider margin than in 1952, with Stevenson's campaign collapsing badly in the final weeks, not helped by the Democratic candidate's controversial speech in Boston's Faneuil Hall suggesting that Eisenhower might not live out another term in office. But it turned out that Harry had made a very personal promise of an Eisenhower endorsement to Leonard Hall, chairman of the Republican Party, also a neighbor, friend, and prized political contact, and he was now doubly furious at his wife, first for endorsing Stevenson without consulting him, let alone asking for his approval (which of course they both knew he wouldn't have given), second for making a fool of him with his big-shot political pal Len Hall.

In the wake of Stevenson's defeat, Patterson, not surprised, though surely disappointed by it, had taken herself down to her hideaway in Kingsland, Georgia, there to stomp about the piney woods, maybe shoot a few quail, drive her speedboat upriver to inspect the cormorants and gators; which is where Harry Guggenheim finally reached her by telephone, after two days of leaving unreturned messages, early one November evening, around the dinner hour. Guggenheim was calling from his own decidedly more baronial establishment at Cain Hoy, roughly two hundred miles to the north, and while no record exists of who said what to whom in that exchange, a record probably wouldn't much matter since Harry always made such a point, especially when angry, of never raising or even changing the inflection of his voice. In essence Harry's brief message to Alicia, surely delivered in his famously, maddeningly toneless baritone was that he wished to see her and would send a little plane to bring her to Cain Hoy. Alicia's equally brief response was that if he wished to see her badly enough, he should get in his little plane and fly down to Kingsland. Harry apparently agreed, whereupon Alicia hung up the phone, then picked it up again, called her assistant, Dottie Holdsworth, on Long Island, and begged her to hie herself down to Kingsland on the next flight.

In the course of their marriage the Guggenheims had evolved an almost Kabuki-like choreography for their fights. Usually it was Harry who made the first move, advancing some complaint or criticism in his cold, civilized voice, which grew ever colder as it became clear that Alicia, far from volunteering to join him in his debating arena of choice, had chosen instead to toss combative, conversational hand grenades in his direction as a form of rebuttal. This seems to have been what more or less occurred in Patterson's house by the St. Mary's, with its faded chintz sofa, large brick fireplace (an Audubon print of wild turkeys hanging above it), with Alicia seated in her favorite armchair, one leg tucked beneath her, doubtless with an ashtray within reach, filled with half-smoked cigarettes, and a nearby tumbler of bourbon.

On this occasion, as Dottie Holdsworth recalled, Harry's maddening manly reasonableness came with a prepared script; she remembered him standing in front of the fireplace, reading aloud from a piece of paper, some kind of document, a list of grievances typed out earlier (perhaps by a secretary in Cain Hoy or New York, since Harry wasn't fond of typing). As he read slowly from the list in his professorial monotone, Alicia, cast as the misbehaving student, seethed in her own kind of noisy silence, expelling puffs of smoke from her Marlboro; when he reached the issue of the Stevenson endorsement, or in his words, "your total betrayal, of both trust and policy" (about number three on his enumerated list of complaints), Patterson began growling, a low, rasping sound as Holdsworth remembered, gathering in volume; and then, as "Harry went on and on, berating her for this and that, disregarding his advice, spending too much money, but mostly about disrespect, disrespect from her, disrespect from the staff, 'a continued campaign of disrespect by the people whose salaries I pay,' she finally slammed her whiskey glass down on the metal tray, a loud bang, and said 'All right, that's it, I want a divorce!' and probably much else since lost to recollection." Dottie did, however, remember what Harry—now seated stiffly at the far end of the sofa—replied: "If you divorce me, you'll lose *Newsday*."

Another feature of the Guggenheim battles was once described by the journalist Hal Burton, a frequent guest at Falaise: "Harry and Alicia could be so charming together, one of those dance teams that could do all the right steps with their eyes closed, when they wanted to . . . but sometimes it was hard to know what was coming next . . . it was like being on one of those beaches where, one moment, the water's calm, the waves rippling quietly, then the next moment there's this violent storm, thunder, lightning, the works, and then just as suddenly it's over, the water's calm again, the waves are back to rippling quietly." This is what seemed to happen after the dramatics in Georgia; for a while all was calm again, the waves rippled quietly, life went on as if nothing had happened. Alicia joined Harry at Cain Hoy for a family Christmas, which included several of his grown children and went off without a hitch, with one of his daughters, Nancy Draper, later writing Patterson about how she "seemed so good and good-humored" with her often-difficult father.

As the new year 1957 began, Harry had numerous irons in the fire to distract him, notably his efforts, as an important new member of the Jockey Club, to reform and revitalize New York horse racing; also his continuing challenges in trying to steer the Solomon R. Guggenheim Museum to completion. Patterson, too, had plenty to occupy herself with at *Newsday*, breaking in new editors, pushing back at New York papers trying to nudge into Long Island. But soon it became clear that this time, not far beneath the surface calm, the business-as-usual accommodations of the Guggenheim ménage, something different was going on.

Harry was the first to take his grievances to a lawyer, and his choice of legal counsel, Leo Gottlieb, the formidable managing partner of the prestigious Cleary Gottlieb firm, was an indication that the Guggenheims' problems had moved beyond the dimensions of a routine marital spat. It turned out that Harry's typewritten list of grievances had not been set aside, forgotten about; on the contrary, with the assistance of Mr. Gottlieb, his original complaints had since expanded, were now more tightly argued and translated into impressive legalese, and on April 11 were hand-delivered to Patterson in the form of a nine-page "legal memorandum." Guggenheim's criticisms were along two main fault lines: first, Patterson's persistent "lack of respect" for "HG's numerous, significant contributions to the success of *Newsday*," a disrespect that took such forms as, "refusing to acknowledge HG's importance in the presence of the staff," and went so far as "to cause HG's name to be removed from the masthead . . . without consultation or agreement"; second, Patterson's misuse of her own editorial power, as in "APG persistently allowing her personal desires, ambitions and friendships . . . to influence what should be impartial editorial positions . . . based on sound, objective judgment." Patterson had guessed a brickbat was coming her way, and on the advice of a friend, Lester Markel, senior editor of the *New York Times*, had recently hired her own lawyer, Louis Loeb, general counsel for the *Times*. But as luck would have it, she was already on her way out of town, far out of town, due to leave on April 13, in two days, to join Adlai Stevenson and eleven others on an eight-week tour of Africa. She had time to send HG's sour, oppressive document over to Louis Loeb's office, get her travel vaccinations, malaria pills, figure out what to pack and not to pack, and head for the airport.

· 69 ·

IT MIGHT BE SAID that Patterson had been in on the start of these airborne "fact-finding missions," as they came to be called, when twenty long years earlier, in 1935, she'd accompanied her father in Max Beaverbrook's chartered de Havilland on a flying tour of prewar European capitals, cooling their heels in embassies, trying to chase down Fascist bigwigs. Since then, airplanes had grown bigger, faster, could fly across oceans; aerodromes were now airports; runways no longer strips of grass, with wind socks fluttering in the breeze, but ribbons of asphalt, with new radio-based traffic controls. Patterson too was in many ways an improved version of the not-quite-educated, scrappy daughter who'd tagged along with Poppa. By now she knew a thing or two herself, in fact quite a number of things of one sort or another, and if she wasn't quite a dominant newspaper figure of the stature of Joe Patterson or Sir Max, she was certainly an editor and publisher of substance. She was also, for better and worse, no longer the youthful, sturdy, tomboy-like female who never minded the wear and tear of travel to difficult places, no longer automatically "the girl" of the trip, the pal and pet of grown men, whose eyes she could always assume were on her even when they pretended to be looking elsewhere. This time around she was an older woman, on her own, part of a larger group, with plenty of competition for the attentions of her once-and-former suitor, the all too distractable Stevenson.

The traveling party assembled in Lisbon, Portugal, where Stevenson's friend, Marietta Tree, her husband, Sir Ronald Tree, and her smart and good-looking sixteen-year-old daughter, Frances FitzGerald, were vacationing in a rented villa. Among the others were Stevenson's law partner, William McCormick Blair, his glamorous wife, Deeda; an African expert and diamond merchant, Maurice Tempelsman; also Stevenson's favorite traveling companion, his pretty, lively, twenty-four-year-old daughter-in-law, Nancy Stevenson. From there they flew south in a chartered DC-4 to Johannesburg, capital of South Africa, at the time firmly in the hands of the Afrikaaners, digging themselves ever deeper into the pit of apartheid. Patterson's account of the trip (which she later published in six installments in *Newsday*) spoke of the grim prisonlike atmosphere in "J-burg," where "the black majority is confined to servitude and life in impoverished shantytowns . . . while the white minority is also imprisoned, in decided more comfortable fashion . . . behind barbed wire, in heavily guarded communities." On the other hand, thanks to Stevenson's presence, the American visitors were made much of by the remaining British colonists, notably Sir Harry Oppenheimer, chairman of the powerful De Beers diamond cartel, who was extravagantly hospitable to Stevenson and his friends, hosting numerous lunches and dinners, flying them for a weekend to his private game reserve, then south to the famous and notorious Kimberley mine, with its elevator drops five thousand feet beneath the surface of the earth, which Patterson insisted on riding down with Nancy Stevenson.

Next they flew north to Salisbury in Southern Rhodesia (now Zimbabwe), less visibly grim than Johannesburg, but with its own colonial disconnects: the smiling, white-uniformed face of British rule everywhere, Land Rover expeditions into more game parks and preserves, a fine polo match between two regiments of the British army, a banquet in honor of Governor Stevenson hosted by Governor General Sir Ian Smith, who toasted Stevenson as "an eloquent beacon of the rule of law," who in turn replied, toasting Sir Ian as "a wise leader who is taking this great mixed-race nation as fast but no faster than wisdom dictates it should be taken to an eventual goal of self-rule." Then north again in their noisy, droning DC-4, first putting down in Zanzibar on the coast; then inland, with lengthy stops in Tanganyika, Uganda, Kenya, all British Crown Colonies, where more governors, high commissioners, also Anglican bishops, and endless colonial officials provided an unbroken sequence of luncheons, dinners, even a black-tie ball at Government House in Nairobi, with fox-trots and waltzes provided by an all-white British dance band flown down from Cairo. "If you stay close to the Colonial Circuit," Patterson wrote later, "it's easy to get the

Smartly dressed for transatlantic air travel,
Alicia about to board a TWA Constellation
for Madrid, on her way to Africa.

impression that Africa is populated mainly by whites who speak Oxbridge English, with a background chorus of black-skinned men and women, some of whom manage the heavy lifting in town, while others can be glimpsed out in the countryside, in the course of a carefully supervised excursion, crafting wooden statues and performing native dances." In Kenya she wrote of her introduction, "at the hands of a well-spoken, boyish, British Army major . . . to several men in colorful caftans and little head caps . . . whom he described as lately imprisoned leaders of the Mau-Mau rebellion . . . who had just completed a program of 'moral rehabilitation.' " In Uganda: "We were promised yesterday a meeting with three African political leaders . . . who showed up today, escorted by the Deputy Commissioner, each expressing gratitude to their British rulers, some of us thought in better English than employed by the Deputy Commissioner, since they had apparently been to a better English university."

Around the third week the group left behind the relative comforts of the chartered DC-4, and switched to ancient Chevrolets, as they continued west toward the Congo, bumping down a long unpaved road, past the Mountains of the Moon, then on even rougher roads as they made their way beneath the great tree canopies of the Ituri Rainforest. Along the way Patterson conscientiously scribbled notes about pygmy villages, more native dances, grazing elephants, a legendary French "white hunter," in whose camp they spent the night, and whose "air of casual glamour," as she wrote, "was somewhat offset by his having just shot himself in the foot." By this stage of the journey Patterson was experiencing several challenges. First, she was feeling less and less well; not the usual intestinal complications of the tropics, but something unspecific, weakening, wearying, perhaps something she'd picked up, she told Nancy Stevenson, the day they'd ridden that steel-cage elevator a mile deep into the hot-cold darkness of the Kimberley mine. She was enough of a veteran traveler not to complain or look for special treatment, knowing none was available; on the contrary, as was her nature, she gamely pushed forward as if nothing was the matter, just a little tired she might say, all too aware that her younger female traveling companions were soldiering on each day—no matter the heat, insects, various discomforts—as if on holiday.

Her other problem, more of an intermittent headwind, was surely not helped by being self-conscious about health, nor by inevitable feelings of competition brought on by daily proximity to younger women, no matter how much they may have genuinely liked and admired her. But as the trip grew longer (even though she was no stranger to long, grueling travel in difficult places), she found it harder to be the person she always liked to think she was: a good sport no matter where or what, a team player. In fact more and more she found herself at odds with the team leader, everybody's beloved "Guv," and while for the most part she kept her alienation to herself, offstage, nonverbal, her notebooks begin to show a barely hidden tone of criticism, a definite impatience at Stevenson's sometimes all-too-facile balancing act, always trying to be a polite, responsive guest at the banquet tables of some of Africa's more authoritarian colonial powers. Not that Patterson herself, in 1957, was in any vanguard of postcolonial thought, or that Stevenson, twice a presidential candidate, and while in Africa still in the public eye, had much room for maneuver. However, as she wrote in one of her notebooks: "It's one thing to talk, with that eloquence which AES does so well, better than anyone, of the need for time in transitioning to native governance, which is obviously what our hosts so much want to hear . . . but do we really need to sound so agreeable, so easygoing about it, and with population ratios everywhere nearly ten-to-one in favor of the blacks . . . it's hard to see where time is coming from."

They spent three steamy days in the Belgian Congo, Joseph Conrad's "Heart of Darkness," mostly in Leopoldville, named after the late Belgian monarch famous for his hand-lopping policies, where Belgian missionaries showed off their school for native children (in one of whose classrooms, twenty or so school-uniformed young Congolese were being taught about Charlemagne), and later, where a brigade of beefy, beshorted Flemish paratroopers, with plenty of rifles and even a few howitzers for good measure, paraded in the stunning heat before Governor Stevenson and the colonial high command. Then across the famously water-hyacinth-clogged Congo River to French Equatorial Africa, and its capital, Brazzaville, where the colony's tiny, fierce Gouverneur Général Léon Pétillon produced the finest banquet of the trip, two hundred guests, mostly European, barrels of Bélon oysters, fresh *asperges*, and a dance band this time flown in from Paris. As Patterson noted: "The Guv's speech brought the house down, as expected, when he made his Father Knows Best remarks, the need to avoid chaos, not to be driven by artificial timetables . . . 'only you know what is best for Africa.' "

While in "Brazza," the travelers heard they had been given a much-anticipated go-ahead for a visit to Lambaréné; this being the site of the little jungle clinic on the Ogone River (four hours west, in the French colony of Gabon) where the saintly Dr. Albert Schweitzer had been ministering to the natives for close to fifty years. At the time Schweitzer enjoyed a huge, iconic, almost mystical reputation in the West as a selfless, wise, providential caregiver to Africans, a paragon of virtue as well as medicine, recipient of the Nobel Peace Prize, *Time*'s "Man of the Year," and so on. For many in the Stevenson group a visit to the "great humanitarian" (as he was invariably referred to in the American press) was viewed as a highlight of the trip. The DC-4 landed downriver, on a dusty, grassy runway shared with grazing goats and scrawny cows (as young Frances FitzGerald noted in her journal), after which the travelers were driven in a couple of beaten-up trucks, plus a new Land Rover lately donated by an American philanthropist, to the doctor's clinic.

Once there, a couple of things became immediately evident to many in the group. First, it was indeed a little jungle clinic, nothing fancy or pretentious; a jumble of outbuildings, some of which were being used for medicine, others for chicken coops and other farmyard activities. Second, the level of medicine being practiced by the good doctor and his mostly native staff seemed astoundingly primitive; not picturesquely country-doctor primitive but often slovenly, unsanitary, in places downright filthy. Third, although Schweitzer went about in his grimy doctor's smock, not the starched, gold-braided uniform of a colonial ruler, his attitude toward his black patients seemed painfully brusque, condescending, bordering on disdain. Patterson, along with most of her traveling companions, noticed right away the striking contrast between Lambaréné's myth and reality, but once again Stevenson seemed to insist on seeing only what he wanted to see, trailing humbly after the great humanitarian as he made his rounds, clipboard in hand, kicking chickens out of the way in the operating room. On their last day at the clinic, Patterson finally lost it with the Guv, asking him furiously if he'd noticed *anything*—not only the farmyard rags all over the dispensary, the chickens in the operating room, the chicken shit all over the tables and floors, the way the saintly doctor literally pushed and shoved patients out of the way, cursing at them in German? As Patterson later remembered it, Stevenson smiled tolerantly at her, as if she were a wayward child, and then told her proudly of his "personal moment" with Schweitzer: how he and the good doctor had been deep in conversation about world peace, a subject needless to say dear to both men, when a tiny insect had landed on Stevenson's jacket. At which point he had made, or rather had begun to make, a typical Westerner's move to brush it off, flick it away—gnat, anopheles mosquito, what have you?—but Schweitzer had reached across and stayed his hand, remarking gravely, "All life is precious." (Not surprisingly this same "All life is precious" insect-protection-routine of the great doctor's turns up in numerous memoirs of Westerners in Lambaréné.) "How *can* you question such a man?" the Guv said to her.

· 70 ·

PATTERSON LEFT THE TRIP one week early, in Ghana, pleading sickness, which was true; also true was her growing worry that, in her seven weeks' absence from the office, Harry Guggenheim would have been unable to resist laying his heavy hand on *Newsday*. But the good news on her return was that Harry's touch had been relatively light: though he had vetoed one proposal from Clurman to expand the paper's business coverage (thinking the idea too specialized for suburban readers), in general he had left Hathway, Clurman, and Patterson's other deputies free to do their jobs.

The bad news was that nothing much had changed in Harry's opposition to his wife's modus operandi, her approach to their supposedly shared business. The complaints raised in the "legal memorandum" were still on the table, had not magically disappeared while she was out of town, traveling in Africa with her friend Stevenson; in fact in some respects his antagonism had hardened. One week after her return, Patterson and Guggenheim had another sizable row, this time over another of Harry's self-described constructive proposals: that they hire a polling and market research company, Gallup, Inc., to survey *Newsday* readers, by telephone or going house to house, in order to find out "in more exact, scientific fashion . . . what information . . . which stories, reports, features . . . our subscribers would want to read about in the newspaper." When Patterson adamantly said no, Harry wrote plaintively to Gottlieb: "This is altogether typical of APG's disrespect and ongoing refusal to accept businesslike proposals." Patterson in turn scoffed and fumed in a letter to *her* lawyer, Louis Loeb: "HG describes himself as a newspaper publisher but clearly has no idea what an editor does . . . an editor is supposed to be out in front of the paper's readers[,] not trailing behind studying poll numbers."

As with many scuffles between husbands and wives, from a certain distance the Guggenheims' conflict could easily be replayed as comedy. But for both of them, close up, it was often a sad and painful time, marked by sharp words and silences, by frigid meetings and heated exits (as when Patterson decamped for several weeks to the house of her friends Phyllis and Bennett Cerf of Random House), and by the shared cloud of defeat that is bound to overhang a couple communicating largely through lawyers. There were moments when a compromise appeared possible. In early October, Patterson agreed to support Harry's "mission statement" for *Newsday*, and soon afterward restored his name to the masthead. But in the next breath, she gave Clurman the go-ahead to publish a political cartoon sharply making fun of President Eisenhower (for being outmaneuvered by the Soviet space program), which Harry considered both unfair and a personal insult, accusing her (via Gottlieb) of "undermining the effectiveness of the President," and once again they were at a standoff.

Over the years, what had consistently rankled Patterson, stuck in her craw, was Harry's dug-in-at-the-heels refusal to cede her full autonomy with *Newsday*—Harry the ruler of the vast Guggenheim empire; *Newsday* such a small piece of it to him, so huge, so everything, to her. But with time passing, with Harry's need for control seeming only to grow stronger not weaker, Patterson could see that this problem was in some ways becoming worse; he not only seemed no closer to selling her his 2 percent, but in fact was pushing for greater control, for using his majority ownership to run the paper his way; his politics, his ideas, his Gallup polls. In early November she wrote Josephine she was "close to throwing in the towel." Later in the month, she went down to Georgia, alone and sad, stomped around in the chill, damp beautiful woods, then typed out a draft letter of resignation from *Newsday*, to take effect on January 1, 1958. "Effective today," she wrote, "I am resigning as editor & publisher of *Newsday*. It is the most painful announcement I have ever had to make, for *Newsday* has been my life's work and I am immeasurably proud of it. But my decision has been painfully simple. . . . We have prospered rather than suffered this far under the theory that journalistic independence and integrity precede purely business consideration. . . . I have chosen to resign because I cannot be part of transforming a living newspaper put out by journalists into a balance-sheet controlled by businessmen." She mailed a copy to Louis Loeb, then decided to stick around in Kingsland and wait for 1957 to run out.

A few days before the end of the year, however, she seems to have called her own bluff, phoning Louis Loeb in New York and asking if something couldn't be worked out. Loeb promptly phoned Leo Gottlieb, who reached Harry Guggenheim in Cain Hoy. The solution that the various great minds came up with was surprisingly simple, brief, and almost anticlimactic after all the Sturm und Drang: a compromise, a peace treaty, not even put in writing or framed in legalese. In the end HG and APG ended their war on a strangely simple, two-part verbal agreement: first, that Harry Guggenheim might express his own views on the editorial page but only above his own signature; second, that at his death, his 2 percent majority would pass directly to Alicia Patterson. Not specified in the agreement, though by no means an afterthought (and generally regarded by all concerned as key to the solution), was the understanding that the young prince, Dick Clurman, would soon be gone from *Newsday*.

· 71 ·

PATTERSON TURNED FIFTY-TWO in 1958, in those days definitely middle-aged, more than middle-aged, certainly a far cry from today, when between sheer youth and senescence there appears to stretch an endless, mostly abstract zone of no age at all. In Patterson's day a woman's fifties was a time for "cutting back," notably on "activities," though in those balmy middle years of the American Century there were few fifty-two-year-old American women, at least in Patterson's social strata, whose "activities" took them much beyond the bridge or canasta tables, or the country club, or shopping and the awkward, begirdled, high-heeled walking that went with it. As always, or whenever possible, Patterson marched herself to a different drummer. While growing up (granted, a lengthy process) as a child of privilege, she had known she was getting a free ride out there in the important world—the world of power, achievement, significance, that almost entirely male world—by hanging on to Poppa's coattails. But over time, and with a little help from HG, she had made a place for herself in that world; she was now one of the very few women publishers, women newspaper editors, women chief executives—CEOs they soon would be called.

As such she took a growing pleasure in being "out there" in the big world, serving on boards, giving speeches, having her opinion sought and published. Equally she appeared to relish what was for her a fairly new activity: introspection, reflection, being alone with her thoughts. Increasingly she traveled south, disappearing into the riverine privacy of her woodsy acreage on the St. Mary's, sometimes with the few friends who "got" the place, for instance George Abbott, the tall, lanky stage and film director with whom she liked to play her fiercely competitive, scramble-for-every-point brand of tennis, then shoot the breeze, drink whiskey as the sun went down. But mostly she went there on her own, happy to walk the woods for hours on end, with the company of Sunbeam, her golden Lab, trotting beside her through eye-filling stands of loblolly pine stretching in every direction; or out in the boat, usually late in the day, those flat pastel hours before sunset, humming upriver over the glassy coffee-colored water, past miles of mangrove, alligators sleeping on the banks, snakes and turtles in the shallows, keeping her sharp eyes alert for the cormorants, egrets, ospreys, blue and (ever-so-rare) white herons she loved to share the river with.

One of her friends described this period of her life as her Epictetus phase: Epictetus being the second-century Greek philosopher who evolved his own version of Stoicism, devotedly if selectively admired across the centuries by such as Marcus Aurelius, Voltaire, Matthew Arnold, J. D. Salinger. Patterson, a lifelong voracious reader (after all, expelled from boarding school at sixteen for having a forbidden copy of *Anna Karenina*), usually maintained a strong Pattersonian aversion to intellectual pretensions, as well as to being preached at or "improved"; nonetheless she had discovered Epictetus at the prompting of a professor friend, while sitting in at one of the early sessions of the Aspen Institute, and found as much to her surprise as anyone's that the old Greek's teachings spoke to her at a compelling level. As a result she now traveled everywhere with a volume of his *Discourses* near at hand, though after too many books lost or left behind en route, she eventually settled on a permanent copy she kept on the table beside her bed in Kingsland. But perhaps her attraction to Epictetus wasn't really so unexpected; the ancient philosopher whose teachings advised against "complaining or making a public display of suffering," who sternly described "grief and pity" as "acts of evil against the soul," was really just another in a long line of voices she had been hearing since childhood, telling her to stop whining, toughen up, and get it together. At any event the little leather-bound volume of Epictetus's *Discourses* remained with her the rest of her life, well thumbed, even underlined.

· 72 ·

AND THEN THERE WAS the trip to Russia, another Stevenson adventure. This was Russia aka the Soviet Union, still secretive, hostile, seemingly as dangerous in its post-Stalin period as before. Ostensibly Stevenson was going there for lawyerly reasons, his trip underwritten by a new client, William Benton of *Encyclopaedia Britannica*, with the quixotic purpose of negotiating copyright agreements with the chronically uncooperative Soviets. But the Guv was still the country's most prominent Democrat, still a potential candidate for president two short years away in 1960; and the Cold War remained the nation's leading political issue. What better way of showing presidential leadership mettle than by journeying to the den of the Russian bear, being photographed with their scowling, enigmatic leaders and peace-desiring citizens?

Patterson and Stevenson by then seem to have traveled a long road from lovers to friends, with various detours and stumbles along the way. If she had irritated him on the African trip, he didn't seem to have noticed, and maybe he hadn't. When he first told her about the Russian expedition, hoping she would come along, she quickly wrote to Bill Blair, who as usual was in charge of the details, promising "at all times to be modest, amiable and prompt . . . causing not the slightest difficulty to anyone" if invited, which she was. Since departure was scheduled for late summer, she brought along her seventeen-year-old niece, Alice Albright. Stevenson took two of his sons, Borden and John Fell. Others were Bill Blair; Ruth Field, the widow of *Chicago Sun-Times* publisher, Marshall Field, and her daughter Fiona; Richard Tucker, a RAND Corporation Soviet analyst, listed as translator.

For anyone with a sense of history, to say nothing of a nose for news, this was an inherently dramatic time to be visiting the Dark Continent of the Soviet empire. A new premier had lately been installed in the Kremlin, Nikita Khrushchev, alternately bellicose and loosely populist, but still a cipher to the West, his every statement and gesture much debated by Sovietologists. Eight months before the Soviets had surprised everyone, not least the Eisenhower administration, by launching the world's first space satellite, the famous Sputnik. There being no direct, or even indirect, airline flights between the United States and USSR, the Stevenson group flew to London, then Helsinki, then into Leningrad, where they were met at the airport by a cortege of Soviet officials and conveyed in tanklike ZIS limousines into the former czarist capital, which Patterson had last visited in 1938 with her father, in the depths of the Stalin era.

The scarcity of airline flights to the USSR was a logical result of the scarcity of tourists, which in turn was due to the almost-congenital Soviet hostility to visitors. It was pointedly difficult to obtain a visa to visit, and once there the government made normal tourism nearly impossible: no wandering around on one's own, no random photography. Patterson had her own ostensible mission on the trip, to write a series of reports on "Life in the USSR," to be published and syndicated by *Newsday*; accordingly she'd thought up a clever way around Soviet censorship, by giving her young niece a tiny camera for the express purpose of snapping under-the-radar pictures of, who knows, secret military stuff, prisons, new space satellites. True, the government minders were everywhere, in the guise of Intourist guides, hotel clerks, even the grim old female "concierges" on every hotel floor, who wrote down in ledgers, like Dickensian bookkeepers, who was arriving, leaving, which room, exactly when, and so on. Unsurprisingly these same minders kept the visiting Americans on rigid, well-defined sightseeing routes, day by day a wearying round of museums, public parks, public buildings in general, especially schools, given that Minister Stevenson was so interested in education.

After Leningrad the group was taken, in the shabby, dusty, almost pleasurable overnight sleeper, to Moscow, where they were installed in the grimy marble splendor of the old Hotel Metropol: the same "concierges" on all the floors, the same ledgers; downstairs, a huge, empty dining room with dim lighting, two waiters in frayed jackets, and impressive, old-fashioned menus, though with most of the items crossed out. In the morning the American visitors would be summoned to the lobby by a new set of identical dark-suited Intourist guides, and led like reluctant children (though too well-mannered to show their reluctance) on a new circuit of museums, more parks, of course more schools, also a puppet version of the *Nutcracker* ballet and a circus, as Patterson later described it, "with many many bears."

Wherever Stevenson showed his face in Russia, his vigilant hosts made sure he was greeted as a visiting dignitary of great stature, the opposition presidential candidate who had campaigned in favor of fewer H-bombs and missiles, greater trust in the USSR, and as such was fawned and fussed over by layers of Soviet officialdom. Stevenson, for his part, tried to tread a careful path between being a responsive visitor, willing to listen to his hosts (in contrast to the belligerent, hectoring, nonlistening of Secretary of State John Foster Dulles), and appearing as yet another Democrat soft on Communism, his every public outing and statement closely witnessed by the sizable cadre of Moscow-based Western journalists and photographers, who clearly had nothing better to do. But even the Guv's well-honed gifts for being a polite guest—sometimes no matter the circumstances or context (as in colonial Africa)—were put to the test by the clumsily primitive Soviet propaganda machine. For instance, on most every visit to schools, museums, innumerable "institutes," Stevenson and his traveling companions would be greeted, on the sidewalk and in the street, by placard-waving throngs of obviously government-hired "welcoming citizens," chanting slogans of peace and opposition to "U.S. warmongering." After a while the normally mild-mannered Stevenson began ordering his driver to drive right through the crowds, scattering the "Greeting Committees," with their identical placards and sullen singsong, as Patterson wrote, "in a decidedly illiberal Cossack manner."

In her own responses to what she saw in the USSR, Patterson didn't exactly switch roles with Stevenson, who as a presidential candidate, twice opposing Eisenhower, had argued for greater trust of the Soviet Union. Patterson never shared the Guv's predilection for trusting the Soviets, for unilateral disarmament, for what she once described as a "too gentlemanly disposition to compromise when there were no other gentlemen in the room," all of which struck her as dangerous. But in her growing disappointment with the conservative anti-Communist obsessions of the Eisenhower administration, she had developed her own aversion to what she saw as a mostly knee-jerk, anti-Soviet state of mind that seemed fast becoming conventional in the American mainstream.

Thus, in the five long articles on her Russian trip she published in *Newsday*, she took a forthright and for the time fairly original line on life in the Soviet state, describing, along with reports of shortages and Soviet obduracy, the many improvements she had noticed since her last visit in 1938. For instance: "The Iron Curtain was officially named in 1950, but it was never so heavy as in the grim years of Stalin's long reign of terror. . . . Today, consumer goods are scarce, shoppers have to line up for groceries . . . but gone too are the liquidations, purges, those many visible signs of overt brutality. . . . It is only a visitor's observation but I would say that pervasive fear has been gradually replaced by wariness, skepticism, distrust . . . which is an improvement." She also went counter to the prevailing habit of belittling Soviet achievements by writing at length about recent Soviet advances in science and technology, as well as about expanding opportunities for women in the USSR. "In Russia," she noted, "where medical care is universal, free, though still backward . . . an impressive sixty percent of the doctors are women," adding tartly, "although when it comes to large numbers, America still remains statistically well ahead in . . . juvenile delinquency and high-school dropouts."

As with the African tour, the Russian trip was long and grueling, covering enormous distances (fifteen thousand miles overall), many time zones, in primitively equipped, comfort-free Aeroflot aircraft, whose perverse schedules invariably required them to depart at one or two in the morning. Mindful of her last experience, Patterson made it a point not to show fatigue even when she felt it, to move briskly, to keep her shoulders back, to be the first one down in the lobby for the morning tour, the first one in the dining room at mealtime. All the same it was a tough slog, even for a student of Epictetus, with nonstop travel, dawn-to-dusk sightseeing; not made any easier by the fact that, in the third week, Stevenson and the other men were whisked away by Soviet officials, flown several thousand miles eastward for a special tour of exotic, seldom-visited Tashkent and Uzbekistan, remote, predominantly Muslim provinces, deemed too genderically sensitive for visitation by American females. As a poor consolation, Patterson, her niece Alice, Ruth Field and daughter Fiona were packed off to cool their heels (and warm their skins) in the Black Sea town of Sochi, one of the new "workers' paradise" resorts, with its pebbly shoreline and beefy, white-skinned, sunbathing Russians, where the American women attempted to negotiate the challenges of nudist and seminudist beaches, with varying success.

The final stage of the trip was a three-day visit to Poland, an Iron Curtain country still under the thumb of the Soviets. Soon after their arrival in Warsaw, they were met at their hotel by *New York Times* correspondent A. M. Rosenthal, who said he was surprised to learn (from Patterson's niece) that Stevenson and his group had no plans to visit the relatively nearby Auschwitz concentration camp, and promptly went to Patterson urging that all of them, though especially Stevenson, make the trip. Patterson agreed and tried to persuade Stevenson, seeing that they had a free day on their schedule. But the Guv begged off, couldn't, wouldn't; he was too tired, didn't want to get sick. Naturally the more he ducked, the more Patterson pushed. "All I want to do is sit under an olive tree and watch the young people dance," he said more than once, quoting a line he probably thought came from somewhere else but was in fact from a popular movie. In the end Patterson let the Guv off the hook, or at least on his own hook, but pointedly took herself, her niece, and Stevenson's two sons to Auschwitz, to wander awhile in the remains of the awfulness, tour its newly opened "museum," paying their respects, as she told them, to the victims of the Holocaust; meantime, the Guv, for lack of olive trees, spent the afternoon on a nature walk, strolling in a pine forest outside Kraków with Ruth Field.

· 73 ·

BY NOW PATTERSON was something of a major player, not only an important publisher, an outspoken editor, also that even rarer *avis*, a female executive in a predominantly male world. Her opinions were sought, her public appearances noted, and if some doors were still closed to her—as a woman she was still excluded from the list of journalists invited to the prestigious annual "Gridiron Dinner" in Washington—many new ones were opening up. Hofstra University, a rapidly growing institution on Long Island, asked her to be a trustee, and she was instrumental in helping to find a new president. In New York, where the Guggenheim Museum had recently opened, with its controversial design and contentious new management, Harry Guggenheim, stepping briefly out of character, actually begged her to come on the board so she might bring her "people skills" to help sort out, preferably fix, some of the Guggenheim's early problems. As a museum board member, in those early days she met often with the gifted, opinionated architect, Frank Lloyd Wright, also with the erudite, opinionated James Johnson Sweeney, the museum's first director, neither man able to stand the other, both men on the verge of quitting in a fury, and somehow brought the two of them close enough together to get the museum's design finished and the first galleries installed. She was asked to give talks, addresses, lectures to audiences of knowledgeable men and women, always conscious of that empty space in her own curriculum vitae, of not herself having gone to college, achieved "higher learning." In October she journeyed to Cambridge, Massachusetts, the heart of the Ivy League, where she gave a packed auditorium of Radcliffe alumnae and undergraduates a brisk earful of her idiosyncratic brand of no-nonsense feminism. Provocatively titled "Can Women Afford a Career?" the speech showed her evolving views on the slow pace of female empowerment: "The reason everyone talks about it is that men hate taking orders from women, they've never had to do it, they don't want to do it now. Of course, that's prejudice plain and simple. Men need to get over that. . . . But at the same time women have sheltered behind their own strong biases and predispositions. . . . For centuries, women have been taught modesty, helplessness, even flirtatiousness as life tactics, and I think we need to get over that too . . . and it all takes time, doesn't it?" She then went over some of the familiar statistics: "Out of 1,700 newspapers in this country we find only sixty-seven women listed as editors . . . and only seven of these women edit papers with circulations over 20,000." But then Patterson took her audience on a somewhat unexpected ride, given that in those days, when fewer than one-third of female high school graduates went on to college, those who did were subjected to two opposing rallying cries: on the one hand those of the traditionalists, guardians of "family values," who insisted that a woman's place was in the home, side by side with (and if possible a little to the rear of) her breadwinner husband; on the other hand those of the new feminists, articulate and sometimes strident, who insisted to ambitious young women (for instance, Radcliffe undergraduates) that they should and could "have it all."

Patterson characteristically took her own tack. "For those of you who are used to thinking in terms of wicked men versus long-suffering women," she told her audience, "let me suggest another way of looking at things. . . . If a woman can't make up her mind whether she wants a career more than marriage, then maybe she shouldn't expect equal consideration in the job market . . . with a man who will stay on the job whether married or single." And: "To have a career is a splendid thing but be advised that it can be a lonely life. It requires sacrifice, and the more important the career almost surely the bigger the sacrifice. . . . To put the thing in plain English, you have to really *want* it." And: "In the end it's not about the degrees you earn, it's about the fire within you, the ambition. If you have it, then nothing is impossible. Go forth and do battle in the male jungle. But if as a woman you're ambivalent, you're not sure, you're on the fence . . . then perhaps our world might be better off if such a woman can proudly accept her sex and the responsibilities that go with it."

· 74 ·

ANOTHER BIG MEDIA SPLASH came in the *Saturday Evening Post*, one of the few remaining giants of print, with close to five million in biweekly circulation. The five-thousand-word piece, a profile in the form of an extended interview, was written by an old friend, the journalist Hal Burton, and titled, *This Is the Life I Love*, "by Alicia Patterson as told to Hal Burton." There she is, in a large black-and-white photo, on one of the magazine's outsize pages: eyeglasses slightly askew atop her head, flecks of gray in her hair, furrows on her forehead; a smart inquisitive face, maybe a bit worn and wary, dark eyes staring right back at the reader.

In long columns of text, the story she told was casual, confident, an often surprisingly personal account of her life as she then seemed (or chose) to remember it, going back to early times, childhood; which, as we have seen, had actually played out in the shadow of alienated, warring parents, with a succession of nannies, *mam'selles*, *Fräuleins*, shifting domiciles, to say nothing of being shipped back and forth across the wide Atlantic, installed in pensions, hotels, boarding schools, institutions of lower and medium learning, Berlin, Lausanne, Rome; all of which jumbled, tumbled narrative she now breezily replayed for the benefit of Hal Burton as a mostly picaresque fable, with her own long-gone, youthful self reimagined as a kind of ugly-duckling antiheroine ("As a child I was not attractive, my hair a mess, my face often sulky"), a trial and burden to both parents and teachers ("I was rarely on time, had no patience for schoolrooms, schoolwork . . . don't know why anyone put up with me"). Of her early adult years, during which she had excelled as a horsewoman, big-game hunter, and pioneer aviatrix, she now wrote dismissively: "My specialty was little more than making a business out of pleasure, my days filled with pointless preoccupations." In six pages of print her mother received but a single mention: "Alice Higinbotham, whose father was president of the 1893 Chicago World's Fair." Sister Elinor was remembered for her "cold, withdrawn beauty and lovely hair"; though more kindly treated was sister Josephine ("We are as close as sisters can be"), also second husband, Joe Brooks, described as "a big-hearted aviator and all-around sportsman . . . who taught me much about the natural world." Not surprisingly the major focus of the article was on *Newsday*, its humble origins and hard-won successes. For the umpteenth time she described the little Hempstead car dealership, the cramped offices, the youthful staff, the bumptious pranks; the lengthy learning curve from amateurishness to scrappy journalism to substantial investigative exposés, in turn leading to awards, prizes, serious circulation numbers.

She was characteristically generous in praise of her staff, finding time and space to honor by name the contributions not only of top editors but also her business manager, comptroller, advertising manager, and even typographical designer. But once again, as if some bad magic stayed her hand whenever the opportunity arose to extend a comparable accolade to her copublisher and husband, to share parenting honors, so to speak, she simply couldn't or wouldn't get beyond a chilly muttering of faint praise; as in, "my husband Harry F. Guggenheim, a businessman and philanthropist, who believes everybody should have a job." More interesting, considering the bleak estrangement that once existed between Alicia and Joe Patterson at his death, was the warmth and intensity with which she now remembered her father: "A wonderful guy, big-hearted, tough, and born to understand what makes people tick; why they laugh and cry and hate and love, and why they buy some newspapers but ignore others," she told Hal Burton. "I gladly admit it, living up to Father, getting his praise, in whatever ways it sometimes came, was always my greatest ambition . . . being his companion was my only real education."

But along with these testaments of daughterly love, there was now a new note, a perhaps belated acknowledgment of a more problematic dimension to their intense relationship. "When I wasn't in trouble on my own," she recalled, "I seem to remember Father was usually brewing some up for me. Long after I had grown up, you could say that he continued to exert an almost hypnotic influence over me . . . and I would have died rather than fail him." Then she recounted the dangerous fishing trip she had made with him to Panama in 1929, when Joe Patterson (who knew she was recovering from surgery) had pushed her beyond her physical limits to the point of serious internal injury. "I sometimes wonder," she now wrote, with an almost childlike bewilderment, "if it might have been possible that Father felt an ambivalence towards me, a mixture of love as well as hate which somehow made him want to push my nervous system to the snapping point?" But even with that open-ended question on the page, she was still Poppa's girl (Who else's could she be?) and quickly backed away from where those thoughts might take her. "All I know," she briskly concluded, "is that it was Father who taught me to be unafraid, not an easy lesson to teach a scatterbrained girl." And not for the first time she retold the old family story about the Spartan boy and the fox—*his* story.

· 75 ·

ALICIA PATTERSON came from people (which is to say, family and forebears) who were no strangers to a number of U.S. presidents, beginning in those far-off, plainspoken, republican days before the White House became a fortress, its occupant a kind of emperor—not exactly friends; who after all is a friend to a president? At any rate some kind of familiar; a footnote in the histories, sometimes more than just a footnote.

First, and perhaps most vividly, had been her paternal great-grandfather, Joseph Medill, still a youngish man, not quite thirty, into whose cramped second-floor office, in the little *Chicago Daily Tribune*'s wood-frame building on State Street, one afternoon in May 1855, had appeared the elongated, ungainly form of the new congressman from the Seventeenth District, Abraham Lincoln, cash-money in hand as Joe Medill always told the story, wishing to sign for a subscription, then making it a point, each time he came up from Springfield, to drop in at editor Medill's office to shoot the breeze and talk a little politics. Medill, already one of the founders of the Republican Party, would soon become a Lincoln familiar (one of the original "Lincoln men" from Illinois), sometime useful adviser, sometime singleminded critic, and a frequent White House visitor until the president's death.

Three years after Lincoln, there was another Illinois downstater in the White House, a failed storekeeper though a more successful military man, Gen. Ulysses S. Grant. Medill and his wife, Kitty, by then prominent figures in Chicago society, found homespun President and Mrs. Grant hard going, but their older daughter, Kate, was the same age as Nellie Grant and the two girls became friends, with Kate a frequent White House visitor; there's an old photo of little Kate Medill, all frills and frowns, seated on President Grant's thick knees, in what is presumably the Oval Office.

Some years later, with Joe Medill by then an old man—bent over with arthritis, hard of hearing, with a foot-long ear trumpet, wintering in the humid warmth of Thomasville, Georgia—he was courted by another Midwestern congressman anxious for the presidency, William McKinley of Ohio. The Medills and the McKinleys became Thomasville friends after a fashion, sometimes taking "constitutional" walks with down-the-road neighbor Thomas Edison; the wives liked one another, more or less. Medill later threw his paper's support behind McKinley, though he never quite forgave McKinley for once refusing to attend an afternoon's Schubert musicale at the Thomasville Inn because the excessively pious Ohioan only allowed himself to listen to hymns.

When McKinley became president, Alicia's paternal grandfather, the ill-fated Robert Patterson (married to Joe Medill's younger daughter, Nellie), then editor of the *Chicago Tribune* as well as a bigwig in the Republican Party, became a frequent visitor to the McKinley White House; there's a photo of tall, handsome, seemingly straight-arrow Robert Patterson and short, glinty-eyed McKinley, seated together on what is probably the presidential yacht, sweating together in the sun, in white linen suits, with their celluloid collars tightly buttoned.

Robert Patterson was apparently on easier terms with a later president, William Howard Taft; he was regularly in and out of the Taft White House, close enough to the huge, mostly good-natured president to send him a lengthy unusually personal letter, essentially blocking an attempt by his bullying sister-in-law, Kate Medill McCormick (the one once sitting on President Grant's knees), to wangle an important ambassadorship for her McCormick husband, claiming *Tribune* support, which Patterson told Taft did not exist. The editor was on especially friendly terms with President Theodore Roosevelt, who once deployed a special presidential train to speed him from Washington to Cleveland in time for the wedding of Alicia's uncle, Medill McCormick. As a footnote, it was Uncle Medill who in 1912 proposed offering the editorship of the *Tribune* to Teddy Roosevelt; a project quashed by her father and her uncle Bertie McCormick, who admired Roosevelt but had their own plans for the paper. (Another family footnote: In 1927, during the presidency of Calvin Coolidge, when the White House had to be vacated for repairs, Alicia's aunt Cissy Patterson offered Coolidge her own Dupont Circle mansion as a substitute, which thus became the temporary White House for six months.)

As for the other Roosevelt, the Democratic Party's FDR, young Joe Patterson and the slightly younger Franklin Roosevelt had been boarding schoolboys together at Dr. Endicott Peabody's school in Groton, Massachusetts. They were not close in youth but later friends, or at least friendly, as Patterson threw his paper's support behind the New Deal, and Roosevelt was grateful for the support, the president and the publisher exchanging countless notes and letters over many years, with many invitations to the White House, summer weekends at Hyde Park, boat rides on the Potomac; until as we saw, Joe Patterson overplayed his hand as a freethinking isolationist (if that is what he was doing), and the relationship did not survive Pearl Harbor.

WHICH BRINGS US to a morning in April 1960, just before noon. A limousine drives up to the entrance of *Newsday*'s offices in Garden City, Long Island, and out steps a young—or at forty-three—still very much a youngish man, whose tousled hair, boyish face, and Boston-Irish-Harvard accent are fast becoming familiar to the country at large: Senator John Fitzgerald Kennedy, not yet president, though trying hard to be, for which he would first need the nomination of the Democratic Party, convening in Los Angeles in three months' time.

Ostensibly the purpose of Kennedy's pilgrimage to *Newsday*'s headquarters is to thank Alicia Patterson for her paper's so-far-friendly coverage of his presidential campaign, especially for its editorials arguing that his Roman Catholicism shouldn't be viewed by voters as an automatically disqualifying issue, not yet a mainstream position. But surely a secondary reason for Jack Kennedy's visit, in many ways his more-pressing mission, which is probably why he came alone, a busy man in the middle of a busy schedule, taking a hired car from New York's Carlyle Hotel to have lunch with a newspaper publisher out in the sticks of Long Island, was that this particular newspaper publisher, in addition to being able to deliver the numbers, the demographics, and so on, in an important market, was also a key voice in the ear of Adlai Stevenson.

The truth was that in the spring of 1960, Governor Stevenson, still the party's popular standard bearer, after two lost elections against the even-more-popular Eisenhower, had apparently not entirely abandoned the idea of a third attempt. Granted he had not yet formally announced; he had assembled no serious campaign staff; besides, he wasn't really campaigning; as he kept telling everyone, his hat wasn't in the ring. And yet he knew there were loyalists still out there, true believers, party faithful, with their "Madly for Adlai" buttons ready to be dusted off and pinned on again. Who could tell what might or might not happen at a deadlocked convention? For instance, a "Draft Stevenson" movement? Stranger things had happened at two in the morning, at deadlocked conventions. And if so, how could he refuse? This characteristic Stevensonian coyness drove the tough-guy Kennedy people crazy. All spring JFK had been pulling inexorably ahead of Minnesota's senator Hubert Humphrey, rapidly becoming the Democratic Party's front-runner; he was popular, a strong campaigner, the party bosses were behind him. However, the final outcome was still in doubt, with Catholicism always a divisive issue, and the Republican vice president Richard Nixon a formidable foe. Worried Kennedy staff kept asking how much longer the ambivalent, indecisive, aggravating Adlai Stevenson would stay on his fence, obviously not in the race and yet unwilling to endorse Kennedy.

With Patterson's brisk informality a good match for Kennedy's own polished casualness, she took him to lunch at Nino's, down the street from her office, bringing along a pack of reporters and editors to share the moment. Predictably the *Newsday* staff (including the often obstreperous Hathway, who remained sober and polite throughout the event), as well as its more-or-less worldly editor, were easily susceptible to the Kennedy charm, and the *Newsday* lunch ran on convivially for several hours. But when it came to the unofficial agenda, Patterson wasn't yet ready to lean on Adlai, to give up on the Guv. She liked Jack Kennedy, politically as well as personally, and told him as much; she said she thought he would make a good president. However, when a private moment occurred toward the end of the long lunch, with Kennedy pressing her for an endorsement, a public commitment (which might be especially useful in the signal it would send to Stevenson), at first she said nothing; then, as the reporter Bob Greene remembered it (and as noted in Robert Keeler's book *Newsday*), she told the young senator: "If anything happens out there, you're definitely my second choice."

· 76 ·

BY "OUT THERE," Alicia meant Los Angeles, site of the Democratic National Convention, already by mid-July its usual sun-bright, high-Fahrenheit, otherworldly self, the nation's recently tabulated Second City, lately edging past Chicago in population, though struggling through one of its periodic slumps, with the Big Studios in various stages of collapse and with Big Television not yet ready for prime time.

As it happened, the Stevenson campaign was also not ready for prime time, with its candidate still not publicly declared, and thus with no official status despite an influx of hundreds of bright-eyed Stevenson Volunteers, who swarmed the lobby of the stodgy downtown Biltmore Hotel (Democratic Party headquarters), where party managers, politely and otherwise, declined to provide office space for a noncandidate. By the Saturday before the convention opened, a solution of sorts had been found by the Volunteers, who took over the top floor of the abandoned Paramount Studios building, right across from the Biltmore on Pershing Square, and due to be demolished in a month's time, from whose grimy windows they unfurled a one-hundred-foot-long, hand-painted banner proclaiming "Stevenson For President" for the benefit of party stalwarts and conventioneers assembling at the Biltmore. Stevenson himself flew into town that weekend, accompanied by his eldest son, Adlai, Jane and Edison Dick, and Marietta Tree, all of whom put up in the pink-and-green, palm-and-stucco fineness of the Beverly Hills Hotel (a fair distance from the dreary downtown), with Stevenson himself installed in one of the hotel's famous poolside bungalows, where on Sunday afternoon he gave tea to Eleanor Roosevelt, FDR's eighty-four-year-old widow.

With the indomitable Mrs. Roosevelt ("the Conscience of the Party," as everyone was always describing her) out poolside in Beverly Hills—doing her earnest, queenly best to light a fire under

Stevenson, urging him to at least offer himself as a possible draft candidate to the convention delegates—some twenty miles away, in her cluttered hotel room in the Biltmore, Patterson was getting herself up to speed at what she'd long considered one of the great kicks of the newspaper business: working a convention, as it was called back in the days before those once shambly, sweaty, smoky, loosey-goosey political assemblies became sanitized and tightened up for television, when convention floors, hotel rooms, and corridors provided an unscripted, often rowdy, garrulous mass of delegates and mostly print reporters, on the prowl for stories, not sound bites. Patterson had brought *Newsday*'s political editor, three reporters, and a photographer with her to Los Angeles, whose assignments she was trying to sort out and orchestrate in the hit-or-miss fashion of those days before cell phones. She was also trying to figure out what, if anything, she might be able to do, at this late stage in the drama, to help her friend Adlai.

The truth of the matter, as she understood it, was that weeks before the convention opened, despite all the chanting Stevenson Volunteers, despite gallant Mrs. Roosevelt, despite the sentimental loyalty of some party elders, pretty much every poll and delegate count pointed to an almost certain Kennedy nomination, probably on the first ballot. Patterson herself had gamely stayed loyal to Stevenson through much of the spring, no matter how strongly Kennedy performed in the primaries. As late as May 31 she had signed an editorial endorsing Stevenson for president on the grounds that he was "most qualified to stand up to the totalitarian powers." But two days before the convention she had bowed to the inevitable, and without explicitly endorsing Kennedy (or ditching Adlai), she had signed another editorial, this time suggesting that "the ideal Democratic ticket would contain a promise of Adlai E. Stevenson for Secretary of State."

Stevenson "at State," a senior member of the new cabinet, wasn't such an unexpected or farfetched proposition. He and Patterson had discussed it often over the years, on their walkabouts in Georgia, in the course of long travels overseas, more notably since his last signal defeat in 1956, when it began to appear as a kind of theme in their endless chatty correspondence, with his finding a variety of thinking-out-loud ways of saying that State was a prize he would be happy to receive, not the Great Prize he had been vainly seeking for a decade but still a worthy satisfying substitute. After all, this was still the heyday of American internationalism, when foreign affairs, foreign policy, foreign news, foreign anything-and-everything was where the action was, the moral goal and career destination for so many of the nation's best and brightest. The question was, Could Stevenson now be realist enough, sufficiently decisive, to seize the chance if it was offered?

Granted, it hadn't yet been offered, but Patterson thought she had a plan, a way of moving the idea along in a manner of speaking. The Kennedys at the time were down the street, two blocks away, in the businesslike Roosevelt Hotel, all of them, Father Joe and Mother Rose, all the brothers, daughters, in-laws, assistants, advisers, a mighty army, taking up most of one of the big hotel floors. One of the *Newsday* reporters out in Los Angeles, Bob Greene, supposedly was on friendly terms with Kennedy's tough-guy younger brother and campaign manager, Robert Kennedy.

Late Sunday afternoon Alicia reached Greene by phone, asked him to find Bobby Kennedy in person, and find out on her behalf what it would take to guarantee the State Department job for Stevenson. Greene made his way to the crowded Kennedy suite at the Roosevelt, found Bobby Kennedy, and asked him Patterson's question. Neither then nor afterward was Bobby Kennedy much of a fan of Adlai Stevenson; moreover the Kennedy camp sensed victory, probably on the first ballot. And yet the Kennedys knew there might be problems: A Draft-Stevenson motion could gather momentum; Stevenson himself might siphon off some of the Illinois delegates. As narrated in Robert Keeler's book, Kennedy told Greene that the campaign could make no firm commitment to Stevenson, but if Stevenson swiftly and decisively withdrew his name as a potential nominee, then threw his support behind JFK, such a decision would certainly be viewed favorably by his brother.

Call it preference or habit, nature or nurture, Patterson was a woman who believed firmly in getting on with it, especially if *it* was something that so obviously needed decision. No sooner did she hear back from Bob Greene as to Robert Kennedy's response—not a definite yes, though not a no, apparently a serious maybe—than she lost no time in sending Greene out again into late-afternoon Los Angeles, now in a taxi speeding down the freeway to the Beverly Hills Hotel, with a hastily handwritten note for Stevenson, the gist of which was that she had just been in contact with Bobby Kennedy, and if Adlai still wanted a chance to be secretary of state, as she knew he did, he needed right then to get out of the race and back John Kennedy, and to do this soon, *now*.

But of course Stevenson's own temperament, equally well honed over the years (as was Alicia's), inclined him just as surely in an opposite direction, toward a determined (and what some had come to see as an almost pathological) avoidance of choice, an avoidance often made easier by the language of high-minded indecision. By the time Greene reached Stevenson's poolside bungalow, the governor was out or inaccessible, and so he left Patterson's letter in the care of a senior aide, with pressing instructions that Stevenson read it immediately when he came in. Then he returned to the Biltmore, where the lobby and corridors were buzzing with the increasing certainty of Jack Kennedy's nomination, and upstairs to where Patterson was waiting, if not for some personal response from Adlai, then at least for some indication on the nightly news that Stevenson had finally terminated his quixotic noncandidacy.

However, by the next morning, Monday, when the Democratic National Convention officially opened for business in the Los Angeles Sports Arena, it was clear from newspapers and news channels, by omission as well as commission, that there had been no change in Stevenson's position. Toward noon a letter was delivered to Patterson from "A.E.S." saying simply, "I know that Kennedy has the votes but in the end I couldn't disappoint Eleanor and Herbert who still think I have a chance, although I know I don't. I'm sure that Bobby and the Kennedy crowd will appreciate my situation."

To the extent that people remember the 1960 Democratic convention, they remember it first for the acclamation of the youthful, glamorous John Fitzgerald Kennedy (with beauteous Jackie beside him, and the whole Kennedy family entourage), and perhaps also for the Kennedy brothers' tough, offstage horse-trading that brought Lyndon Baines Johnson aboard as vice president. But then, in that zone between not quite forgotten and not really remembered, save as a strange elegiac footnote, was Adlai Stevenson's final appearance on the big political stage. On Tuesday night, in the lull before the nominating speeches, with nothing still theoretically decided, when Governor Adlai E. Stevenson of Illinois was introduced and stepped onto the platform, there erupted in the auditorium a literally unprecedented twenty-seven whole minutes of applause and cheers and waving placards and parading in the aisles; no one could remember the equal of such a demonstration, and the fact is there's never been one since. And then the Guv stepped to the microphone, almost hesitantly so it seemed, with the huge crowd expectantly hushed (with Patterson looking on from the press section, with the Kennedys in their hotel room watching on TV), and said in effect . . . nothing: a few softly graceful words of thanks, how touched he was, how undeserving and so on, and then made a small mild joke, and was gone, without so much as a murmur about the Kennedy tsunami that everyone knew was about to overwhelm the convention. Back in the Kennedy suite at the Roosevelt Hotel, Robert Kennedy was heard to say: "My God, the man still can't make up his rabbit-assed mind."

· 77 ·

PATTERSON WAS NOW FIFTY-SEVEN, not young, not that old, on the whole feeling pretty good; seemingly no more endemic, soul-sapping bouts of weakness, no more existential weariness. She still kept Epictetus by her bed in Georgia, though by now layered under other books, more a talisman to keep the room safe than a life preserver. Besides, she wasn't down in Kingsland all that much; one week in the fall, ten days in spring.

Mostly, she was busy.

Newsday was humming, still growing, achieving heft both in journalistic substance as well as circulation numbers. Profits also meant more and better hires, in all departments. Twice, or maybe more, she'd made up her mind to fire the rough-edged, still-incorrigible Hathway; but each time she'd backed away from getting rid of someone whose talk and walk and pretty much everything about him reminded her not only of her own paper's plainspoken origins but also of the rough-and-tumble "Front-Page" school of newspapering she'd grown up with. As a kind of compromise, she steadily signed on a cohort of young, smart, matter-of-factly college-trained journalists: editors who could think as well as make decisions, reporters who could cover local crimes as well as national stories.

Things were even okay, fairly stable, in the copublisher arena. True, the bitterly contested Kennedy-Nixon campaign hadn't made for an easy time, with Harry legally entitled to write and run (which of course he did) his horrible, sour, scaremongering pro-Nixon editorials on the very same page as her closely reasoned, New Frontier arguments for JFK; and it obviously didn't help things that the election had been so close, down to the wire: in the end stolen by those thugs in Cook County, as Harry angrily averred; fairly decided by tough Chicago politics, as she defiantly explained. But by now this was old ground between the two of them, old news; she might still blow off steam to anyone who'd listen, sister Josephine probably at the top of the list, but there didn't seem to be that much heat in the steam anymore.

Speaking of Josephine, her oldest son, Joseph Albright, a recent Williams College graduate (homage to Joe Brooks), was now rising in the ranks at *Newsday*; her older daughter, Alice, veteran of the trip to Russia, more or less amicably bullied by her aunt Alicia into going to Radcliffe instead of Wellesley, was currently the first female elected to the editorial board of the *Harvard Crimson*.

Patterson was somewhat sad but mostly realistic about the Guv, who of course was never seriously in the running for JFK's secretary of state (why would an energetic president want a "rabbit-assed" secretary of state?), but who had found some salve for his pride in the fine-sounding though decidedly less consequential post of ambassador to the United Nations—just how inconsequential, how far down the totem pole, he would ruefully discover come April 1961, when as a result of being deliberately kept out of the loop by the Kennedys on the Bay of Pigs debacle, he was forced to stand before the General Assembly of the UN (an institution he had helped found) and tell a series of palpable lies about United States involvement.

Her own relationship with the new president got off to a fine start a few months after his inauguration, at which time he had famously declared, "Ask not what your country can do for you, ask what you can do for your country." But with Kennedy soon running into a headwind of obstacles at every turn, Patterson helpfully tossed him a softball, writing a public "Letter to the President" editorial in *Newsday*, asking him to "Spell out for the American people, many of whom wish nothing better than to respond to your call and to do something for our country . . . exactly what you think must be done . . . what actions we should take . . . where we need to sacrifice . . . ?" Kennedy responded quickly to Patterson's editorial with his own lengthy "Letter to Mrs. Alicia Patterson," which *Newsday* naturally ran with much fanfare, spread out over two pages, as did the *New York Times* and *Time*, which titled its story "Alicia's Pen Pal." Unfortunately Kennedy's reply was not one of his speechwriters' more graceful or memorable efforts, full of earnest presidential boilerplate about "the needs of citizens to support our national defense . . . and strive for excellence at home," but a rapport of sorts had been created between "the President and the Publisher," as the media played the story for a while.

A few months later Patterson's connection to the new president kicked into an even higher gear, providing a number of tangible benefits to both *Newsday* and the Long Island communities it served. The matter at issue was the fate of Mitchel Field, a military airfield commissioned back in 1917, during World War I, on eleven hundred acres of what was then little-used farmland in sparsely populated Nassau County. Over the years several obvious problems had arisen with this arrangement, notably the building boom that now surrounded the once-little rural airfield (where both Alicia and her father had learned to fly) with residential structures great and small, along with the dangerous challenges of new aircraft trying to use an increasingly outdated facility.

There were also two competing solutions: The one favored by Alicia and her *Newsday* editors was to close the field and use the substantial acreage for the expansion of Hofstra University and a local community college; the rival plan, supported by the local chamber of commerce (also by Harry Guggenheim) was to close Mitchel as a military base but reopen it as an airfield for business aircraft. The situation seemed to be stuck in one of those almost-deliberate bureaucratic limbos, even after the especially alarming crash of an air force bomber, which resulted in the death of two airmen while narrowly missing a housing development. With the Federal Aviation Authority seemingly unwilling or incapable of coming to a decision, Patterson asked one of her editors, Bill Woestendick, to phone Kennedy's office and request an appointment to discuss the problem. Pierre Salinger, Kennedy's press secretary, remembered the request, which he passed on to the busy president, expecting to be told to schedule something in the usual two or three months' time. Instead (as reported by Bob Keeler), Salinger recalled the president saying, "Let's do it right away. Ask her to come down for lunch tomorrow."

Patterson was sufficiently excited by the sudden invitation to forgo the customary shuttle flight from LaGuardia, with its possible delays, and instead arranged to be driven down (with Woestendick), leaving Falaise just before dawn. On arriving at the White House she and Woestendick were shown into the family quarters, where the president soon joined them, cheerfully reminding Alicia of her earlier hospitality to him at Nino's. They had Bloody Marys together and then went into the family dining room for lunch (which Alicia remembered as ending with ice-cream cake), in the course of which many subjects were discussed: the hazards of presidential press conferences; an imminent steel strike; the pros and cons of young Teddy Kennedy's political ambitions; Jackie Kennedy's imminent trip to India.

Finally, the subject of Long Island's development came up, and of Mitchel Field in particular. Alicia had a number of talking points written out on a notebook in her hand, but after listening for no more than a few minutes Kennedy pushed himself away from the table in his back-friendly rolling chair, reached for a phone, and said (as Woestendick remembered), "Get me Jeeb Halaby," referring to Najeeb Halaby, the head of the FAA. A moment later the president said into the phone, "Jeeb, we don't need Mitchel Field, do we? Let's shut the damn thing." Then he put the phone down, pushed himself back to the table, and said, "It's closed." As Najeeb Halaby remembered the exchange: "Actually, closing Mitchel was a very complicated issue, with many loose ends. But she had convinced him to skip the loose ends and just do it. She was a very persuasive and powerful woman."

· 78 ·

FOR MUCH OF HER LIFE Alicia Patterson liked to present herself as a proudly, briskly unsentimental woman, almost an antisentimentalist, averse to kitsch, what she called gooey feelings, nostalgia, and so on, all of which helped her get along so well with tough-guy, wisecracking, mostly male newspaper people, to say nothing of the smart, cynical, sophisticated Manhattan crowd. Nonetheless, as her closest friends—the "Gunners" of old, sister Josephine, and very few others—well knew, her own past, with its soup of vague and vivid memories, with its powerful and sometimes deafening tribal music, was of huge and inescapable consequence to her, especially as she grew older.

Thus (although there's no record one way or the other on the matter), when she had her White House moment, so to speak, hanging out with young JFK, the nation's thirty-sixth president, shooting the breeze, doing a little business around the lunch table, then given a brief presidential walk-around ending up in the always-imposing Oval Office, it's hard to believe she didn't register, somewhere beneath her no-nonsense, newspaperwoman's exterior, all sorts of tugs and tidal pulls, proverbial mixed feelings, to say nothing of raw, daughterly emotions, remembering her long-gone-but-never-forgotten Poppa, Capt. Joseph Patterson of Battery D, whose own muddled, complex, misguided interactions with the nation's thirty-second (and original triple-initialed) president, FDR, had ended so painfully, disastrously, almost exactly twenty years ago; on that same blue carpet, in that same Oval Office, though now without secretary Grace Tully's desk in the back of the room.

The new Publishing Patterson, with her newfound, modest White House access, tried to keep things simple; and for a while Alicia's Kennedy connection produced some nice, positive results, both for Long Island as well as *Newsday*'s standing in the area, a community of now more than two million people. With Mitchel Field supporters overruled, the base was soon closed, and the land became available for residential and educational development. Soon afterward the president stepped forward with help on another problem that Patterson had raised in her lunchtime meeting at the White House, in this instance directing the air force to channel new contracts to Republic Aviation, an important Long Island aircraft manufacturer lately threatened by order cancellations and employee layoffs. In fact the years 1961 and 1962 represented a high point for *Newsday*, in terms of the paper's growing advocacy and influence, helping to push Long Island in both a popular and progressive direction; with one of its most significant accomplishments being the creation of the Fire Island National Seashore, a hotly contested and at the time controversial piece of environmental legislation that in the end succeeded largely (as most sources agree) because Patterson not only took up the matter person-to-person, face-to-face with the secretary of the interior, Stewart Udall, who had been inclined to decline the project, but was at the same time willing to fight for it despite the defiant opposition of an old friend, the powerful New York State Public Works Commissioner Robert Moses (*The Power Broker* of Robert Caro's fine biography), who strenuously opposed it.

MEANTIME, THE FORMER GUV, now Mr. Ambassador, hadn't disappeared, not a bit of it; besides, even though each of them sometimes drove the other crazy, they were too old to disappear on one another, too much like kin, kissing or nonkissing cousins, who finished each other's sentences, corresponded continually, with Patterson often playing the lean-on-my-shoulders wifely role that was largely absent in her own marriage. In August 1962 she did something unusual for her, took a real holiday, the way other people did, not a "working vacation," not a Spartan-boy, beat-yourself-up, fact-finding, discomfort-seeking mission to the Third World. She went to Europe. First, as part of a Stevenson-centered gathering of old friends, to Lake Como, north of Milan, where Stevenson's old Harvard Law School roommate, Francis T. P. Plimpton (founding partner of Debevoise & Plimpton, and now a special representative at the UN) and wife, Pauline, hosted a two-week house party at their elegant hillside, lakeside villa: delicious al fresco lunches, interesting excursions, and in the evenings more good food, better wine, and all that talk, *conversazione*, between those softly, sleekly powerful East Coast Liberal Democratic rajas and their tart, clever wives, among whom Joe Patterson's daughter surely by now felt almost at home. Then, on to Athens, part of a smaller group, again including the peripatetic Stevenson, assembling at the hallowed Hotel Grande Bretagne, followed by a leisurely tour of the Greek islands, aboard the stately motor yacht (formerly J. P. Morgan's) chartered by Agnes Meyer, publisher of the *Washington Post*, the stately newspaper into which the late Cissy Patterson's lively, unreliable *Times-Herald* had been merged. This was the next-to-last trip Stevenson and Patterson would make together, on the whole a happy one; Stevenson teased Alicia for traveling without a valise full of spiral-notebooks, Patterson chided the increasingly portly ambassador for his unadventurousness, for example taking a taxi to the top of Santorini instead of riding donkeys up the hill with the rest of them.

THEIR LAST TRIP CAME in late May 1963; both of them flying off together from New York's still-named Idlewild Airport, bound first for San Francisco; a night at the Fairmont, then down the winding coast highway to Big Sur, where Stevenson's newest grandchild was to be christened, at a family ceremony where she'd been asked to serve as godmother, an invitation that seemed to surprise even her by how much it mattered. The christenee was John Fell Stevenson's firstborn—John Fell, the youngest of Stevenson's sons, was perhaps the warmest, most responsive of the three boys, someone she had long known and felt close to, had bonded with on long overseas trips (as to Russia), and who now had seemingly chosen *her*, over all the rest of Adlai's ladies, to be this honored, surrogate-mother figure for his and wife Natalie's new baby. It was another kind of happy time for her, she who usually managed to be on the outskirts of family life, even when trying to participate after her fashion. The sun shone, as it should; the breeze blew, just the right amount, across the yellow-green meadow high above the Pacific. When she talked with Josephine soon after, she described the rare sweetness of the long afternoon, with its easy warmth, play of affections, multigenerational family bustle, that ancient pagan-churchly ritual, holding Adlai's tiny grandson in her arms.

AND THEN (how else really to put it?) the roof fell in.

· 79 ·

ONE IS TEMPTED TO SAY that roofs don't fall in all at once; there's usually a preliminary creaking in the rafters, a warning snowfall of plaster or whatever; and perhaps if we were actually talking about a roof and not a person—a woman, *this* woman, Alicia Patterson—there might have been some visible warning, some easy-to-notice sign.

A FEW WEEKS AFTER returning from Big Sur, she flew off again, this time to Chicago, where she picked up her eighty-two-year-old mother—Mrs. A. H. Patterson, tiny, white-haired, frail and steely at the same time—and drove north with her, back to Lake Forest, eight miles north of the old town, with its Tudor-style storefronts, avenues of Palladian great houses, to the heavyset, nineteenth-century brickwork cluster of Lake Forest College, where Patterson was scheduled to receive an honorary degree at that year's commencement exercises: *she* (as Alicia more than once pointed out to her mother, who didn't really need reminding) who had been tossed out, asked to leave, by so many schools and hadn't even been to college. And while Lake Forest might not be Harvard or Yale, or even the University of Chicago, the institution still carried powerful meanings for both mother and daughter: founded in 1881 by Alicia's other significant great-grandfather, the Reverend Robert Patterson, the charismatic minister of Chicago's Second Presbyterian Church, coeval of Joseph Medill in the great early days of the city. On that mild, sunny June afternoon, Alicia's mother sat on one of the hard little folding seats, in the front row of the commencement audience, and watched with quiet pride as Second Daughter, the difficult one, the one who was always somehow making waves, this time received the kind of sound, correct, dignified honor (unlike those always problematic, slightly show-offy magazine covers or journalism prizes) that had always meant so much to Alice Higinbotham

Patterson. "I think she finally approved of me," Alicia later said to Josephine.

YEARS LATER, what Dottie Holdsworth best remembered from that frantic yet strangely slow-motion drive through midmorning Long Island Parkway traffic, from Falaise toward the Triborough Bridge, then across the bridge and down the East River Drive to Doctors Hospital, was of her friend and boss, Alicia Patterson, alarmingly pale and weak on the backseat beside her, sometimes slumped over, seemingly passed out, but then struggling to sit up, now suddenly wide awake and talking to her with that familiar intensity, with her trademark husky briskness, about this new book she'd just been reading on the 1840s Irish famine (*The Great Hunger*, by Cecil Woodham-Smith), which Dottie must also absolutely, without fail, read as soon as she herself was done with it. The date was June 30, barely ten days after her return from Lake Forest; and the reason for Patterson's pallor and weakness, for the emergency nature of the drive into the city, was that the night before she had begun bleeding again, hemorrhaging from her insides, apparently trying to deal with it on her own, calling no one, letting nobody know; but then during the night bleeding out so badly that she'd been found in the early morning on her bathroom floor, lying in a pool of blood, by her maid, Nan, who phoned Dottie, who in turn (over Alicia's faint protestations) contacted her Long Island doctor and set the trip in motion.

By the time Patterson entered Doctors Hospital, she'd already lost roughly one-third of her normal blood supply, and was in a sufficient state of shock that she not so much entered the hospital as was carried in by Dottie and her driver, Noel Dean. She was taken first to intensive care and for twenty-four hours was given massive blood transfusions, three full units, plus intravenous feedings, which began to restore her to a "convalescent condition." By the afternoon of July 1 she was considered well enough to be moved upstairs to one of the large rooms on the tenth floor, where she now reclined (in her own nightgown and bed jacket), fatigued though grumpily cheerful, receiving a steady parade of visitors, many from *Newsday*; also Josephine, summoned earlier by Dottie from Wyoming, niece

Alice from Washington, and Harry Guggenheim arriving from Cain Hoy in South Carolina, all of whom were under the impression (as was the patient herself) that after a few days of rest and recuperation she would be on her way back to home and office.

There were now two doctors on the case: Dr. William Rawls, her regular physician, who had come back early from his vacation; and a Doctors Hospital specialist, Dr. Gere Lord (a former chief of surgery at the NYU Medical Center), both of whom were concerned about their well-known alternately charming and combative patient. The cause of the bleeding, both doctors agreed, was surely an ulcer—a "bleeding ulcer"; the problem was what to do about it. Since the hemorrhaging had stopped with the transfusions, and her general condition showed a return to near-normalcy, Dr. Rawls first proposed to Patterson that if she'd seriously promise to change her lifestyle—that is, reform her "habits" (within the modest parameters of the day) as to eating more nutritious foods and cutting down on cigarettes and alcohol—she might be able to avoid one or another of the then-standard surgical fixes. But Patterson, who liked quick fixes, solutions, action, almost as much as she disliked "goody-goody" diets and virtuous self-denial, surprised the avuncular Rawls by instantly opting for surgery. "Who wants to live on mashed potatoes and skim milk?" she said to Dottie Holdsworth, who, in the absence of visitors, sat in a chair near Alicia's bed reading aloud to her from Agatha Christie.

Less surprised than Dr. Rawls was Dr. Lord, who had proposed surgery in the first place. He appreciated that Alicia wanted to have the problem fixed, and he didn't anticipate any difficulties with the surgery, a gastric resection (or removal of a small part of the stomach), which was at the time the standard medical solution to aggressive ulcers, a procedure he had performed hundreds of times before with consistent success. Thus, soon after her go-ahead, on the morning of July 2, she was taken down to the fourth floor, anesthetized with sodium pentothal, and opened up. Lord quickly located the ulcerated area, which was—as he expected it might be, after checking the records of her 1952 surgery—at the juncture where her small intestine had been reattached to the stomach. He performed the resection without difficulty, removing roughly one-third of her stomach, then reattached a healthier part of the intestine (the jejunum), and sewed her up again.

In the recovery room on the same floor, Alicia soon regained consciousness, though the effects of the heavy anesthetic kept her groggy. Dr. Lord looked in on her from time to time, checked the nurses' charts, and informed Josephine and Harry upstairs that Alicia was coming along well, as expected, and should be back in her room on the tenth floor in a few hours. But around five o'clock a nurse notified the surgeon of an unexpected, and certainly unwanted, development: Blood was showing up in the drainage tube from her stomach. As Gere Lord told *Newsday* biographer Robert Keeler many years later: "This was extremely unusual, and had not happened before in my experience." At first they tried to stanch the bleeding with a saline solution, but this didn't work; in fact the bleeding only seemed to be getting worse. At this point, Lord (now joined by another surgeon, Dr. William Hinton) decided that their best move was to reopen the patient and attempt to suture or somehow block the flow of blood.

At ten o'clock in the evening of July 2, barely twelve hours after her first surgery, Patterson was returned to the operating room for what her doctors cautiously hoped might be a quick repair job. But when they opened her stomach for the second time they saw what Lord described as "massive, widespread and inexplicable bleeding of the stomach lining." Lord said that he briefly considered a gastrectomy, or total removal of the stomach, but rejected the plan as too extreme, too dangerous and burdensome for the patient. Instead he and Hinton decided on a more moderate solution: a vagotomy, or removal of the vagus nerve in the lower abdomen, which regulates blood flow to the stomach. This they did, or tried to do, a difficult undertaking in the best of circumstances, since the vagus nerve has numerous fibers, each one small and hard to find. By midnight or so they had done what nerve removal they could, patched her up again, and sent her back to the recovery room.

But the bleeding never stopped. Around nine o'clock in the morning, with Patterson glassily pale, weak, and barely conscious, the two surgeons decided—reluctantly, as a desperate measure—to make one more attempt to root out the hidden tributaries of the vagus nerve. For the third time in less than thirty-six hours Alicia was taken back into the operating room and opened up. On this occasion Dr. Hinton was lead surgeon; he and Lord removed such nerve fibers as they could find, also her spleen, which Hinton thought might be contributing to the bleeding. For the third time they sent her back to the little recovery room, and hoped, apparently without much confidence at that point, that the problem had been solved. When Josephine (the only visitor admitted) looked in on her later in the afternoon, Alicia was pale as a ghost but managed a weary smile. Josephine sat by her bed for a while, talked to her of this and that; at one point Alicia looked across at her younger sister. "Tell me true," she said, employing traditional sister-speak. "Am I going to die?" And Josephine, who later remembered she actually didn't think so, it was so impossible to think, said: "No, you're not."

BUT SHE DID, later that night. "At 11:25 p.m. July 2, 1963," as indicated in the hospital records. Dr. Lord's old files note the cause as "Unexplained and unstoppable bleeding." She was fifty-six years old; too young, although maybe not for a Spartan.

EPILOGUE

ONE OF THE ALL-TOO-FEW benefits of dying too soon—in fact, pretty squarely in her prime—was that Alicia Medill Patterson Guggenheim (who over the years, at odd moments, had given formal thought to such matters) pulled a big crowd for her funeral: not merely a church-full but a cathedral-full. On a bright, windy July morning, close to one thousand people pressed into the Episcopal cathedral in Garden City, Long Island (her choice)—still-stunned *Newsday* staff; family, friends and acquaintances; plus a fine showing of politicians, editors, and publishers. As per her wishes, the outside of the cathedral was arrayed with a colorful amplitude of flowers; inside there were thick layers of orange roses covering her coffin; a choir chanting psalms and lustily bellowing Protestant hymns, concluding with her favorite, "The Battle Hymn of the Republic," which left scarcely a dry eye in the house. Two months later, a second rite took place, this one orchestrated by Harry Guggenheim: a quiet, sad little assembly on the banks of the St. Mary's, with her family gathered on the lawn beneath the great oak tree that stood (and still stands) between the house and the river, its branches heavy with Spanish moss, and under which her ashes were buried beneath a simple plaque, whose tender inscription ("A beautiful and spirited lady lived on this land, and under this oak tree she watched the river that she loved.") had been composed by Harry, who seemed truly to miss his lively, quick-witted sparring partner now that she was gone.

AS TO ALICIA'S MASTER PLAN for the future of *Newsday*—a work in progress that consumed much time and energy as well as generating handsome legal fees (and which seemed to have at its core some varying degree of ownership sharing among Josephine's children)—needless to say, her persistent and combative yearning for Harry's crucial 2 percent had been predicated on the expectation of his dying first. Upon Alicia's death, Harry took over as sole publisher, and also editor, and for seven years by general agreement continued to run *Newsday* as a successful and respected newspaper. To nobody's surprise, he quickly got rid of Alan Hathway. But then in 1967 he surprised a good many people, possibly even himself, by turning over the job of publisher to young Bill Moyers, while staying on as editor in chief. Moyers was not only young but a Democrat; he had been a well-regarded press secretary to President Lyndon Johnson. But he was smart, astute, politically moderate, and personally appealing; sufficiently so for Guggenheim soon to regard him as "family" and even include him in his will. But as the Vietnam War split the country into opposing camps, Harry (more and more feeling his age and natural conservatism) came to view Moyers's still-moderate-though-antiwar position as a betrayal, and fired him from both the paper and his will.

In 1970 Harry sold *Newsday* to the then-conservative *Los Angeles Times-Mirror*, under whose distant ownership it continued to flourish, extending itself into greater New York, first with a Queens edition, then a stand-alone Manhattan daily, *New York Newsday*. However, in 2000, as an early symptom of the challenges that newspapers would increasingly face in the Internet era, the *Times-Mirror* sold itself to the *Chicago Tribune*, with the result that for a few years Alicia Patterson's little garage start-up became a subsidiary of the giant Midwestern monolith created by her ancestors, and which for generations had continued both to enrich and to devour them. Eventually even the once-mighty *Tribune* was forced to declare temporary bankruptcy, and in 2008 *Newsday* was purchased for $680 million by the cable television conglomerate Cablevision. Its current headquarters are still on Long Island in Melville, New York, about twenty miles from Garden City. At present writing, *Newsday* is sold throughout the New York metropolitan area, though its focus is back to Long Island. Its weekly circulation is the eleventh-highest in the country, the largest among suburban newspapers. Since its inception, *Newsday* has won twenty-two Pulitzer Prizes and has been a finalist in nineteen additional entries.

AUTHORS' NOTE

While we have tried to make our account of Alicia Patterson's eventful, idiosyncratic life reasonably brief, even untome-like in the telling, in keeping with our subject, we would like the reader to know that the narrative, facts, details, and so on in this volume derive from a proverbial storehouse of research material: privately held family correspondence, library collections, books and manuscripts (some unpublished), photographs, newspaper and magazine archives, etc. A substantial resource has been the Papers of Alicia Patterson, originally part of the Estate of Alicia Patterson Guggenheim, later augmented by the Papers of Josephine Patterson Albright (made available by the heirs of Josephine Patterson Albright): a compendium of personal and official correspondence, documents, memoranda, photographs, and published and unpublished journalism. Other valuable sources have been the Joseph Medill Patterson Manuscript Collection, Donnelley and Lee Library, Lake Forest College; the Papers of Adlai E. Stevenson, Seeley G. Mudd Manuscript Library, Princeton University; the Papers of Colonel Robert R. McCormick, First Division Museum, Cantigny Park, Illinois. Also "Joseph Medill Patterson: Right or Wrong, American," by Joseph M. P. Patterson, undergraduate thesis, History Department, Williams College, 1958; and "Alicia Patterson Profile," by J. M. Flagler, *The New Yorker* (unpublished manuscript), 1963. Last but by no means least, the authors wish to acknowledge their indebtedness to Robert F. Keeler, author of the masterful *Newsday: A Candid History of the Respectable Tabloid* (William Morrow, NY, 1990), who also generously provided Alice Arlen with extensive research materials, letters, documents, interview tapes relating to Alicia Patterson, Harry F. Guggenheim, et al., from his own files and *Newsday* archives.

BIBLIOGRAPHY

Arpee, Edward. *Lake Forest, Illinois: History and Reminiscences, 1861–1961.* Lake Forest Historical Society, 1979.

Baden-Powell, Sir Robert. *Pig-Sticking.* London: Herbert Jenkins, Ltd., 1924.

Baxter, David O. "The Chicago Tribune." *Fortune*, May 1934.

Berg, A. Scott. *Lindbergh.* New York: Berkley, 1998.

Bessie, Simon Michael. *Jazz Journalism.* New York: E. P. Dutton and Co., 1938.

Caro, Robert. *The Power Broker: Robert Moses and the Fall of New York.* New York: Vintage Books, 1975.

Cashman, Donald. *A Fierce Discontent: The Rise and Fall of the Progressive Movement in America.* New York: Oxford University Press, 2003.

Clendenen, Clarence C. *Blood on the Border: The United States Army and the Mexican Irregulars.* London: MacMillan, 1966.

Chapman, John. *Tell It to Sweeney.* New York: Doubleday, 1961.

Chernow, Ron. *Titan: The Life of John D. Rockefeller, Sr.* New York: Random House, 1998.

Chisholm, Ann, and Michael Davie. *Lord Beaverbrook.* New York: Alfred A. Knopf, 1993.

Clary, David A. *Rocket Man: Robert H. Goddard.* New York: Hyperion, 2003.

Coolidge, Harold J., Jr. *Three Kingdoms of Indo-China.* New York: Thomas Y. Crowell, 1933.

Cooney, John. *The Annenbergs.* New York: Simon & Schuster, 1982.

Crane, Richard Teller. *Autobiography.* Chicago: Privately printed, 1927.

Cromie, Robert. *The Great Chicago Fire.* Nashville, TN: Rutledge Hill Press, 1994.

Crosby, George D. *Fishing in the Chagres River.* Burford, UK: Davenant Press, 1937.

Davies, Joseph E. *Mission to Moscow.* New York: Simon & Schuster, 1941.

Davis, John L. *The Guggenheims: An American Epic.* New York: William Morrow, 1978.

Engels, Vincent. *Adirondack Fishing in the 1930s.* Syracuse, NY: Syracuse University Press, 1978.

Gallagher, Brian. *Anything Goes.* New York: Times Books, 1987.

Gibbons, Edward. *Floyd Gibbons: Your Headline: A Biography.* New York: Exposition Press, 1953.

Gizycka, Eleanor. *Fall Flight*. New York: Minton, Balch & Co., 1928.

———. *Glass Houses*. New York: Minton, Balch & Co., 1926.

Guggenheim, Harry F. *The Seven Skies*. New York: G. P. Putnam's Sons, 1930.

Hoyt, Edwin P., Jr. *The Guggenheims and the American Dream*. New York: Funk & Wagnalls, 1967.

Jackson, Kenneth T. *Crabgrass Frontier: The Suburbanization of the United States*. New York: Oxford University Press, 1985.

Jonas, Manfred. *Isolationism in America, 1935–1941*. Ithaca, NY: Cornell University Press, 1966.

Kahn, E. J. Jr. *The World of Swope*. New York: Simon & Schuster, 1965.

Keeler, Robert F. *Newsday: A Candid History of the Respectable Tabloid*. New York: William Morrow, 1990.

Kinsley, Philip. *The Chicago Tribune: Its First Hundred Years*. 3 vols., New York: Alfred A. Knopf, 1943.

Langille, Leslie. *Men of the Rainbow*. Chicago: O'Sullivan Publishing House, 1933.

Lawson-Johnston, Peter. *Growing Up Guggenheim*. Wilmington, DE: ISI Books, 2005.

Lomask, Milton. *Seed Money: The Guggenheim Story*. New York: Farrar, Straus, 1964.

Martin, John Bartlow. *Adlai Stevenson of Illinois*. Vol. 2. New York: Doubleday, 1976.

Martin, Ralph G. *Cissy*. New York: Simon & Schuster, 1979.

McKeever, Porter. *Adlai Stevenson: His Life and Legacy*. New York: William Morrow, 1989.

McKnight, Gerald. *Verdict on Schweitzer*. New York: John Day Company, 1964.

Medill, Joseph. "A Talk with Abraham Lincoln's Friend." *Saturday Evening Post*, August 5, 1899.

Miller, Donald. *City of the Century*. New York: Simon & Schuster, 2003.

Miller, Kristie. *Ruth McCormick: A Life in Politics*. Albuquerque: University of New Mexico Press, 1992.

Monaghan, Jay. *The Man Who Elected Lincoln*. Indianapolis: Bobbs-Merrill, 1950.

Nissenson, Marilyn. *The Lady Upstairs: Dorothy Schiff*. New York: St. Martin's Press, 2007.

Patterson, Alicia. "Behind the Iron Curtain: U.S.S.R. Journal." *Newsday*, beg. Sept. 1958 (five parts).

———. "Berlin Airlift." *Newsday*, beg. Dec. 1948 (five parts).

———. "Fox Hunting in Leicestershire." *Liberty*, 1929.

———. "Report on Africa." *Newsday*, beg. Sept. 1957 (six parts).

———. "Report on the Middle East." *Newsday*, beg. Oct. 1956 (five parts).

Patterson, Alicia, with Hal Burton. "This Is the Life I Love." *Saturday Evening Post*, Feb. 21, 1959.

Patterson, Joseph Medill. "Confessions of a Drone." *Independent*, Chicago: Aug. 30, 1906.

———. *Little Brother of the Rich*. Chicago: Reilly and Britton, 1910.

———. *Notebook of a Neutral*. New York: Duffield & Company, 1916.

———. *Rebellion: A Play in Four Acts*. Chicago: Reilly and Britton, 1911.

———, ed. *Socialist Party Platform*. Chicago: Socialist Press, 1908.

Rascoe, Burton. *Before I Forget*. New York: Literary Guild, 1937.

Robinson, Jerry. *The Comics*. New York: G. P. Putnam's Sons, 1974.

Rothschild, Hannah. *The Search for Nica*. New York: Alfred A. Knopf, 2012.

Rue, Larry. *I Fly for News*. New York: Albert and Charles Boni, 1932.

Salvatore, Nick. *Eugene V. Debs: Citizen and Socialist*. Chicago: University of Chicago Press, 1984.

Schlesinger, Arthur M., Jr. *Journals, 1952–2000*. Penguin Press, 2007.

Seldes, George. *Lord of the Press*. New York: Julian Messner, 1938.

Smith, A. Ledyard. *Excavations at Altar De Sacrificios*. Cambridge, MA: Peabody Museum of Archaeology and Ethnology, 1972.

Smith, Richard Norton. *The Colonel: The Life and Legend of Robert R. McCormick*. Boston: Houghton Mifflin, 1997.

Strevey, T. E. "Joseph Medill and the Chicago Tribune, 1860–65," Ph.D. thesis, History Department, University of Chicago, 1930.

Sullivan, Mark. *Our Times*. New York: Scribner's, 1933.

Tebbel, John. *The Marshall Fields*. New York: E. P. Dutton, 1947.

Unger, Irwin, and Debi Unger. *The Guggenheims*. New York: HarperCollins, 2005.

Waldrop, Frank C. *McCormick of Chicago*. Englewood Cliffs, NJ: Prentice Hall, 1966.

Weeden, Edward St. Clair, *A Year with the Gaekwar of Baroda*. Boston: Dana Estes & Co., 1911.

Wendt, Lloyd. *Chicago Tribune: Rise of a Great American Newspaper*. Chicago: Rand McNally, 1979.

Wendt, Lloyd, and Herman Kogan. *Bosses of Chicago*. Bloomington: Indiana University Press, 1974.

Wertenbaker, Charles. "The Case of the Hot-Tempered Publisher." *Saturday Evening Post*, May 12, 1951.

Williams, Paul. *Dupont Circle*. Charleston, SC: Arcadia Publishing, 2000.

Wilson, Edmund. *The Thirties*. New York: Washington Square Press, 1958.

Wister, Owen. *Out West: Journals and Letters*. Chicago: University of Chicago Press, 1957.

INDEX

(Page references in *italics* refer to illustrations.)

Abbott, George, 137, 138, 297
Abu Bakar, HRH Ibrahim 'Bu, 107, *107*
Adirondacks, Brooks's fishing camp in, 96–7, 140–1, *141*, 149
Aeronautical Foundation, 153, 155, 182
Africa:
  Alicia's 1957 trip to, 286–94, *289*, 299
  Belgian colonial rule in, 291
  British colonial rule in, 288–90
  North, Alicia's 1932 flight across, 117–18
  Schweitzer's jungle clinic in, 291–3
Albright, Alice (niece), 299, 300, 303, 320, 328–9, 333
Albright, Ivan (brother-in-law), 201, 210, 225, 234, 240
  portrait of Joe Patterson by, *202*
Albright, Joseph (nephew), 320, 333
Albright, Josephine Patterson (sister), *see* Patterson, Josephine
Aldridge, Albert, 253, 254–5
Algonquin Round Table, 123, 158
Allen, Tommy, 269
America's Cup (1938), 137
Annenberg, Max, 155, 156, 158, 159, 167, 189, 190
Arvey, Jake, 211, 212
Aspen Institute, 298
Associated Press (AP), 269
Ausable River, New York, Brooks's fishing camp on, 96–7, 140–1, *141*, 149
Auschwitz, 303
Australia, Alicia's 1930 travels in, 99–102, 111
Backer, George and Helen, 225–6
Baruch, Bernard, 137
Battle of Britain, 164, 182–3
Bay of Pigs invasion (1961), 320
Beaverbrook, Max Aitken, Lord, 127–9, *128*, 130, 287
Becker, Fred, 92, 93, 95
Belgian Congo, Alicia's 1957 travels in, 290, 291
Benton, William, 299
Berlin airlift (1948–49), 219–23, 236–7
Blair, Deeda, 287
Blair, William McCormick, 249, 287, 299
Blevins, Captain, 221
Boston Herald, 76
Boyden, Philip, 95
Brooks, Joseph W. ("Big Joe"; Alicia's second husband), *95*, 95–7, 98, 108–16, 117, 137, 138, 150, 166, 307, 320
  Alicia accompanied to Europe by (1935), 127, *128*
  Alicia visited in hospital by, 256
  disconnectedness in Alicia's marriage to, 114–15, 136, 143, 145–6
  divorce of, 145–6, 147, 150, 167
  engagement and wedding of, 108–13, 145
  fishing camp of, 96–7, 140–1, *141*, 145, 149
  honeymoon of, *113*, 113–14
  Joe Patterson's financial support of, 114, 116, 124, 125, 135, 146
  Joe Patterson's friendship with, 96–7, 110, 145, 146

Brooks, Joseph W. ("Big Joe"; Alicia's second husband) *(continued)*
  planes crashed by, 108, 109, 110, 113–14
  shortcomings and failures of, 96, 123, 124, 126
Brooks, Stan, 269
Broun, Gertrude, 123, 181
Broun, Heywood, 123, 137, 158, 181
Bukharin, Nikolai, 132
Bullitt, William C., 132
Burton, Hal, 306–8

Cablevision, 334
Cain Hoy Plantation, Charleston, South Carolina, 150, 166, 168–74, *170*, 233, 250, 256, 260, *278*, 283, 285
  Guggenheim's creation of, 169
  horse-breeding and -racing operations at, 197, 219, 246, 263
  visited by Alicia's father and stepmother, 168–74
Caribbean, Alicia and her father's 1929 "air-cruise" to, 92–4, *93*, 193, 244
Carnarvon, SS, 99–100, 106
"Case of the Hot-Tempered Publisher, The" (Wertenbaker), 238, *239*
Catholicism, Kennedy's presidential aspirations and, 311, 312
Cave, Henry, 254–5
Cerf, Bennett and Phyllis, 181, 295
Chaliapin, Boris, 272
Chambliss, Ned, 51–2
Chase, Howard, 104
Chase, Libby:
  Alicia accompanied to India by (1932), 117–18, 121–2
  Alicia accompanied to Indochina by (1930–31), 99–104, 106
Chicago Daily News, 205, 211
Chicago Morning American, 3–7, *4*, 21, 26, *26*
Chicago Tribune, 6, 27, 28, 44, 45, 68, 116, 148, 156, 274, 310, 334
  isolationist stance of, 165, 178, 180
  Joe Patterson's job as commissioner of public works and, 21–2, 25
  Joe Patterson's work for, 10, 11, 13–14, 15, 20–1, 23–4, 35, 54, 55–6, 57
  Patterson and McCormick family's takeover of, 46–8
  tabloid venture of, 60, 61–3, 124, 200; *see also Daily News*
  "Workingman's Magazine" of, 15, 17, 19, 20
Childs, Marquis, 194, 247
Churchill, Winston, 127
Clurman, Richard, 270, 282, 294, 295
  Alicia's relationship with, 278
  firing of, 296
  as *Newsday*'s editorial director, 276–9
  Time cover story and, 272, 273, 275
Cochran, Jacqueline, 182, 183, 186
Codman, Mrs. Russell (sister), *see* Patterson, Elinor Medill
Codman, Russell (brother-in-law), 71
Cold War, 131, 226, 299
  Berlin airlift and, 219–23
Collier's, 29, 226
Colson, Nub, 212
Communism, 130, 257, 301
  Alicia's 1937 trip to Soviet Union and, 131–4
  witch hunts of 1950s and, 134, 250
Communist Party USA, 132
Congo, Alicia's 1957 travels in, 290, 291
Conwell, Georgie, 242
Coolidge, Calvin, 175, 310–11
Cooper, Lady Diana (formerly Lady Diana Manners), 70, 128
Cotillo, Salvatore, 149

Cowles, Sage, 72
Crane, Florence Higinbotham (aunt), 36, 37, 58, 64, 89, 113
Crane, Richard Teller (uncle), 36–7, 89
Croydon Aerodrome, London, 128, *128*
Curtiss Field and Flying School, Long Island, 88–90, 182

Daily Express (London), 127–8
Daily Mail (London), 60
Daily News (originally *Illustrated Daily News*), 83, 84, 114, 116, 135, 159, 167, 173, 180, 198, 280
  Alicia's book reviews for, 125
  Alicia's interview pieces for, 126
  Alicia's low-level reporting job at, 75, 82
  Beaverbrook's reprinting of isolationist editorials in, 127
  Joe Patterson's death and, 200
  launch of, 60, 61–2, 63, 73, 124, 156, 161
  Roosevelt criticized in editorials of, 147, 161, 164, 167–8, 177–9
  Roosevelt's anger at, 177–9
Daily News building, New York, 135
Daily Socialist, 28–9, 30, 35, 42
Dark Star (thoroughbred), 263
Davenport, Miss (nanny), 185, 188, 201
Davies, Joseph E., 132, 133, 192
Davis, Al, 188–9, 190
Dean, Noel, 328
Debs, Eugene V., 28, 35, 36, 42, 124
DeKoning, Rose Mary, 266
DeKoning, William, 264–70
  Dudar's five-piece series on, 266–7, 270
  Hathway's motivations for investigation of, 265–6
  Pulitzer Prize awarded to *Newsday* for stories on, 270, 271, 273, 277, 280
  second round of stories on, 268–70
  shortcomings in *Newsday*'s original series on, 267–8
  Time piece on *Newsday*'s stories about, 270, 272
  Yonkers Raceway shootout and, 268–9
Democratic Convention (1952), 248–9
Democratic National Convention (1960), 314–18
Dewey, Thomas, 269
Dick, Edison, 241, 314
Dick, Jane, 241, 281, 314
Dietz, Howard, 137
Discourses (Epictetus), 298, 319
Doctors Hospital, New York, 252
  Alicia's death at, 328–31
  Alicia's 1952 illness treated at, 251–7, 258–9
Doolittle, Jimmy, 95, 182, 183
Draper, Nancy (daughter-in-law), 285
Dubois, Wyoming, Alicia's sojourns at Albright ranch in, 238, 240–2, 273
Dudar, Helen, 266–7
Dulles, John Foster, 281, 301
Dunne, George, 21, 22, 25, 26
Duranty, Walter, 132

Early, Steve, 174, 175, 176, 177, 178
Edison, Thomas, 310
Editor & Publisher, 86, 197
Eisenhower, Dwight D., 281
  Alicia's admiration for, 205, 236–7
  Alicia's disappointment with first term of, 281
  Alicia's interview with, 247, 248
  as presidential candidate, 205, 236, 246–7, 248, 257, 259, 260, 281–3, 301, 312
  Soviet space program and, 295, 300
Epictetus, 298, 319

Falaise, Sands Point, Long Island, 142, 166, 197, 203, 209, 238, 272
  Alicia's first visit to, 138–9
  Guggenheims' first fight at, 156–7
  Koenigswarter children at, 184–5, *185*, 186, 187–8, 200–1
  Stevenson's visit to, 233, 234
Fascism, rise of, 127–30, 147
Fay, Joey, 267, 268
Federal Aviation Authority (FAA), 321, 322
feminism, no-nonsense, of Alicia, 258, 304–5
Field, Fiona, 299, 303
Field, Ruth, 281, 299, 303
Fire Island National Seashore, 324
Fitzgerald, F. Scott, 135, 138
FitzGerald, Frances, 287, 292
Fosdick, Dorothy, 241
Foxcroft School, Middleburg, Virginia, 67
foxhunting, of Quorn at Melton Mowbray, England, 79–80, *80*
French Equatorial Africa, Alicia's 1957 travels in, 291–2
"From Across the Atlantic," 127

Gabon, Schweitzer's jungle clinic in, 291–3
Gallup, Inc., 294, 295
Germany:
  Alicia's childhood sojourn in, 49–53
  Alicia's 1935 trip to, 128–30, 236–7, 287
  Alicia's trip to, during Berlin airlift, 219–23
  rearmament of, 129
  rocket research in, 155
Gershwin, George, 137
Gest, Morris, 70
Gibbons, Floyd, 92, 93–4
Gizycki, Count Josef "Gigy," 15–18
Goddard, Robert H., 152–5
Gottlieb, Leo, 285–6, 294, 295, 296
Grandi, Dino, 129
Grand Union, 250
Grant, Nellie, 309
Grant, Ulysses S., 309
Great Britain, 147, 161
  Alicia and her father's 1935 trip to, 127–8, *128*
  foxhunting in, 79–82, *80*, 119
  isolationists in, 127
  war materiel supplied to, 161, 164, 167–8
  in World War II, 164
Great Depression, 123–4, 135, 207
Greene, Bob, 268, 313, 316–17
Gridiron Dinner, Washington, D.C., 304
Guggenheim, Gertrude (mother-in-law), 166, 184
Guggenheim, Harry F. (Alicia's third husband), 145, 150–1, 193, 201, 213, 233, 235, *237*, 246, 259, *278*, 297, 307, 321
  Alicia's battles with, 156–7, 283–6, 294–6
  Alicia's death and, 333–4
  Alicia's decision to leave, 238, 240–3
  Alicia's first encounters with, 138–9, 142–4
  Alicia's illnesses and, 256, 260, 329, 330
  and Alicia's minority 49% interest in *Newsday* (and his own crucial 2%), 199, 237–8, 271, 280, 295, 296, 333
  Alicia's plan to join Wings for Britain quashed by, 182–3, 186
  Alicia's political differences with, 165, 282, 319
  Alicia's role in managing households with, 166
  alienation in Alicia's relationship with, 210, 225–6, 227, 235, 236, 237–8, 242–3, 246
  anti-Semitism and, 142, 146–7

aviation and, 142–3, 182–3
civilian life resumed by, 195–7
Clurman hiring and, 276, 279
deemed unlikely mate for Alicia, 150–1
endorsements for presidential candidates and, 249, 257, 281, 282, 283
family background of, 142
Guggenheim Museum and, 285, 304
homes of, 166; *see also* Cain Hoy Plantation, Charleston, South Carolina; Falaise, Sands Point, Long Island
honeymoon of, 152–5
horse-breeding and -racing of, 143, 197, 219, 246, 260, 262–3, 285
infidelity of, 194
Jewish immigration and, 184, 185
Kennedy-Nixon campaign and, 319
lawyers consulted during marital discord of, 285–6, 294, 295
Levittowns disdained by, 209
military commission reactivated by, in World War II, 186–7, *187*, 190, 194–6
mother-in-law's relationship with, 201–2
national magazines' pieces on *Newsday* and, 227, 238, 242, 244
Newsday management and, 157, 158–9, 190, 196, 197, 229, 230–2, 276, 279, 280, 286, 294–6, 333–4
newspaper acquired by, 151, 155, 156–7, 158
physical appearance of, 162–3
rocket research and, 153–5, 197
tennis playing of, 230
Time cover story and, 272–3, 274–5, 276
unaware of Alicia's romance with Stevenson, 225, 242, 250
wedding of, 152
Guggenheim, Solomon, 196
Guggenheim, Solomon R., Museum, New York, 285, 304
Guggenheim Brothers, 196–7

Halaby, Najeeb, 322
Hall, Leonard, 283
Harvey, Daggett, 72
Hathway, Alan, 189–90, 196, *239*, 246, 260, 274, 294, 313, 319, 334
Clurman's arrival at *Newsday* and, 277, 278, 279
DeKoning story and, 265–6, 268, 269, 270, 271
in *Newsday*'s collaboration with Levitt, 208, 209
Hauck, Janet, 163, *212*
Hempstead Garden, Long Island, 265
Higinbotham, Harlow (grandfather), 5, 36
Higinbotham, Rachel (grandmother), 5, 10, 21, 36
Hinton, William, 330, 331
Hitler, Adolf, 128, 129–30, 164, 170, 192, 272
Hofstra University, 304, 321
Holdsworth, Dottie, 252, 256, 261, 268, 284–5, 328, 329
Holocaust, 303
Hood, Raymond, 135
Hooft, Hans, 106–7, 111–12
Humphrey, Hubert, 312

Illinois Democratic Party, 211
Illinois Historical Society, 252–3
Illinois National Guard, 57, 59–60
Illustrated Daily News, *see Daily News*
India:
Alicia's 1932 travels to, 117–22, *118*, *121*, *122*, 123
pigsticking in, 117, *118*, *119*, 119–20, 123
tiger hunt in, 107, 117, 120–2, *121*, 123

Indochina:
Alicia's 1930–31 travels in, 100, 103–6, *104*, *106*
tiger hunt in, 103, 104–6, *106*
Vietminh rebels in, 103, 104
Inger (maid), 10, 38
Italy, Alicia and her father's 1935 trip to, 128–30
Ives, Buffie, 212, 236, 241

Jewish immigration, 183–5
Johnson, Lyndon B., 317, 334
Joseph Medill Trust, 148, 199

Kahn, Otto, 70
Keeler, Robert F., 160, 265, 313, 316, 321, 330
Keeley, James, 13
Kefauver, Estes, 281
Kennan, George F., 133
Kennedy, John F., 315, 319, 320–2
Alicia's meeting with, at *Newsday* headquarters, 311–13
Democratic Convention and, 316–18
issues of interest to Long Island and, 321–2, 323–4
"Letter to Mrs. Alicia Patterson" by, 320–1
Kennedy, Robert, 316–17, 318
Kennedy, Theodore, 322
Kentucky Derby, 262–3
Kenya, Alicia's 1957 travels in, 288–9
Khmer tribesmen, 104–5
Khrushchev, Nikita, 299–300
King, Mary S. (later Mrs. Joseph Patterson; stepmother), 54, 64, 83, 86, 110, 116, 147–8, 162, 163, 180
Alicia's disdain for, 125
Cain Hoy visit of, 168–74
Joe's death and, 198
Joe's decline and, 192–3
Joe's legitimization of his situation with, 147–9
Kingsland, Georgia, *see* St. Mary's River, Georgia, Alicia's retreat on
Koenigswarter, Patrick and Janka de, 184–5, *185*, 186, 187–8, 200–1

Labor Lyceum, Long Island, 264–5, 266, 267
Lake Forest, Illinois, 39–40
Lake Forest College, Alicia's honorary degree from, 327–8
Lambaréné, Gabon, Schweitzer's jungle clinic in, 291–3
Laos, Alicia's tiger hunt in (1931), 104
Lasker Advertising Agency, 115
Lend-Lease Bill, 164, 167–8
Leonard & Co., 140
Levitt, Bill, 208–9
Lewis, Snakes, 269
Liberty (amphibious flying boat), 92–4, *93*
Liberty (magazine):
Alicia's articles for, 81–2, 83, 84–5, 87
Alicia's overseas assignment for (1930–31), 97–108, *104*, *106*, 110–11
Tribune Company's ownership of, 84, 123
Libertyville, Illinois, Patterson house and farm in, 32–43, *41*, *78*
Alice's flight from (1908), 36–8
donated to Catholic convent, 215
family reunion at (1947), 201–6
farming at, 33–4, 42
house and garden at, 33, 34, 40
Joe's purchase of, 32–3
Joe's writing at, 34–5, 42–3
Patterson family's return to town from, 44, 48
Patterson family's role in area around, 39–40
sale of farmland at, 202
Stevenson's reconnection with Alicia at, 204–6, 235, 259

Lincoln, Abraham, 309
Lindbergh, Charles A., 142, 153
Little Brother of the Rich (Joe Patterson), 35, 37, 42–3, 46
Loeb, Louis, 286, 294, 296
Long Island:
  Alicia's Kennedy connection and, 321–2, 323–4
  building boom on, 207–9, 229, 280
  DeKoning's operations on, 264–70
  Guggenheim estate on, *see* Falaise, Sands Point, Long Island
Lord, Gere, 329–30, 331
Los Angeles Times-Mirror, 334
Luce, Clare, 251

Mme. Gautier's École Internationale (Switzerland), 64–5
Manners, Lady Diana (later Lady Diana Cooper), 70, 128
Mapel, Bill, 158–9
Markel, Lester, 286
Marshall Field & Co., 21, 29, 72
Marx, Harpo, 137
McCormick, Kate Medill, 14, 27, 44, 45, 131, 309, 310
  Tribune management and, 47, 48, 62
McCormick, Medill (uncle), *16*, 310
McCormick, Robert R. ("Bertie" or "the Colonel"), 6, *16*, 45, 46–8, 59, 75, 78, 116, 131, 149
  isolationism of, 165, 178, 180
McCormick-Patterson Trust, 148, 199
McGregor, Mr. (gardener), 34, 40, 202
McIlwaine, William, 277
McKinley, William, 310
McMein, Jack, 137, 138
McMein, Neysa, 123, 126, 135–6, 137, 138, 158, 193
Medill, Joseph (great-grandfather), 6, 14, *16*, 22, 26, 44, 309–10
Medill, Kate, *see* McCormick, Kate Medill
Medill, Kitty (great-grandmother), 309
Meeker, Harold, 94, 114, 244, 246
Meet the Editors, 250
Melton Mowbray, England, foxhunting in, 79–82, *80*, 119
Mercer Field, near Trenton, New Jersey, 186–7, 190, 194, 230
Mescalero Ranch, Roswell, New Mexico, Guggenheims' honeymoon at, 152–5
Mexico:
  Joe Patterson's 1914 trip to, 55–6, 57
  squirmishes against Villa on border of, 57, 58
Meyer, Agnes, 325
Mill, Hugo, 193
Miracle, The, 69–71, *70*, 128
Mitchel Field, Long Island, 321–2, 324
Mitchell, Billy, 95
Moi tribesmen, 105–6, *106*
Morton, Carol, 143
Moses, Robert, 324
Moulton, Walter, 157
Moyers, Bill, 334
Mukerji, Mr. (Second Officer), 100
Murrow, Edward R., 164
Mussolini, Benito, 128, 129, 130

Nassau Review-Star, 188
NATO, Alicia's interview with Eisenhower at, 247, 248
Nehenta Bay, USS, 194, 195
New Deal, 116, 147, 192, 208, 311
Newhouse, Samuel, 156, 158
Newsday, 156–63, 168, 193, 201, 210, 221, 226, 227, 234, 236, 237–8, 246, 250, 264–80, 285, 307, 315, 316, 319
  acquisition of, 155, 156–7, 158
  after Alicia's death, 333–4

Newsday (continued)
Alicia and Harry's battles and, 283–6, 294–6
Alicia's account of Berlin airlift in, 222–3
Alicia's account of her African travels in, 288–90
Alicia's account of her Russian travels in, 300–3
Alicia's daily activities at, 166–7
Alicia's draft letter of resignation from, 295–6
Alicia's illness and, 260–1, 262, 268
Alicia's Kennedy connection and, 321–2, 323–4
Alicia's minority 49% interest in (and Harry's crucial 2%), 199, 237–8, 271, 280, 295, 296, 333
circulation of, 188, 196, 201, 209, 226, 280
Clurman's role as editorial director of, 276–9
copy desk introduced at, 277
DeKoning story and, 264–71
delivery of, 159, 167
Eisenhower interview in, 247, 248
endorsement of presidential candidates in, 249, 257, 281, 282, 283, 319
first press run of, 159–61, *160*
Guggenheim's role in management of, 157, 158–9, 190, 196, 197, 229, 230–2, 276, 279, 280, 286, 294–6, 333–4
"His" and "Hers" editorials in, 165, 319
Joe Patterson's visit to, 162–3
Kennedy's "Letter to Mrs. Alicia Patterson" in, 320–1
Kennedy's pilgrimage to headquarters of, 311–13
Long Island's building boom and, 207–9, 229, 280
market research for, 158
naming of, 159
national conventions covered in (1952), 248–9
new building in Garden City for, 229–32, 233
polling and market research for, 294
Pulitzer Prizes won by, 270, 271, 273, 277, 280, 334
run by Alicia during war, 183, 187, *187*, 188–90, 196, 197
Saturday Evening Post piece on, 238, *239*, 242, 244
staff hired for, 158–9, 188–90, 276–9, 280, 319, 334
tabloid format of, 156, 159
Time pieces on, 226–7, 238, 270, 272
typeface and design for, 159
Washington bureau of, 278
Newsday (Keeler's book), 160, 265, 313, 316, 321, 330
Newsweek, 226, 247
New York American, 113
New York Herald Tribune, 209, 251
New York Newsday, 334
New York Post, 219
New York State Crime Commission, 268, 270
New York Times, 76, 132, 209, 251, 260, 303, 320
New York World, 126, 138
New York World-Telegram, 269
Nixon, Richard M., 319
Noble, Ray, 128
Normandy, Alicia's 1948 visit to war sites in, 220–1
Northcliffe, Edward Harmsworth, Lord, 60

O'Hara, John, 114
Oppenheimer, Sir Harry, 288
Orient Princess, 107–8

Paley, Babe, 251
Panama, Alicia's 1929 travels with her father in, 93–4, 193, 308

Parker, Dorothy, 158
Pasley, Fred, 173, 174, 175, 176, 177–8
Pasley, Virginia, 256
Patterson, Alice Higinbotham (mother), 27, 31, *31*, 32, 36–8, 41, 52, 58, 61, 62, 73, 86, 89, 98, 113, 222, 306
  Alicia's illness and, 256
  Alicia's marriage to Brooks and, 110, 113, 114
  Alicia's marriage to Simpson and, 75, 77, 83, 110
  Alicia's 1947 visit to, at Libertyville, 201–6
  Alicia's relationship with, 58, 148–9, 167, 203, 275, 327–8
  divorce of, 148, 149
  Elinor's debut and, 67–8
  European sojourns of, 22–4, 48–51, 64–5
  Guggenheim's relationship with, 201–2
  Joe's farming and, 31, 32, 33, 34, 36, 40
  Joe's remarriage and, 148–9
  Libertyville house given away by, 215
  marital unhappiness of, 9, 20, 21, 22, 34, 48, 49, 53, 54, 57, 64–5, 148
  mothering style of, 58, 65–6, 188
  pregnancies and childbearing of, 11–12, 25, 28, 29, 30, 54–5, 57
  Time cover story and, 272–3, 275
  wedding of, 3–7, *4*, 9, 10
Patterson, Alicia Medill, *115*, *125*, *160*, *187*, *212*, *237*
  abdominal pains, internal bleeding, and ensuing illness of, 94, 244–6, 251–62, 290, 294
  Africa trip of (1957), 286–94, *289*, 299
  as aviatrix, *87*, 87–91, *88*, *90*, 97, 182–3, 321
  "Baby" as nickname for, 30, 52, 53, 55
  Berlin trip of (1948), 219–23, 236–7
  birth of, 29, 30
  books reviewed by, 125
  cancer diagnosis of, 253, 254–7
  Caribbean "air-cruise" of (1929), 92–4, *93*, 193, 244
  childhood of, 31, *31*, 33, *34*, 38, 40–2, *41*, 46, 49–55, 58, 62, 63, 64–6, 69
  death of, 328–31, 333
  debutante party of, 71, *73*
  divorced from Brooks, 145–6, 147, 150, 167
  divorced from Simpson, 78, 83, 94, 95
  European sojourns of, 49–53, 64–5, 127–30, 287, 324–5
  family and forebears' relationships with U.S. presidents, 309–11
  first overseas assignment of (1930–31), 99–108, *104*, *106*, 110–11
  as fisherwoman, 96, 140–1, *141*, 240
  funeral of, 333
  geopolitical views of, 134, 165, 180–1, 274
  honeymoons of, 79–83, *113*, 113–14, 152–5
  honorary degree received by, 327–8
  as horsewoman, 62, 63, 67, 79–81, *80*, *84*, 143, 240
  hospitalizations of, 251–7, 258–9, 260, 328–31
  hunting adventures of, 103, 104–6, *106*, 107, 117–22, *118*, *121*, *122*, 123, 171–2
  India trip of (1932), 117–22, *118*, *121*, *122*, 123
  inheritance of, 199, 200
  Jewish immigration and, 183–5

Patterson, Alicia Medill *(continued)*
lauded as major figure, 304–8
miscarriage and inability to have children, 81, 94, 114
newspaper acquired for, 151, 155, 156–7, 158; *see also Newsday*
New York's cosmopolitanism and, 180–1
no-nonsense feminism of, 258, 304–5
photographs of, *31*, *34*, *41*, *73*, *76*, *77*, *80*, *84*, *87*, *88*, *90*, *93*, *97*, *104*, *106*, *113*, *115*, *118*, *121*, *122*, *125*, *128*, *141*, *160*, *187*, *212*, *237*, *239*, *275*, *278*, *282*, *289*
physical appearance of, 41–2, 72, 162
planes owned by, 97, 108, 109, 110, 113–14, 141
political clout of, 321–4
propensity for abstraction or "deep thinking" lacked by, 181, 298
Pulitzer Prize and, 270, 271, 273, 277, 280
rebellious activities of, 55, 58, 66, 274
romantic relationships of, 72–8, 95–8, 106–13, 138–9, 142–7; *see also* Brooks, Joseph W.; Guggenheim, Harry F.; Simpson, James, Jr.; Stevenson, Adlai
Saturday Evening Post profile of, 238, *239*
schooling of, 55, 58, 63, 64, 65–7, 90, 207, 274, 304, 327
Soviet Union trip of (1937), 131–4
Soviet Union trip of (1958), 299–303
Spartan stoicism of, 200, 201, 308, 331
Time cover story on, 271–5, *275*, 276
war effort and, 182–3, 186
wed to Brooks, 108–13, 145
wed to Guggenheim, 152
wed to Simpson, 75–8, *76*, *77*, 110, 193
Patterson, Eleanor Medill ("Cissy"; briefly Countess Gizycka; aunt), *16*, 70, 149, 198, 215–16, 311
death of, 216
Joe's relationship with, 175
Washington Times-Herald and, 178, 180, 216, 325
wedding of, 15–18
Patterson, Elinor Medill (later Mrs. Russell Codman; sister), 30, 67–71, 73, 78, 86, 113, 192, 198, 200, 201, 256, 307
Alicia's relationship with, 69
birth of, 11–12
childhood of, *11*, 22, 23, 30, 31, *31*, 33–4, 38, 40–1, 42, 44, 46, 49–55, 58, 62, 63, 64, 65
debutante party of, 67–9
marriage of, 71
as Tragic Nun in *The Miracle*, 69–71, *70*, 128
Patterson, James ("Jimmy"; Joe's illegitimate son), 83, 110, 116, 125, 148, 149, 198
Patterson, Josephine (later Mrs. Fred Reeve, and then Mrs. Ivan Albright; sister), 9, *77*, 98, 110, 113, *115*, 140, 147, 198, 210, *212*, 225, 227, 228, 295, 320–1, 323
Alicia's illness and, 253–4, 255–6, 258, 260, 261, 262
Alicia's final illness and death and, 328, 330, 331
Alicia's letters to, 75, 201
Alicia's relationship with, 150, 167–8, 307
Alicia's sojourns at Wyoming ranch of, 238, 240–2, 273
birth of, 54–5, 56
childhood of, 58, 63, 64, 65, 69
Europe trip of (1935), 127, *128*, 287

family reunion of 1947 and, 201, 203–4, 205, 206
father's relationship with, 192, 200
India trip of (1932), 117–18, 120, *121*, 121–2
isolationism of, 180
Patterson, Joseph Medill (father), 3–39, *16*, *26*, 42–67, 117, 135, 189, 240
Albright's painting of, *202*
Alicia's first writing assignments for, 81–2, 83, 84–5, 87
Alicia's flying lessons and, 87, 88, 89
Alicia's marriage to Brooks and, 108, 109–10, 111, 113, 114, 115–16, 135, 145, 146, 147, 150
Alicia's marriage to Simpson and, 75, 77, 78, 83, 110, 193
Alicia's *Newsday* venture and, 159, 160–1, 162, 163, 193
Alicia's overseas assignments and, 97–8, 99, 110–11
Alicia's relationship with, 64–5, 66, 87–8, 115, 124–5, 126, 159, 167, 168, 193, 200, 203, 274, 297, 307–8
as aviator, 86–7, *90*, 321
Brookses financially subsidized by, 114, 116, 124, 125, 135, 146
Brooks's friendship with, 96–7, 110, 145, 146
Cain Hoy visit of (1941), 168–74
Caribbean "air-cruise" of (1929), 92–4, *93*, 193
as Chicago's commissioner of public works, 21–2, 25–6, 27
Cissy's wedding and, 15–18
death of, 198, 200, 204
as Debs's campaign manager, 35, 36, 42
decline of, 191–3, 198
as "deep thinker," 181
Depression-era successes of, 123–4
divorce of, 148, 149
European sojourns of, 22–4, 48–53, 127–30, 287
as farmer, 30–5, 36
as father, 10–11, *11*, 28, 30, 42, 52, 54, 56, 62, 63, 200
father's death and, 44, 46–7
Guggenheim's Jewishness problematic for, 146–7
illegitimate son of, 83, 148; *see also* Patterson, James
as Illinois legislator, 10–11
infidelity of, 64–5; *see also* King, Mary S.
isolationism of, 127, 147, 161, 164–5, 167–8, 175, 177–9, 180, 181, 192, 311
as journalist, 10, 11, 13–14, 15, 17, 19, 20–1, 23–4, 26–9, 30, 34–5, 42, 46–7, 55–6
left-wing politics and, 13–14, 20–2, 25–9, 30, 35, 36, 42
marital unhappiness of, 9, 20, 21, 22, 34, 48, 49, 53, 54, 57, 64–5, 148
military service of, 57, 59–60, 61, 96, 164, 173–4, 175
as novelist, 35, 37, 42–3, 46
Pearl Harbor attack and, 172–4
planes given to Alicia by, 97, 141
remarriage of, 147–9, 150
as Renegade Heir, *26*, 29, 191
rise of Fascism and, 127–30
Roosevelt's relationship with, 116, 124, 164–5, 311, 323; *see also* Roosevelt, Franklin D.
Soviet Union trip of (1937), 131–4
tabloid launched by, 60, 61–2, 63, 73, 124, 156, 161; *see also Daily News*
as war correspondent, 55–6, 57, 58
Washington, D.C., mission of (December 1941), 174–9
wedding of, 3–7, *4*, 9, 10
Patterson, Mary King (stepmother), *see* King, Mary S.

Patterson, Nellie Medill (grandmother), 9, 14, 27, 28, 55, 60, 62, 65, 175, 310
  Alice's correspondence with, 21, 23, 24, 32, 37, 54
  Cissy's wedding and, 15–18
  husband's death and, 45
  Joe and Alice's European sojourns and, 22, 23, 24, 48–9, 50, 51
  Tribune management and, 47, 48, 62
Patterson, Rev. Robert (great-grandfather), 14, 39, 46, 327
Patterson, Robert Wilson (grandfather), 6, 10, 13, 14, 20, 27, 310
  Cissy's wedding and, 16–17
  death of, 44–6
Pearl Harbor attack (1941), 172–4, 175
Peckham, Stan, 159, 160, 165, 196, 201, 238, *239*, 279
Pershing, John, 57, 59
Pétillon, Léon, 291
pigsticking, in India, 117, *118*, *119*, 119–20, 123
Pirie, Robert S., *77*
Plimpton, Francis T. P. and Pauline, 324–5
Poland, Alicia's travels in (1958), 303
Post, Marjorie Merriweather, 132
Pratap Singh Gaekwar, HRH, *119*
Prince of Wales, 80, 82
Pulitzer Prize, 270, 271, 273, 277, 280, 334

Quorn Hunt, 79–80, *80*, 119

Radcliffe College, 304, 305, 320
Radek, Karl, 132
Rascoe, Burton, 25–6
Rawls, William, 253, 254, 329
Reeve, Fred, 148
Reilly & Britton, 37, 42
Reinhardt, Max, 69
Republican Convention (1952), 248
Republican Party, 6, 13, 309, 310
Republic Aviation, 324
Rhodesia (now Zimbabwe), Alicia's 1957 travels in, 288
River Club, New York, campaign-launching dinner for Stevenson at (1952), 249–51, 258
rocket science, Guggenheim's support for, 153–5, 197
Rogerson, Cliff, *239*
Roosevelt, Eleanor, 314–15, 317
Roosevelt, Franklin D., 149, 183, 192, 311, 323
  Alicia's support for, 165
  American-Russian relations and, 131, 132
  criticized in *Daily News* editorials, 147, 161, 164, 167–8, 177–9
  Joe Patterson's distancing from, over antineutralist policies, 164–5, 167–8
  Joe Patterson's early support for, 115–16, 124, 174, 192, 311
  Joe Patterson's final meeting with, 174–9
  Pearl Harbor attack and, 172, 173, 175
Roosevelt, Quentin ("The Colonel"), 99, 103
Roosevelt, Theodore, 6, 176, 310
Roosevelt Raceway, Long Island, 267, 269
Rosenthal, A. M., 303
Rue, Larry, 221–2, 223
Russian Revolution (1905), 23–4, 131

St. Louis, SS, 183
St. Mary's River, Georgia, Alicia's retreat on, 150, 201, *212*, 238, 240, 295–6, 319
  Alicia and Harry's battle at, 283–5
  Alicia's introspection at, 297–8
  Alicia's recuperation at, 260–2
  Stevenson's 1948 visit to, 212–14

Stevenson's 1956 campaign planned at, 281
St. Timothy's School for Girls, Baltimore, 65–6, 67
Salinger, Pierre, 321
Sands Point, Long Island:
Alicia and Joe Brooks's summer rental at, 125, *125*
Alicia's modernist Raymond Hood house at, 135, *136*, 146
social scene in, 136–9
Saratoga Springs, New York, 141–4
Saturday Evening Post, 29, 99, 226
Alicia profiled in, 238, *239*, 242, 244
extended interview with Alicia in, 306–8
Savoy-Plaza Hotel, New York, Guggenheims' apartment in, 166
Schiff, Dorothy ("Dolly"), 219, 220, 221, 222, 235
Schlesinger, Arthur, 281
Schweitzer, Albert, 291–3
Sea Island, Georgia, Alicia and Joe Brooks's honeymoon on, 113, *113*
Sikorsky Aviation, 92
Simpson, James, Jr. (Alicia's first husband), 72, *74*, 74–81
Alicia's divorce from, 78, 83, 94, 95
Alicia wed to, 75–8, *76*, *77*, 110, 193
honeymoon of, 79–81, 83
Simpson, Mr. (father-in-law), 75, 77, 79, 80
Simpson, Mrs. (mother-in-law), 75, 77
Singapore, Alicia's 1931 travels in, 99, 106–7, 117
Singapore Times, 107
sladang, brought down by Alicia with single bullet, 105–6, *106*
Smith, Ledyard, 72, 73–7, 94
Alicia's 1927 travels to Guatemala with, 75–7
Smith, Richard Norton, 45
Smith, Sir Ian, 288
Soames, Harry, 101–2
Socialist Party, 35, 42
South Africa, Alicia's 1957 travels in, 288
Southeast Asia, Alicia's 1930–31 travels in, 99–108, *104*, *106*, 110–11
Soviet Union, 192, 295
Alicia's 1937 trip with her father to, 131–4
Alicia's 1958 trip to, 299–303
Berlin airlift and, 219–23
Hitler's advance into, 170
Revolution of 1905 and, 23–4, 131
"show trials" in, 132–3, 134
see also Cold War
Spartan boy, story about fox and, 200, 201, 308
Sprague, J. Russell, 269
Sputnik, 300
Stalin, Joseph, 132, 133, 192, 220, 272, 302
Stevenson, Adlai, 72, 210–18, 222, 224–5, 226, 227–8, 233–7, 238, 240–5, 280–3, *282*, 324–6
Africa trip of (1957), 286–93, 299
Alicia as godmother to grandson of, 325–6
Alicia's failed "elopement" with, 238, 240–2, 243–4
Alicia's "last letter" to, in case of her death, 252–3, 258
Alicia's last trips with, 324–6
Alicia's reconnection with, at Libertyville, 204–6, 235, 259
Alicia's retreat on St. Mary's River visited by, 212–14
Alicia's romantic liaisons with, at Albright's studio, 210, 225, 234
Alicia visited in hospital by, 256, 258–9
as ambassador to United Nations, 320
campaign-launching dinner at River Club for, 249–51, 258

Stevenson, Adlai *(continued)*
divorce of, 233
grand consolation tour of, after 1952 defeat, 260
as gubernatorial candidate, 212, 214, 215, 216–18, 219, 259
Guggenheim unaware of Alicia's romance with, 225, 242, 250
immobilized by both professional and marital indecision, 205–6, 210–12, 216, 246–8, 259, 281, 317, 318
Kennedy's presidential aspirations and, 312–13
Newsday's endorsement of, 281, 282, 283
other women in life of, 241, 281
political aspirations of, 211–12, 236, 259–60
as possible Secretary of State, 315–17, 320
as presidential candidate, 228, 236, 237, 246–51, 257, 258, 259–60, 281–3, 299, 301, 312–18
Soviet Union trip of (1958), 299–303
Stevenson, Adlai, Jr., 314
Stevenson, Borden, 299
Stevenson, Ellen Borden, 204, 211, 214, 215, 224, 233
Stevenson, John Fell, 299, 325–6
Stevenson, Nancy, 287–8, 290
Sullivan, Kathleen, 194
Sweeney, James Johnson, 304
Swenson, Mrs. (cook), 38
Swope, Herbert Bayard, 126, 137–8

Taft, Robert A., 247, 248
Taft, William Howard, 310
Tempelsman, Maurice, 287
Tempersley, Eugene, 107, 117, 118, 119, 120, 121
tennis, Guggenheims' enjoyment of, 230
Thierry, Lieutenant, 104
This Is the Life I Love (Patterson, as told to Burton), 306–8
Three Spear Ranch, Dubois, Wyoming, Alicia's sojourns at, 238, 240–2, 273
tiger hunting expeditions:
in India (1932), 107, 117, 120–2, *121*, 123
in Indochina (1931), 103, 104–6, *106*
Time, 92, 247, 251, 292, 320
cover story on Alicia in, 271–5, *275*, 276
pieces on *Newsday* in, 226–7, 238, 270, 272
Tipton's Auction House, Saratoga Springs, N.Y., 143
Tolstoy, Count Leo, 30–1
Tree, Marietta, 251, 260, 281, 287, 314
Tree, Sir Ronald, 260, 287
Tribune Company:
Liberty and, 84, 123
see also Chicago Tribune
Truman, Harry S., 197, 212, 215, 216, 228, 233, 257, 259
elected president, 217
reelection bid declined by, 247
Tucker, Richard, 299
Tully, Grace, 176, 177, 178
Twain, Mark, 49
Tyree, Walter, 172

Udall, Stewart, 324
Uganda, Alicia's 1957 travels in, 288, 289–90
United Nations, 195, 233, 320
University School, Chicago, 55, 58, 64

Veracruz, Battle of (1914), 55–6
Versailles Treaty (1919), 129
Vietminh rebels, 103, 104
Vietnam War, 334

Villa, Pancho, 57, 58, 93
von Braun, Wernher, 155, 197

Wardell, Sir Michael, 130
Washington Times-Herald, 178, 180, 216, 325
Waugh, Evelyn, 127
Wechsler, James, 250
Wertenbaker, Charles, 238, *239*
White, Stanford, 14
Whitney, Jock, 137
Willkie, Wendell, 165
Wilson, Woodrow, 56
Wings for Britain, 182–3, 186
Wirtz, Willard, 281
Woestendick, Bill, 321–2
Wood, Albert, 208, 229–31
World, 32
World War I, 57, 96, 127
- Guggenheim's military service in, 186, 194
- Joe Patterson's military service in, 59–60, 61, 173

World War II, 164–5, 170
- Alicia's trips to Europe on brink of, 127–34
- Battle of Britain and, 164, 182–3
- Guggenheim's military commission reactivated in, 186–7, *187*, 190, 194–6
- Guggenheim's return to civilian life after, 195–7
- housing needed after, 207–9
- isolationism in years before, 127, 147, 161, 164–5, 167–8, 175, 177–9, 180, 181, 192
- Joe Patterson's decline during, 191–3
- Joe Patterson's Washington, D.C., mission and, 174–9
- Pearl Harbor attack and, 172–4, 175

Wright, Frank Lloyd, 304

Ycaza, Manuel, 263
Yonkers Raceway, shootout at (1953), 268–9

ABOUT THE AUTHORS

Alice Arlen is the author of *Cissy Patterson*. For many years, she was a successful screenwriter: among her credits are *Silkwood* (cowritten with Nora Ephron), nominated for an Academy Award; *Alamo Bay*; *Cookie*; *A Shock to the System*; *Then She Found Me*; *The Weight of Water*. She is the niece of Alicia Patterson and (until her death in March 2016) lived in New York.

Michael J. Arlen was for thirty years a staff writer and television critic at *The New Yorker*. He is the author of many books, including *Thirty Seconds*, *An American Verdict*, *Exiles*, which was short-listed for a National Book Award, and *Passage to Ararat*, which won a National Book Award.

A NOTE ON THE TYPE

This book was set in Fournier, a typeface named for Pierre Simon Fournier fils (1712–1768), a celebrated French type designer. Coming from a family of typefounders, Fournier was an extraordinarily prolific designer of typefaces and of typographic ornaments. He was also the author of the important Manuel typographique (1764–1766), in which he attempted to work out a system standardizing type measurement in points, a system that is still in use internationally.

Composed by North Market Street Graphics, Lancaster, Pennsylvania
Printed and bound by Berryville Graphics, Berryville, Virginia
Designed by Iris Weinstein